YOID
NATION

The Truth About Britain's Yob Culture

FRANCIS GILBERT

Visit the Portrait website!

Portrait publishes a wide range of non-fiction, including biography, history, science, music, popular culture and sport.

If you want to:

- read descriptions of our popular titles
- buy our books over the internet
- take advantage of our special offers
- enter our monthly competition
- learn more about your favourite Portrait authors

VISIT OUR WEBSITE AT: www.portraitbooks.co.uk

Please log onto francisgilbert.co.uk or yobnation.com to post your own stories and see photographs of the author's travels through our yob nation.

Many of the names in the book have been changed – and locations slightly altered in a couple of instances – to protect the innocent and the guilty.

First published in 2006 by Portrait
an imprint of Piatkus Books Ltd
5 Windmill Street
London W1T 2JA
e-mail: info@piatkus.co.uk

The moral right of the author has been asserted

A catalogue record for this book is available from the British Library

ISBN 0 7499 2669 4

Text design by Paul Saunders

Typeset by Palimpsest Book Production Limited,
Polmont, Stirlingshire
Printed and bound in Great Britain by
William Clowes Limited, Beccles, Suffolk

This book is dedicated to Sunday nights in the pub with my father and my brother, and my friendship with Carlo Roberts.

Contents

Acknowledgements

I would like to thank all the people who agreed to be interviewed for this book. All my interviewees were terrific. I would in particular like to thank David Cracknell, Kirsty Smith, Rupert's friend Tim and Tim's sister, Jane Harris, Gary Wildman and D.S. Simmons, Gillian Ford, Martin Sixsmith, Bronwen Peacock, Stephanie Harrison, Phil and Julie Hughes, Sarah Robinson, Darren and Danielle Forrester, Jenny Turton, Jamie James and Jean Herbert, who all went out of their way to help me with various interviews and research. Thank you!

My agent Ivan Mulcahy was instrumental in helping me flesh out my ideas, and Alan Brooke, my editor, played an essential role in editing my drafts and encouraging me.

Marq Bailey, who photographed many of the interviewees and places written about in the book, proved to be crucial in assisting me with many of my interviews.

My wife's support was indispensable and without it the book would not have been written.

Important note
Mike Batten, who is chairman of the London Borough of Redbridge bench of magistrates and makes a number of comments in the book, wishes to make it clear that his views are not the views of the bench of magistrates but his personal observations.

Prologue

' What's your problem, you cunt?
I can fucking do what the fuck I want
here, cunt. '

1979 - Beaten but not frightened

'Blood burst out of his eyebrow. He reached for his handkerchief as the boys ran screaming and laughing into the street.'

My father kicked at the glass on the tarmac, sending it scuttling against the wire fence. I jumped up into the air, heading the football at him. He smiled and caught the ball. The Saturday sun shone on his face, illuminating the incipient crow's feet around his eyes.

'Hey, you're not supposed to catch the ball! You're supposed to kick it!' I yelped, rushing up to him and trying to snatch it away.

'I know how to play football!' he protested.

He didn't really – even though I was a smallish 11-year-old, I always beat him at three and in. I could dribble the ball through his legs. It was a stretch to imagine I was Johann Cruff and he was a great defender.

Perhaps it was because he was so bad at football that I felt protective of him. Or perhaps it was because my parents were divorced and I saw so little of him, living as I did with my bad-tempered and volatile mother. Anyway, in my 11-year-old vision of the world, anyone who didn't know much about football was in need of help.

My brother went in goal and I began my onslaught, dribbling around my father's legs, and enjoying my skills as he half-heartedly tried to get the ball off me.

Then there was a whizzing and sizzling on the tarmac, and a firework exploded next to the ball. Three youths, white boys scuffling around in trainers, snarled with laughter from behind the hoods of their green parkas. One of them chucked another firework in our direction. It fizzled and snapped at our feet. My brother and I retreated, but my father, in a tough-guy Marks and Spencer anorak, approached the teenagers.

'You can't do that! That just isn't acceptable! It's utterly intolerable!' he blustered. I shrank back, and my stomach tightened. My father's outraged received pronunciation seemed very out of place in this grotty Kentish Town playground. I was a veteran of some fairly rough playgrounds. I knew the hue and timbre of trouble. My father, an academic and businessman, did not.

'What's your problem, you cunt? I can fucking do what the fuck I want here, cunt,' a pale-faced youth replied steadily.

My father gave the boy one of his most vehement stares. 'You shouldn't speak like that. What you've done is intolerable,' he said.

'Ah, fuck off,' the kid said. Then he began to walk away with his friends, sniggering. But as he did so, he suddenly wheeled around on the heels of his trainers and whacked my father in the face.

My father screamed out, 'Hey!'

Blood burst out of his eyebrow. He reached for his handkerchief as the boys ran screaming and laughing into the street.

Once they were safely in the distance, my brother and I started shouting, 'Hey!'

My father mopped his brow and raised his free hand into the air. 'Hey! Come here! You can't do that.'

With this clarion call, all three of us gave chase, running after my father's tormentors. All of us knew deep down that this was probably not a wise idea, but the youths were sufficiently far away for us not to worry too much. Our lame pursuit enabled my father to keep his dignity intact. The parkas vanished into a warren-like council estate and were never caught.

Today, my father would never chase after someone who had assaulted him. Today, people are scared. Fear of being severely hurt by louts is endemic in the culture. Most of us are too cowardly to argue. We cowering people know that it would be very unwise to protest if attacked because we might lose our life as well as our wallet and our dignity.

In September 2004, my father was mugged near where he lives in a far smarter part of north London, Chalk Farm. In a dark side road next to the trendy Greek restaurant Lemonia, he was approached by two youths. When he was asked for his money, he handed it over as quickly as he could. He didn't pursue them.

My father was quite right not to tussle over his wallet. Home Office statistics published in 2005 showed that violent crime has risen very sharply in recent years. There were 1,159,400 violent assaults against people in 2004.[1]

But it's more than statistics that make the people of Britain worried about being attacked today. It is personal experience . . .

The night bus home - 1999

'Oi, have you got a quid?'

I staggered out of the nightclub and drifted onto the train. The seats were ripped and the windows were covered in graffiti, but I didn't feel intimidated.

I am a Londoner and expect nothing less from my public services. I was not the 11-year-old who watched helplessly as his father was smashed in the face. I was 31 and had lived and worked in London most of my life. I had taught in some of the roughest schools in the city and felt at home in the dirtiest streets – too comfortable perhaps.

There were other people around and I felt secure enough on this late-night train to put my feet up. I dozed. I dreamt that the nightclub was not the noisy, thumping hole that I had been happy to leave. Instead, soothing music stroked my soul there and charming maidens with enigmatic smiles drifted by. There had been no pogo-ing louts or brash, thundering girls in lumpy tops.

I was just about to be taken from the club on a mysterious gondolier when I woke up with a jolt. Oh no, the train was terminating here! And it was the last train! I looked around and saw that I was at the benighted Leytonstone station. I scrambled off the train and managed to catch a night bus on Leytonstone High Street. I congratulated myself on my luck: I might have waited an hour for the bus. It smelt really badly of vomit downstairs, so I climbed the stairs and positioned myself in a seat tucked away behind the stairwell.

Even in my drunken state I registered the fact that there were about five black boys sitting at the very back of the bus. A tiny squirt of adrenalin suffused my veins. I dismissed my fear as racism. Besides which, I had taught kids like this for years. They were all harmless kids when it really came down to it.

I clamped on my Walkman earphones and pressed play. Neville Jason reading Proust's *In Search of Lost Time* enlivened my mind. I was walking on the shimmering beach, watching the lithe bodies of Albertine and her friends in their bathing costumes. The sea of Proust's prose washed over me, I could feel the sand beneath my feet, I could touch the strands of Albertine's wet hair, and I could taste the glorious blue sky.

A rough hand shook my shoulder. I sat up. A face, washed-out in the bright light of the bus, zoomed down upon me. It was one of the boys from the back of the bus.

'Oi, have you got a quid?' My reaction was immediate. I snapped back that I didn't. I bitterly resented the way in which my sublime vision of Albertine had been interrupted. I was also very afraid.

In a split-second I calculated my options. The other kids were approaching my seat rapidly and there was one of them right in front of me. If I stayed where I was I would be trapped in a couple of seconds because I could see that the kids would block the stairwell. Then I would be totally finished. There was no one else on the top of the bus. They would be able to treat my head like a basketball and bounce it off the scratched perspex windows until it split open.

So I bolted. I pushed past the boy who had asked me for the money and just managed to edge in front of them on my way to the stairs. At the head of the stairs I clocked them properly, staring right into their eyes. Hungry eyes. Surly eyes. Predatory eyes. Their cheeks were sculptured out of ebony. They were thin and wired with a nasty energy.

I rushed down the stairs and thought that they were following me. Maybe they were so confident that they were aiming to mug me in front of everyone else in the bus? I lunged at the driver behind his plastic, reinforced screen and yelled, 'They're trying to mug me! They're going to get me!'

He was ruddy-faced man, with a thick mane of dry, wiry white hair. He unclipped his counter immediately and stepped out into the bus. 'Where are they? It's those fuckers!' he shouted in a strong Irish accent. 'I know all about them. They've been fucking around since we left the depot.' He walked up menacingly to the stairs and shouted, 'Right, you lot, get off the bus! That's it! You didn't pay and now you need to *get off*!'

I felt a bit worried for him. He was just a chunky old Irishman, and they were strong and young. But his anger had the desired effect, and they all came tumbling out of the bus, not looking into the bus driver's eyes as they left. He dusted down his hands as the last one left and then climbed back into the driver's seat. The door clapped shut and it appeared that we were going to be on our way, completely unscathed.

Just as he was about to drive away, however, the leader of the gang pressed the emergency door button outside the bus and sneaked back on. I was sitting right next to the exit. Suddenly, I felt his fist plunging into my eye. There was a flash of blinding light and a massive spinning feeling in my head. I felt blood gushing out of my eye. I rose to my feet, blood dripping onto the floor, and saw that the kid had gone.

'I got hit,' I said, reeling towards the bus driver.

He grimaced and then said, 'I'll call an ambulance, and the police.'

'Don't,' I said. 'I'm all right. I just want to get home.'

He shook his head. 'You're bleeding. And the police need to see this. They need to see what happens on this bus every night. It needs to be reported.'

He phoned them from the driver's seat and I sat on the chair next to him. The front door of the bus remained open as we waited for the emergency services to arrive. A few kids got on as I held a bloody tissue to my head.

We all waited. And waited. After about ten minutes an ambulance arrived. The paramedics rushed on, took a look at my eye and asked me a few questions in order to ascertain whether I had concussion or not. Then they left.

The police still hadn't arrived. Once again we waited. After about five more minutes, the kids who had got on the bus shortly after the mugging asked the driver what was going on. He told them that we were waiting for the police to speak to me, and that he wasn't going to move until they did. This made the two kids turn on me.

'Why don't you get off the bus, man? Can't you see that you're holding the whole bus up?' one of them said. He was a tight-eyed boy with light black skin and pursed lips.

I shook my head and averted my eyes. I wanted to melt away. I clung onto the plastic armrest of my seat. I was frightened. I didn't want to get off the bus. The darkness of Stratford was lapping at the lip of the bus entrance. I knew that I would drown the moment I stepped outside. Maybe those boys were waiting for me? There was no way I could wait for the police at the battered, lonely bus stop. I would die there.

Suddenly, a tired-looking black lady came to my rescue. 'Why don't you leave the poor man alone? Can't you see he just got blinded in the eye? What's the matter with you, boy?' The kid squared up to the lady. 'He's fucking holding up this bus and he should get off. Get off, you hear me?'

I was terrified of getting another beating. I hung my head down and remained silent. Luckily, the lady continued to defend me. 'Just leave him alone. The police will be here soon.'

Eventually they did arrive, but not until after the lady and the boy had argued at length about the merits of me getting off the bus. A man in a bright fluorescent coat asked me whether I was all right, and said that it probably wasn't worth a statement. I nodded and he left. Finally, the bus started up again. I stood next to the driver all the way, and when I got off I ran home without once looking up. I was shaking when I opened the front door. My eye hurt like hell and I was still very, very frightened.

I was one of the lucky ones.

The undercover cop's story

'They are animals. There is nothing human about them at all.'

A few years later the attacks in the Stratford area escalated considerably. One group of youths from Stratford evolved into Britain's biggest 'steaming' gang, who called themselves 'Lords of Stratford Cru'. They only properly registered on the police's radar in September 2003, when they knocked two Asian youths unconscious on a Liverpool Street train and stole £500. Later, a woman in her twenties was repeatedly punched in the face after one of the gang groped her. A youth held her in an armlock while his mates smashed her face with their fists. The day after this incident, a female student was followed by 15 gang members and brutally beaten at Hackney Downs station. She was grabbed, punched, kicked to the floor and 'groped all over'. The victim said: 'What they did to me will stay with me for my whole life. They're animals – there's nothing human about them at all.'

Five members of the gang were caught when 19 of them boarded the N25 night bus at Whitechapel in October 2003. The bus driver called the police when they began robbing the passengers on the top of the bus. The majority of them escaped through the bus's emergency door at Bow Church DLR station, but the police managed to apprehend five of them.

These five were essentially 'Stratford tourists' because none of them actually came from the area: most of them were from the suburbs of north-east London. But Stratford became their 'manor' because it was a central meeting point for all of them, and is configured in such a way that gangs can easily assemble there. It has all the classic requirements for the modern gang: it is close to lots of buses and trains; it has a labyrinthine but slightly run-down shopping centre; it has parks and takeaways; and it includes several areas where gangs can roam around looking intimidating.

They were each sentenced to five years in a youth offenders' institution. Judge Henry Blacksell summed up the case by saying: 'It was, in my judgment, an aspect of this offending that you enjoyed the humiliation of your victims. You picked on people who were weak and vulnerable . . . and not content with taking their property you beat them up. You targeted them. It was gratuitous violence.'

Over a year after some of the Lords of Stratford Cru were sentenced, I met Detective Superintendent Simmons and DC

Gary Wildman in Stratford. We crossed the main road, walked through the shopping centre and sat down in a café right opposite to where I was attacked in Stratford. I shuddered to remember that dark night, but I was glad to be with these two, who felt like the right guys to be with in Stratford.

Detective Sergeant Simmons agrees that I could have been attacked by some of the 'LOS' – his acronym for the gang – but points out that it could been any of number of other gangs. 'There are a lot of them around here,' he says, 'and the situation is getting worse.'

He is a well-built man in his late thirties, with gym-trimmed arms and shoulders, dressed casually in a T-shirt and jeans. He wears a leather bracelet and looks pretty tough. I learned later, from another colleague of his, that he is well known in the British Transport Police for being fit and brave. 'When the situation gets rough,' his colleague confided in me, 'you'll be glad to have Steve Simmons on your side.' His partner, Wildman, is a larger man in a checked black shirt, sunglasses and jacket. He is the quieter of the two.

'The LOS were a large gang, formed mostly of African kids,' says DS Simmons. 'But we suspect one of them, from a West Indian family, was just along for the ride. The idiot went and got himself caught when he probably had little to do with the carnage that the LOS committed elsewhere. It was a personal tragedy for him because he was an Essex youth team cricket captain. That's the thing with these gangs – you get a lot of wannabees, a lot of hangers-on, who tag along for a night or two just to see what is going on. The real hard core of the group were from places like Sierra Leone, Nigeria and Somalia and were hardened offenders.

'They weren't actually that hard to catch, because like all these gangs, they were creatures of habit. Most youth gangs go to the same locations, wear the same clothing, and do the same mindless things night after night, week after week, month after month. Like just about everyone else, the LOS were obsessed with American street culture: they wore the baggy pants, the bling-bling jewellery and the designer label trainers. Their motivation for mugging people was almost certainly to get money to buy this sort of shit – although the LOS, like a lot of the gangs we are investigating now, took things a step further.'

Gary Wildman nods at this point and adds, 'What is frightening about these guys is that they enjoyed really kicking the shit out of people who had *already handed over their stuff.* This is the most worrying thing. They enjoyed watching people being totally humiliated. One of the guys who was attacked by them still can't go back to work. The beating he got has ruined his life. And the black girl was the victim of the most degrading kind of assault. If this series of robberies had not been stopped when it was, I'm sure we would eventually have ended up with a murder enquiry. They had no morals, and no concept that others have feelings or rights. They are just ruthless . . . and on their own, complete cowards.'

Detective Sergeant Simmons becomes visibly angry, and says, 'They are just shit. A lot of people come from bad backgrounds, but they don't do that kind of stuff. And I'm sorry, but I just don't go along with the view that we should try and understand them better. I know Gary takes a bit of a different view – that we need to appreciate where they are coming from. Yes, I know that a lot of them live in squalid conditions – but I am getting less and less sympathetic as I grow older and see more of this stuff.'

There is a pause as we all reflect upon the suffering wrought by the gang on their victims. I am surprised by the level of sympathy felt by the police for the victims of street robberies. At least there are some people out there who care.

'It was pretty straightforward catching the LOS,' says Simmons. 'We knew their whereabouts, because they were creatures of habit. They would usually start off at Dalston Junction, and then board certain buses like the 86 or the 242. The night we caught them we got some excellent CCTV footage. We could clearly see their faces on camera. There was no problem with identifying them. You see, this is why gangs like them are so hard to convict. You know who they are. They know who you are. But for a case to go to court, you need a very high level of proof. Often witnesses are too frightened to come forward to testify, so you either need to get a very good description of their clothing, or CCTV footage which is very clear. A lot of the time, the gangs are wearing hoods, bandanas or baseball caps so that they can't be IDed by the CCTV, and so a lot of that footage can be worthless. Also, they deliberately wear the same clothes so that you can't prove who is who, and often exchange clothing with each other throughout the day.'

But are gangs like the Lords of Stratford Cru the shocking exceptions?

DS Simmons shakes his head vehemently. 'It is getting worse, a lot worse. The violence is more in the open now, and it is much more extreme.

> The trouble is the crime figures are very misleading. Added to which, just before the election, the government pumped millions into solving street crime, with a special focus on robbery offences. They flooded the streets with coppers. And crime did dip down. But now that the election is over the money has gone, and we're back to square one.
>
> You've also got to remember that in the late seventies, when I first started working as a policeman, robbery didn't exist in the form that it does today. The most common type of robbery was a guy in a balaclava with a sawn-off shotgun trying to take off a bank, a Securior van or a betting shop. And that wasn't that common then. Now it is even less common because the security around places

like that is so much better. The organized gangs are into other crimes. They can't hack the hassle of getting past so many alarms, and guards and safes. They're selling drugs, or racketeering or pimping.

Meanwhile, the kids are left on the streets. And they are the most dangerous types of people – particularly some of the kids we are seeing here in London today. We've got a particular problem at the moment with Somali youths. These are refugees from war-torn Somalia who have come straight from a war zone. Some have been trained from an early age as boy soldiers. Now we have quite a few who are roaming around the capital. They don't give a second thought about using extreme violence and, rather like the LOS, they enjoy inflicting pain upon people for absolutely no reason.

Many of these gangs don't have names because they are not organised. They are just groups of people who hang around the same places, at the same times, in the same clothes, speaking the same lingo, doing the same things. And the thing is, human nature being what it is, all it takes is one or two psychos to lead a whole group. What usually happens is that the psycho will give their victim a slap to start the fun off, and the others will imitate him. 'Happy slapping' is a good example of this. These kids love to take pictures on their mobiles of people looking distressed and being abused. We're now frightened that the craze, which is sweeping through London, could escalate to more sinister levels.

After the slapping comes the more serious violence: the lead 'psycho' will go one step further by kicking the victim in the face, or maybe stabbing him, or if it is a pretty girl by having a feel around. The others copy him. He'll then goad them on to do more, often leading by example. And before you know it, your victim, who has probably handed over his mobile phone or whatever, is basically kicked to fuck. The psycho, you see, has to establish that he is the dominant male by being more violent than the rest.

DS Simmons stops here and looks me in the eye. He is thinking carefully about how best to make his next point. A world-weary, deadpan smile comes to his lips.

You know, I had to laugh when I went on holiday. I was on safari, and we were in a jeep in the bush, when suddenly we saw a lion's head pop out from behind a tree. None of us had seen him before this. It was like magic. He'd appeared from nowhere. And then suddenly, before we knew it, another head popped out, and another and another. And there, in the matter of a few seconds, before us was a whole pride of lions, primed and lethal.

That's how these gangs operate. They are predatory. They stalk their victims. They spot them at bus stations, or in tube stations or shopping centres, and they follow them secretly, often not appearing like they are in a gang, and then, when they've got their target in a relatively empty place, they pounce.

Some of the worst violence we've seen recently is with new recruits being blooded into a gang. This is where the new recruit has been given a target to prove himself or herself with. The rookie often feels the need to inflict some serious violence upon their chosen victim so that they can truly feel part of the gang.

This is another reason why you shouldn't trust the crime figures. Most crime goes unreported. We're investigating a very violent series of muggings that were carried out by a gang called the 'Paki Panthers' at the moment. The nickname is theirs, not ours, by the way. We are very careful in the force now with racial issues. Anyway, we know that the Pakistani community in the east London estate where the Panthers come from knows who these boys are. They know, but they won't help us at all. We have gone to the victims but they are too terrified to give us a statement. These kids have to exist on the streets, and they know if they grass up the Panthers, they'll be dead. And the elders of the community, who used to have power over the youth, have totally lost control. It's a scary situation.

Introduction

' Violent crime has increased tenfold since 1979.[2] '

A nation of yobs?

'Yob - a noun, a colloquialism from the mid-19th century, which is back slang for BOY. Originally it meant a boy. Now, an uncouth, loutish, ignorant youth or man; especially, one given to violent or aggressive behaviour, a hooligan.' *The Shorter Oxford Dictionary*

Inspiring fear in the public is perhaps one of the central reasons why gangs exist. The Lords of Stratford Cru gang, who possibly attacked me in London, did not actually steal vast quantities of money, but concentrated upon thieving mobile phones, small change and cigarettes. However, extreme violence was used in the pursuit of such booty. The street names of the gang members partly explain why they were so violent: 'street tags' like Killer, Pacman and Driller. They suggest that the boys felt they were living in their own 'computer game', but that the thrill of this game was that it was real and that they had a ready-made audience: the terrified public. Their muggings were theatrical; they needed an audience to validate what they were doing; they needed to feel that they were inspiring fear.

This impulse towards theatricality is what distinguishes the yob from the criminal. The genuine criminal is a secretive creature, carrying out his nefarious activities in a clandestine fashion: he does not want to be seen because he does not want to be caught. His goal is usually to better himself materially. He is quite different from the yob, whose primary purpose is not to get money but to shock a captive audience.

This was what disturbed me most when I reflected upon my interview with Simmons and Wildman: the fact that these boys enjoyed being watched. It was something that I found hard to understand. What kind of person got a kick out of beating the hell out of someone so publicly? There is something almost fetishistic about it. Even though I had been attacked in London, even though my father and brother had been mugged, even though I didn't know anyone who hadn't suffered some kind of violence or crime in London, I still couldn't reconcile my picture of London with what Simmons and Wildman were telling me. They were painting the picture of a war zone, where feral gangs were turning the streets of London into their own bloody theatre.

In fact, various crime statistics indicate increasing chaos. One set of statistics issued by the Home Office reveals that violent crime has increased tenfold since 1979, with 94,960 violent crimes against the person being record in 1979 compared with over one million in 2004. However, the British Crime Survey (BCS) reveals a 14 per cent drop in violent crime since the mid-1990s.[3]

As DS Simmons pointed out, the crime statistics are not reliable. Successive governments have a vested interest in showing declining figures. Even the massaged figures of the BCS, though, revealed in 2004 that there had been a 7 per cent increase in violent crime since the previous year.[4] What is beyond doubt is that a huge number of violent crimes go unreported, and that people's perception is that things are getting worse. Everyone I spoke to during my research for the book, from police officers to magistrates to gang members, felt that there is a lot more violence now.

Most tellingly, a Home Office survey showed that one in five people are now fearful of crime. This 'fear' factor interested me most: it was incontrovertible. People feel that there has been a general decline in behaviour throughout Britain. In the British Crime Survey of 2000, a third of people felt that antisocial behaviour was a major problem in their area, with vandalism and teenagers hanging around the streets being cited as major causes of worry and anxiety. The majority of people also felt that things were getting worse.[5]

When I reflected upon the whole of my life after my interview with Simmons and Wildman, I began to see that the
problem with yobbery was much wider than teenagers
hanging around on the streets.

It isn't just vicious youths like the Lords of Stratford Cru
who are yobs. The British have become more brutal. More
and more people, from our government to our celebrities on
TV, revel in their rudeness, using the techniques of bullying
and harassment to establish their dominance over others,
and often delighting in making their victims suffer. As a
result, many of us feel under siege: harangued by gangs in
the street, bullied at work, puked at by lager louts on our
nights out, emotionally blackmailed by adverts and
programmes on television, lied to by our politicians and
pushed around by ruthless money men in the City.

In fact, the more I investigated the issue, the more I
concluded that the gangs on the street were only part of the
problem. As I researched the book in more depth, I realised
that my initial hunch was correct: some of the worst yobs
are the people who are the most powerful.

After years of being in the political wilderness, New Labour
came to power intent upon manipulating the media for its
own ends: it openly bullied and intimidated anyone who tried
to criticise the party, or to expose its shortcomings. The techniques of the football hooligan were employed in order to
crush its opponents.

Similarly, in the media and the City, perhaps the two other
currently most powerful institutions in the land, it is now
the yobs who are in charge. The media has openly promoted
the values of the yob. Since the 1970s it has transformed our
culture with the way it has openly encouraged the public to
be violent and abusive. Meanwhile, the money men in the
City, who are perhaps the most powerful people on earth,
ruthlessly and publicly destroy their enemies.

My book is divided up so that I can compare and contrast

the habits of yobs on the street with people who enjoy much more power. I have structured the book so that the yobs in a Scottish street gang can be juxtaposed with what is happening in Whitehall or the City. The first section is called 'Victims and Perpetrators'; it looks at the origins of British yobbery, and points out the links between the victims of yobbery and the perpetrators of it. I then move on to look at the ways in which yobs plan and parade their yobbery in 'Briefing Rooms' and 'Parades'. The largest section of the book is entitled 'Battlefields', and is about the ways in which yobs cause conflict. The following section, 'Sitting Ducks', focuses upon a number of poignant stories that highlight the distress and trauma that yobbery causes. Finally, I look at what various organisations, people and thinkers are doing to combat the problem, and offer some concluding thoughts of my own.

CHAPTER ONE

Victims and Perpetrators

' I was too drunk to know exactly what was going on, but there appeared to be a guy racing at me on a motorbike pointing a lance in my direction. '

Truly blooded

'Then I pissed myself.' Army officer

Of all the institutions in British society, the army remains the one where yobbery has been enshrined for centuries.

'I was a little nervous but quietly confident as I combed my short-cropped hair in the mirror,' said Rupert as he explained to me what happened to him at his first officers' mess: his first big ceremonial dinner with his regiment. 'I felt I had got all my mess kit just right: highly bulled George Boots, polished for hours to look like a mirror, black, skin-tight trousers with a red stripe, a black waistcoat and a red jacket adorned with various insignias of my infantry regiment.'

'Everything was calm in the "subby's annex"; these were ten rooms at the back of the officers' mess – subalterns live, eat and sleep in the mess – where the junior officers were billeted. I dusted down my jacket and walked towards my doom.'

Rupert is a middle-class lad, a 22-year-old platoon commander in the Warminster area. He went to a comprehensive in Middlesex, and then Durham University, and spent a year training at the Royal Military Academy Sandhurst (RMAS). He had completed his 'passing out' parade and been awarded his commission from the Queen. Now he had his first command: an officer in charge of a whole platoon. Even though he was quite experienced in the army, nothing had quite prepared him for what happened at his first mess.

I chatted with some of the senior officers in the ante-room as I drank a pint of lager. I noticed that the older officers were sipping their drinks, but the younger ones were chucking down the pints, and encouraging me to do so. Everyone was very friendly. We all laughed about the usual stuff: cars, girls, and 'chuckers' – polo.

Suddenly the conversation stopped. The mess sergeant shouted, 'Dinner is served! And remember, please, once you sit down you can't stand up!'

To be honest, this took me by surprise. I rushed to the bogs before I entered the dining room. Being 'Mr Vice', I was the last one to be seated. ('Mr Vice' is the name given to the most junior officer in the regiment.)

The regimental silver gleamed underneath the vast twinkling chandelier. It was all quite a sight. We were surrounded by pictures from history, the Battle of Waterloo being the most striking at the far end of the room. The colonels and majors sat in the middle of the table, while the subbies were at both ends.

I could see that something was wrong immediately, because as soon as I went to pick up my knife and fork, they flew away from me! I tried to reach out for them, but they had vanished entirely. I looked around at everyone, and saw that no one was smiling or looking at me. I asked for my knife and fork back in a jokey voice, but still I was ignored.

I opened up my napkin and suddenly found out that I was covered in a vast quantity of flour. I stifled a cry. It had covered my skin-tight trousers, more or less ruining them. It was then that I noticed that I was sitting in something a bit slippery, a little squelchy. I put a finger on the chair. Someone had pasted it in Marmite.

'OK, you chaps, what's going on here?' I said, trying my best to smile.

But again, there wasn't much of a reaction. Indeed, no one seemed to be paying any attention to me. The guy sitting next to me told me not to worry, and poured me a drink. I glugged it down, feeling a little unnerved by the pranks. But then my lips began to feel a bit strange; they became totally numb. I pinched them and didn't feel a thing.

When the first course arrived, a spoon magically materialised, but as I began to eat the soup, I found that I was being slapped about the head with something wet and scaly. Someone had fixed a fish onto the end of a fishing line, and was able to navigate it so that it slapped me about the head. I tried to snatch it, but it got yanked away before I could grab hold of it and chuck it at the subby sitting opposite me. I could tell from his secretive grin that he was the one who had organised this torture.

My meal was agony because every dish had been over-loaded with chillis, even the ice cream, added to which I was beginning to need the toilet really badly. I knew it was a rule that no one was allowed to leave the table.

Once we finished the meal, the colonel stood up to give a speech. I could scarcely concentrate upon it because my bum was covered in Marmite, my lips were numb from the Novocaine on every glass I had drunk from, I was dying for a piss and my mouth felt like it was on fire from the chillis. The colonel chuntered on and on. I felt like I might pass out: I was definitely on the verge of pissing myself.

Then, suddenly, someone's phone went off. I jeered. Everyone knew that mobile phones in the dining room were absolutely banned. I was alarmed when I felt my own chair vibrating. Everyone was looking at me. Someone had taped my phone to my chair.

The colonel, who was still in mid-flow, was furious. 'Right, get the axe off the wall and destroy the offending object!'

My lip trembled. An axe would destroy the SIM card; I'd lose all my numbers, and I didn't have them backed up. I wanted to plead with the colonel not to do this, but instead I took the phone from under my seat and handed it over. The officers cheered as they watched it being smashed to smithereens by the fireside.

It was then that I pissed myself. Long rivulets of piss running down my trousers.

The chaps were merciless after the meal. I got called

all sorts of names. 'Piss-pot', 'Pisser', 'Piss-snot' and so on. I tried to get cleaned up in the toilets, but I knew that my trousers wouldn't dry for the rest of the evening. The flour had mingled with the piss, and my trousers looked shocking.

Back in the bar, everyone was laughing about what had happened to me. Apparently, everyone had been in on it. They seemed to be most proud of the 'fish slapping' episode, which had taken some organisation.

I drank some more and started to get a bit angry. 'You fuckers, you smashed up my phone and then made me piss myself,' I said.

They fell about laughing, and demanded that I fought a duel. It was time for some motorbike jousting.

The next thing I knew I was being put on a motorbike in the ante-room, and given a lance someone had ripped off the oak-panelled wall. I was too drunk to know exactly what was going on, but there appeared to be another guy racing at me on another motorbike pointing another lance in my direction. I slid off my motorbike before I could get hit, but in doing so, I managed to break the lance by smashing it into the oak panelling.

The next morning, I woke up with a broken lance in my bed, and a bucket covered in puke by my pillow.

My head throbbed as I went down to breakfast. Everyone seemed wonderfully friendly. To my surprise, I didn't feel humiliated at all. It was like I had finally joined the club. I was blooded now. I was the initiated. And next year I would be doing it to someone else.

The army is one of the last of the great British institutions that still has ritualised acts of yobbery woven into its fabric. While other institutions, like the public schools, have abolished ritualised bullying such as 'fagging', the army has retained a few, such as the one above. 'It used to be the case that the army had many more of these kinds of humiliation rituals,' said Clive Winstanley, an officer in the infantry. 'Most of them have regrettably gone now, but the officer's first mess still stands proud as a time when a new guy gets a jolly good going-over! There used to be loads of others, which were much more uncivilised, but this is one of the last remaining ones. The thing is that the army really needs rituals like this because you need to learn how to take punishing jokes when you're a soldier. It prepares you for the surreal, awful comedy of battle.

'When you've gone through some ritual joshing around you feel much more part of the platoon afterwards: you feel like you've bonded with everyone, and that you're all in it together, which is a vital feeling if you know your life is going to depend upon these people. Every new recruit – from squaddie to officer – has to be blooded.'

Speaking to squaddies, who are predominantly from working-class backgrounds, I learnt that some of their initiation rituals were rather more brutal. Terry Smith, who was a squaddie for ten years and served in the first Gulf War, told me: 'The army is like any organisation full of men, like the police or the firemen; it has these initiation ceremonies. You wouldn't be a man if you didn't go through it. Everyone has to do it, and you should do it with a smile on your face even though you are bricking it. The worst one I suffered, and then did to a lot of other guys, was the pillowcase on the head trick. This is where the guys are ironing their clothes in the barracks, and suddenly someone jumps onto you, holds you down and shoves a pillowcase over your head. You then feel something very, very warm next to your head, and you realise that it is an iron. A red-hot iron. I was so frightened I had to stop myself from pissing my pants. It's partly the shock, you see. You're not expecting it. You were just doing something that seems totally safe – ironing your clothes – and now this. Anyway, what the guys do is swap the hot

iron for a cold one, take the pillowcase off and slam the iron
on your head. Then you really do piss yourself! And everyone
else pisses themselves laughing.'

Tim, who is an officer in the infantry, explained to me
that it was very important to make a distinction between the
types of yobbery that go on in initiation ceremonies and rowdy
celebrations, and the much more serious criminal yobbery
that has been highlighted in the press recently. 'In recent
years the army has suffered from some very negative publicity
in the press over cases that are still yet to be conclusively
resolved,' he said. Tim was very reluctant to talk about specific
cases, but it was clear that the deaths of four young soldiers
at the Deepcut army barracks in Surrey between 1995 and
2002 were at the back of his mind, as well as the accusa-
tions of abuse levelled at the army in Iraq.

There are two very separate things. There's the initiation
ceremonies that go on in the army, which makes it rather
like a society like the Masons: the army has its own rituals
of inducting recruits into it. And then there is criminal
behaviour. The initiation ceremonies are about testing
someone's mettle, their ability to laugh at themselves. That
is quite different from the chronic bullying and abuse that
may have gone on. You have to remember that the army
is 100,000 strong: you're bound to have your criminal
element within it. In that sense, it only reflects British society
today – which has its fair share of violent criminals. The
army as a whole despises those criminals, and does its
level best to kick them out, but inevitably some still get
through. Even in the finest orchards there are rotten apples.

The culture in the British army is unique because it is
like joining a big family that has an incredible history, which
goes back hundreds of years. This history is enshrined in
its rituals like the officer's first mess. When you are being
tested in the dining room, you are being watched very

carefully. Everyone is seeing whether you can take the strain and carry on grinning. And if you can, you're part of the family.

At his best, the average British squaddie has a great facility to laugh at himself partly because he has gone through all these weird ceremonies and, as a result, has acquired a good sense of humour. This means that when things go 'tits up', the British squaddie has an amazing ability to carry on, to improvise in the worst situations.

For nearly a millennium, the army has felt that it has an image to live up to. Its members have aspired – and still aspire – to be brutal in battle and brutal in play. As a result of its numerous escapades over the years, the army is partly responsible for generating Britain's yobbish image as an aggressive, bullish nation, which is full of people who drink heavily and get into fights.

This is an image that has been cultivated for centuries, since Henry V's British army defeated the French at the Battle of Agincourt in the 14th century. In Shakespeare's homage to Britain's great warrior king, the French king talks of Henry V being 'bred out of that bloody strain/That haunted us in our familiar paths'; he speaks of Britain's 'victorious stock', and tells his men to 'fear/The native mightiness' of the warrior king. In many ways, Henry V is the character who all British yobs consciously or unconsciously aspire to be like: hard-drinking, single-minded, bloody-minded, ruthless and victorious. The number of books, plays and films that Agincourt has inspired is a testament to just how seriously and obsessively the British take pride in this conquering king. In many ways, Henry V still personifies the aspirations of the British: feared by his enemies, but loved by his chums; jokey and drunken in play, but merciless and violent in combat.

While the image of Henry V was an emblem of the mighty

British during the Elizabethan and Jacobean periods, the colonialists in the 18th and 19th centuries invoked the John Bull stereotype in order to instil fear in their colonial subjects. Created as a satire on the British identity by Dr John Arbuthnot in 1712, John Bull went on to become a national personification of Britain. He was popularised by prints depicting a fat man in tailcoats with breeches and a Union Jack waistcoat. He wore a low topper hat on his head and frequently a bulldog yapped at his heels. Central to his power as an image was the notion that he was a hard-drinking, bullish, no-nonsense character who would beat the crap out of his enemies, but have a pint with his mates. He was part and parcel of the British Empire: aggressive but jovial, domineering but friendly. He was a yob, openly parading his great capacity to imbibe alcohol, and his fierce temper.

The dismantling of the British Empire in the post-war period left the nation's identity in question, however. We no longer had so many reasons to be so aggressive: we weren't invading anyone else's territory, we weren't constantly engaged in wars and we weren't very keen to assert our superiority over anyone.

It is perhaps no coincidence that the rise of the stereotype of the British football hooligan has coincided with a decline in the power and influence of the military. This stereotype is a corrupted version of the John Bull character. Whereas John Bull had a purpose to his yobbery – namely to subjugate his enemies so that they might comply with his colonial edicts – the football hooligan has no such purpose. He has only John Bull's aggression without his mission.

More recently, as the police have sought to curb the worst excesses of football hooliganism, new stereotypes have arisen that are even more suggestive of the aimless and purposeless aggression of the British. The comedy show *Little Britain* has created a new character who has come to personify our yob nation of the 21st century: Vicky Pollard. This teenage girl, played by Matt Lucas, is a delinquent who lives in the town of Darkly Noone. Like John Bull, she is a fat, hard-drinking character who exudes aggression. However, she does not have Bull's decency or sense of fair play, swapping her baby for a Westlife CD and shamelessly stealing off the state and other people. Arbuthnot's satire at least had some redeeming features, but there are none to Vicky Pollard, who is a welfare-dependent money-grubber. Implicit in the comedy is a serious critique of our society: our welfare state has produced a generation of teenagers who view themselves as the victims of other people's machinations. The joke in the show, of course, is that other people are the victims of them.

Most importantly, these are stereotypes that have entered the bloodstream of the nation. They are massively popular and widely discussed because they reflect our pointless aggression. Their popularity and pertinence tell us implicitly that the centuries of ritualised violence the British have inflicted upon the new generations has continued, even though we are no longer a nation at war, or a state seeking to subjugate the colonies. The reasons for our ritualised violence have disappeared, but our inbred aggression has not. We continue inflicting misery upon each other – as I have seen in my work as a teacher.

School

'I don't know what has happened to him. He's so rude now. He uses terrible language. And he shouts at me.'

I found the small boy crying in a corner of the playground. His sandy hair was covered in dust, and one of his hands was streaked in blood. I felt a surge of pity seeing him there, lying helpless on the ground.

'What happened?'

The boy turned round and I recognised him as one of my year seven pupils, Chris, a shy, quiet boy who struggled to keep up with the book we were reading in class.

The boy wiped the snot away with the sleeve of his over-sized school uniform. He was the picture of victimised, pathetic innocence.

'Nothing,' he said. 'It was nothing.'

'Are you sure?' I asked. 'Those kids weren't bullying you, were they?'

'No, no, I just fell over,' he said.

He looked at me pleadingly; he really didn't want me to persist with my questioning. 'You do know, don't you, that we won't tolerate bullying in the school. There's an anti-bullying policy.'

Chris gulped.

'I already tried that,' he said angrily. 'And look where that got me.'

Anger stabbed at my chest. I felt determined the school had to get the bastards that had beaten him up. I said, 'We'll do something. We'll get them. I promise.'

He shook his head vehemently. 'Don't. Just don't. It's no good. It's no fucking good.'

I was shocked that he swore, but decided to let it go. He got up off the ground, and together we walked back to the school. I could sense that a lot of pupils were watching us now. Chris had been left abandoned in the playground before. Initially, the bullies had rushed away from him as soon as they saw that I was approaching. Now they were gathering. I could see the disguised grins on their faces.

'All right, sir, how's it going?' one of them shouted at me.

His tone and posture indicated that this apparently inno-cent question was a challenge; he was actually asking whether I was going to do anything about Chris getting beaten up.

'Do you know anything about this?' I said, striding angrily up to him.

He immediately became aggressive. 'What you saying? What's your problem? I didn't do nothing and you're poking your finger at me.'

Chris had slunk off by now, disappearing into the throng of the corridor. I looked into the bully's face. I was shocked at how quickly his apparent bonhomie had transformed into real menace. I backed off.

Later, I told the head of year at the school what had happened, and she sighed. 'Oh my goodness, poor old Chris, they're doing it again, are they?' She promised to take some action, but she was a very busy woman and I am not sure whether she ever did follow up this incident. The bullies had already been excluded for a few days for beating up Chris. How many more exclusions would it take? Besides which, the school was now under pressure from the government and the local authorities to reduce the number of exclusions.

A week later, she told me that because Chris had refused point blank to 'grass' on the bullies, she could do nothing. We both knew that Chris had paid the price for getting the bullies excluded and didn't want to pay it again.

Over the next two years that I taught at this suburban comprehensive in outer London, I noticed a change in Chris. He stopped trying at his work, and became louder and brasher in his manner, more confident perhaps. He joined his tormentors in the playground in year eight, and began to get into trouble.

At a parents' evening over a year after I found him bleeding in the playground his mother appeared very anxious. 'I don't know what has happened to him,' she said. 'He's changed. He's so rude now. He uses terrible language. And he shouts at me. He says the most awful things. It's definitely the children he hangs around with. He goes out with them in the evenings, and I dread to think what they get up to.'

'He does seem more confident,' I said, thinking of his worrying tendency to shout out in lessons now.

This cheered her up a little. 'Yes, I suppose there's that,' she said. 'And he does seem to be holding onto his stuff now. Last year, things were always going missing from his bag: he was always losing his dinner money. Now that doesn't happen.'

After that parents' evening, I talked to Chris about what was going on. He was quite giggly, sniggering about what he got up to. 'Oh, I go round with the crew, don't I? I mean, we get into fights don't we?'

Chris was in many ways typical of the children who get involved with serious antisocial behaviour: he was struggling at school, he was being bullied and his parents had lost control of him.

Research published by the University of Edinburgh in 2004 indicates that 'victimisation predicts delinquency three years later . . . the more often victimisation is repeated, the more strongly it predicts delinquency'.[6] Most tellingly, the researcher, D.J. Smith, found that children who were bullied regularly at the age of 12 were most likely to be delinquents when they were 15 years old. This was because these children, like Chris, often attempted to befriend their bullies, and ended up moving in the same circle as them: a cycle of victimisation and offending then occurred.

Jamie James, 29, who has a long criminal record, explained to me what first set him on the path to being a serial offender.

Schools can be a breeding ground for yobs. One person can influence loads of other people. If the cocky one starts bigging it up, and proves himself to be successful, then everyone else can follow. When I was at primary school, I was getting bullied. Bullied very badly. Being picked upon. Called names. I didn't know what to do about it, until an older boy told me that I should be fighting back. He showed me how to look after myself: how to punch, how to give as good as I got. I really looked up to this boy, Ryan, because he saved me from so much misery. You see, I took on my bullies. I whacked them in the face with the moves that Ryan had shown me. They didn't touch me then. After that, after I had proved myself, Ryan introduced me to a lot of people who went on to form part of the gang that was to lead me into so much trouble later on at secondary school.

When I was in school I was a nightmare. Once, I tried to get away from some prefects and climbed up onto the roof and fell through a skylight, smashing it up. I thought I was going to get roasted for this. I shouldn't have been mucking around on the roof. But instead, I got a lot of sympathy because I made out the whole thing had been an accident. I thought it was the best thing on earth. I got two weeks off school and the kudos of smashing up the school property. I loved the glory. I didn't give a toss about school, really. I wanted to get expelled because all my mates were hanging around on street corners, up to no good. I wanted to have a proper excuse to be on the streets. But there was a teacher at the school who refused to expel me no matter what I did. I suppose I should be grateful to him now because he ensured I was educated at least a little bit.

Jamie James's case is a variation upon what D.J. Smith found – a bullied boy finding answers in another group of offenders rather than looking to the teachers at his school to solve the problem. James now runs a youth organisation that tries to help gang members sort their lives out, and feels that his experiences are fairly typical. 'Having interviewed hundreds of gang members now, I can safely say that nearly every gang member has been seriously bullied to begin with.'

If we accept James's point, then recent statistics issued by Childline are worrying for a number of reasons. This charity reported that there was a 42 per cent rise in the number of children calling their helpline about bullying in

2004, with 31,000 children calling them compared with nearly 21,000 the previous year.[7] These are shocking figures and indicate a growing discipline crisis in our schools, but they also suggest that we may be creating a problem that could increase exponentially if something is not done soon. Victims go on to become perpetrators, who pick on more victims, who then create perpetrators, and so on, in an ever-downward spiral.

Victims of their parents or are parents their victims?

'When my dad learned about all the crimes I had been involved in, he punched me in the face.'

The most common stereotype of the delinquent child is that his parents bully him. The kitchen-sink dramas of the 1960s promoted the view that parents enduring very severe social deprivation vented their frustrations upon their children, who then went on to vent their spleen on the streets. There is undoubtedly a strong element of truth in the stereo-type. D.J. Smith's study *Parenting and Delinquency at Ages 12 to 15* concluded that inconsistent and harsh punishments meted out upon a child by a parent significantly contributed towards delinquency.

Interestingly, however, contrary to the stereotype, there is no direct link between a parent's wealth and a child's propensity to offend. In other words, just because you come from a poor background doesn't necessarily mean that you will be more likely to be an offender. The ability of a parent to inculcate good social skills in a child is more important.[8]

'When my dad learned about all the crimes I had been involved in, he punched me in the face,' Jamie James confessed to me.

I asked Jamie why he didn't punch him back, and Jamie explained that he had been brought up to have absolute respect for his parents. While Jamie had nothing but praise for his parents, I sensed that he had grown up in a very disciplinarian environment where thoughts and feelings were not discussed at all. Apparently, his father didn't know about the havoc he had been causing on the streets of Bexley Heath until Jamie was 16, despite numerous arrests and cautions.

I grew up in a very strict household, where you always obeyed your dad. If you didn't, you'd stay in your room. We'd have to put our hands up in the air and one leg on the floor. That don't sound bad but when you've been doing it for 15 or 20 minutes your arms and legs start wanting to die. I was very scared to tell my dad what was going on because I would be in so much trouble. If my dad had found out what I was doing from such an early age, he'd have sent me somewhere like to my grandad's in the Caribbean.

As soon as I left my dad's house, I felt that was it. I could do what I wanted. I was free as a bird! I felt that no one could catch me. Well, no one that is except my dad, who occasionally ventured out of the house to see what was going on in the street. The funniest example of this was when my dad nearly caught me on a motorbike racing away down the street. Me and my mate had been behaving like yobs, making a big noise with the bike, revving it up and down the road. Anyway, my dad, not knowing that it was me, came belting out of the house, steam coming out of his ears. Our dog came running out as well. Suddenly, I found my dog yapping at my heels. The dog recognised me, but my dad didn't because I was quite a long way off and wearing a balaclava. He was really mad about the noise and started chasing after the yobs on the bike. It was agonising because the bike wouldn't get going properly, and my dog nearly dragged me off it. But luckily, just in the nick of time, the bike started up and we raced away. My dad phoned the police to say that there were boys riding up and down the hill. But he never caught me. He never caught me. Ever. It was only when the police contacted him about one of my crimes when I was 16 that he found out. It was then that he hit me.

Another former street robber that I talked to told me about how his mother had died when he was 11, and his father had brought them up 'by hand'. 'He was a tough man, my dad,' Phil told me. 'There was no backchatting with him. You got a whack round the back of the head if you said anything rude, or you didn't do what you were told. There was no messing around at all.'

Much like Jamie James, Phil was very reluctant to be critical of his father. 'I was brought up to respect him, and I still do,' he said to me. 'You see, although there wasn't much money around the house, he always made sure that I got what I wanted: trainers, jewellery, clothes. He shelled out for me. I can't complain.'

Both Jamie and Phil were the victims of poor parenting: households where emotions were expected to be buried away under the floorboards, and where very severe beatings were given for relatively small offences. Perhaps most importantly, administering corporal punishment does not teach a child the power of empathy or rationality: children do not learn to consider other people's feelings, they only think about the consequences. When the consequences are removed in a different environment – such as the street or at school – then the child believes that they can do anything. Which is exactly what both Phil and Jamie thought outside their home environment.

At the other end of the scale is the hapless parent who is bullied by his or her children. For me, Chris's mother fell into this category. When I spoke to her when Chris was in year nine she appeared frightened of the consequences of reminding Chris of the right way to behave. 'He just goes into these great rages and shouts at me,' she said in a low whisper on the phone. 'I don't know what to do. He is so aggressive and moody all the time. It's quite frightening, really.'

I have no doubt that since humans have been living on this earth there have always been moody teenagers, but the situation of the child that bullies the parent is a relatively new phenomenon. Often it happens in single-parent families, but I have come across it in households where there are two parents as well. Adults are no longer viewed by society at large as trustworthy figures, and this distrust fatally undermines a weak parent's authority.

'One of the major problems we get at the magistrate's court with youth offenders is parents not setting any boundaries at all for their children,' says Mike Batten, who is chairman of the London Borough of Redbridge bench of magistrates, and chair of a judicial issues group that oversees the whole of north-east London. 'Either because they are scared of them or because they are not concerned about them, they allow their children, who are often as young as 12, to stay out on the streets at night until one or two in the morning. These very same children have often been very sheltered as younger children; not allowed out in the park because of over-exaggerated worries about paedophiles and strangers. As a consequence, they haven't really been socialised to behave in public spaces. And they cause chaos with their fighting, under-age drinking and vandalism.'

An incident recounted to me by the cultural commentator Kate Colquhoun is instructive of the sorts of contradictory messages parents are sending their children in a world where parents view their children as victims of a pernicious, perverted adult world.

I think that parents often send very mixed messages to their children now, and that this leads to a confusion of values. I'll give you a small illustration of this. A few years ago, I saw a four-year-old child drop a sweet wrapper on the street. I said, in my nicest possible voice, 'Come on, darling, pick up that sweet wrapper.' The child looked at me and blinked. I don't think she had ever been told to do that before. She scuttled into the shop where her mother was buying some sweets and beer, and told her what had happened. The mother came striding out of the shop, and started screaming at me, 'You shouldn't fucking tell my child off, you fucking cunt. Who do you think you are, you stuck-up cunt?'

I stood my ground. I hate being bullied like that. I replied that I was only asking her to do what I would ask my own children to do. She snorted. And then, as a final riposte, she turned on her own child and yelled, 'You make sure you throw your own fucking sweet papers in the bin next time.' I find this encounter interesting because it is indicative of what I think is wrong with Britain today. There are no common rules, except that everyone should mind their own business. We are much more isolated than we used to be. And this depresses me because it allows a free reign to bullies who feel that they can say and do anything without censure from the wider community.

The public feels that it no longer has the right to interfere. This is a cross-class phenomenon. Recently, I encountered the child of an upper-class parent bullying a little boy in a playground – I was acquainted with the parent and the child – and felt that it was appropriate for me to tell the boy to stop hurling balls at his intended victim. When he ignored my request, seeing that a fuming parent was standing beside me, I raised my voice and told the boy to stop it, reminding him that what he was doing was totally out of order. The ball throwing stopped after this, but his parent was angry that I had admonished his son like this, and stormed over to me, saying that he was furious and that he was certain I would never speak to my own child like that. I apologised for raising my voice and was about to explain that I probably would speak to my own child like that if he was behaving in that way, when the parent grabbed hold of his charge in a vicious and violent manner, and disappeared from view. There was no chance for a rational discussion, no chance for me to justify my actions, just an angry departure.

Children are victims of this paranoid parenting, but they also exploit their own parents' fears. One pupil of mine, irate that I had complained that she was missing all her deadlines for handing in work, told her mother that I was bullying her. The mother, a social worker, phoned me and said, 'You know, threatening to throw my daughter off the A level course because she hasn't done some work is tantamount to psychological abuse, and there is legislation which prohibits these sorts of threats. I believe you are trying to harm my child's mental well-being, and may well take steps to remedy this situation if you are not careful.'

I was astonished by this threat but, after reflection, realised that it was a logical extension of the presupposition that all adults are abusers of children.

So we can divide parents into three categories. Firstly, there are the authoritarian parents who brook no dissent and send their child out into a much more liberal world, which causes the child to think that he can do what he wants. Having lived in a world of fear, his conscience is chronically under-developed: there is only what he can get away with and what he can't. Secondly, there is the opposite of this, the parent who has no boundaries and rules, leaving his child to be the victim of his own desires. This sort of child drifts around in a haze, very unclear about what he should or should not be doing. He is very prone to be a victim of the culture of his school. Thirdly, there is a mixture of both of these two types of parent: this is the authoritarian parent who believes that nobody but him or her can impose any boundaries upon their child, the parent who is suspicious of all adult authority except his own. This last type of parent is the worst because the child is left fatally confused. The child absorbs his parent's aggression and suspicion of rules and regulations, and of other adults in general. Schools are seeing more and more of these troubled children.

Victims on the streets

'You know, we get hurt and killed and we are scared but you gotta keep moving.'

In Swinton shopping centre, I talked to a group of 14-year-old boys about their lives in this troubled suburb of Greater Manchester. They were sitting on a bench that was right opposite the boarded-up Yates' Wine Lodge where Frank Buckley, a 47-year-old father of two, was murdered in an unprovoked attack by a gang of youths over a year before in 2004. They knew all about the murder, and the youth who was convicted of it. 'You get a lot of gangs roaming about here,' one boy, Terry, told me. 'You have to be very careful.'

It was clear from talking to them that they had all been the victims of various assaults. 'I was walking down near the town hall one night when we was chased by a gang of about 30, with their hoods up. They had sticks and bats. They were going to mash us up,' another boy, Peter, told me. 'Another time near the town hall, one of that gang drew a knife out, and asked me for a pound. "You got a spare quid mate?" he said. "Or do you want to chew on this knife?" I gave him my money. I didn't want to die!'

The other boys told me about a litany of assaults they had

all experienced at school. 'Some of the girls like to poke you in the eye, or the lads like to "keck you"; get you from behind and pull up your pants so that they go right into your crack hole! But that isn't as bad as them pulling your pants down, or happy slapping you. It's scary at school. That's why you have to move around in your own gang. Otherwise you die,' Terry told me.

It was clear, however, that the boys gave as good as they got. A local man walked past us as I was interviewing the group; he was in his early thirties and looked very muscular and suntanned, but he got the treatment from the boys. 'Oi, fucker, you think you're tough, or what?' one of the group shouted at him.

He ignored them and moved on, seemingly used to such abusive comments. It was very obvious that while everyone in the group had been a victim of yob culture, they were also dishing it out. Superintendent David Baines, who is the police chief in charge of the Swinton area, told me that because many of the schools and parents had lost their authority over the children in the area, inevitably the children were looking for other ways to protect themselves. 'A lot of children think that being in a gang is a form of protection from the abuse,' he said. 'With the breakdown of parental authority, the gang becomes a form of family. This is why I am very vigilant about letting my own teenage daughter out at night. I know what goes on round here. I know how easy it is for teenagers to get sucked into yob culture if they are allowed out to go drinking and clubbing late at night. My daughter complains bitterly about not being allowed out, but I know I am doing what is best for her. Too many parents have lost control of their children and allow them to roam around the streets, getting drunk and getting into fights. And don't think this is just a working-class phenomenon: it affects middle-class families as well. We have plenty of middle-class children being arrested for yobbish behaviour.'

The problem with having a gang as your protector is that it is frequently abusive to its members. In Carbrain, Cumbernauld, a satellite town of Glasgow in Scotland, I talked to a gang member who spoke of the trauma of having to fight other members of the gang in order to prove himself. 'It's like you have to be initiated,' said Taj, an articulate, thoughtful 17-year-old who was hanging around with his gang outside the local off-licence. He was a mixed-race boy with a smiley, welcoming face and a sensitive, perceptive air about him. He had a bottle of Buckfast in his hand, and offered me a swig of this cheap alcoholic drink before he explained what he meant. 'The Carbrain gang makes its members have a serious fight before they become members of the gang. That means you have to smash someone's face in, or get your face smashed in. I fought my friend here.'

Taj's friend grinned. It was very clear from his grin who had won the fight. His mate, George, tussled Taj's hair, and said, 'He's one of us now!'

Later, Taj opened up to me more fully, explaining the full extent of the horrors he had endured in the Cumbernauld area.

Personally, yes, I have been a victim, but that ain't new, everyone here will have been a victim. You know, I've took beatings and been jumped or chased a long time before I was involved in gangs. It's just a day-to-day thing here for someone to try and rob or stab you. My first time was when I was at a firework show near Westfield when I was 12 and some guy pulled me around a corner and put a knife to my neck. I didn't even have any money! I had nothing to give him! So I'd say every gang member and every one here has been a victim in some way. I'll break it down for you. Round here you got young teams and young teams are the gangs from different areas, and in the young teams hold many different types of criminal, from the muggers, to the bigger robbers, to the dealers. If you ain't making much dealing you're damn sure in a tough spot because we all gotta eat. That's a social problem, that, because we grew up here and have had to adapt or get hurt. It's hard to get a good job so you have to resort to crime. You know, we get hurt and killed and we are scared, but you gotta keep moving. And a lot of people don't see or look for the reasons behind what we're doing; they just look at the dirt and make their own decisions. No one's forced to join the gang but most people do. A lot of the things we do look like senseless violence, but normally someone owes someone money or their friend or family does. Just two days ago there was seven people at my friend's house looking for me. I wasn't in the house, but I walked by and they tried to get me, but his dad dragged me away. It was my fault; I beat someone up. He called me 'a black fuck' twice and I flipped and kicked him twice in the face. I ain't trying to sound hard, I just want to give you a real and graphic picture of how we are living around here. I think the reason we are violent is because to make a living here you need to be and it becomes a part of our personality. There's a saying for it around here: 'Maybe we crazy, but this is the way we came up'.

It isn't just in the socially deprived areas of Britain where this phenomenon can be observed. It occurs even in the most surprising groups. I interviewed a lesbian woman who joked about the way in which gay people can victimise each other, but there was an undercurrent of yobbery to her story that was alarmingly similar to what I learnt in Swinton and Carbrain. This is what Vanessa, a 19-year-old student, told me.

I was at Hyde Park Corner, enjoying myself with my girl-friend, Anastasia, on a gay pride march. We wanted to have a good time, but there was this butch lesbian standing behind us. Me and my student mates all started calling her Dykey McDykison because she looked like a man with lots of facial hair. It was great fun making fun of her.

I said to her face, 'Sort it out, mate, I can't work out whether you are a bloke or a girl.'

My friend Carl joined in with: 'A bit of colour wouldn't kill you, neither would make-up! And when was the last time you got laid?'

At first she took it quite well, but then she started hitting on my girlfriend, so I said, 'Hands off, she's not yours, you great big lesbian.'

At this, she raised her arms in the air, and waved them about like a football hooligan, growling at us, 'It's all in the fun of Pride, why don't you just leave it?'

Carl went, 'Fuck off.'

My girlfriend started dissing Dykey McDykison by saying, 'She's not even in my league. I wouldn't worry about it.'

But Dykey got defensive and started going on about how her last girlfriend was a right 'stunner'.

We all laughed at this, 'Wasn't she a man called Dave?' We howled with laughter. It is great making fun of really dykey lesbians because they live up to all the stereotypes. It's weird if you go to G-A-Y – you'll see all the guys sipping white wine spritzers and the women downing pints like real geezers. Nearly all the women have short, horrible spiky hair, loads of earrings in one ear, leather wrist-bands, combat pants and Doc Martens. The stereotypes are true in my view.

So the big butch dyke goes, 'If you little bastards don't shut up, I'm going to stab you.'

She had a knife we'd seen her use to cut her leather wrist-band.

At this point, we started to get worried, but I replied, 'If you stab us, I am going to glass you, you big bitch.'

For a minute or two there was a stand-off, as we stared at each other in silence. I had a bottle in my hand, ready to crack it against her neck if she approached me with her knife. After a few minutes another lot of my student mates, Claudia and her friends – Kara and Soul – arrived, and helped me to intimidate the woman enough to get her to go away without any actual violence.

You have to be careful with lesbians, especially if you are one. Lesbians are competitive. They are like men. Not like gay men. They are all like butch 'he' men. They go for the prettiest girl. And it's all or nothing. It's not about feeling a lot of gay solidarity, about feeling that you're fighting prejudice together; it's about looking after yourself and your partner. It is a world where you have to keep your wits about you to avoid losing either your girlfriend or your life because lesbians will do what is necessary to get what they want. You have to fight back.

I found my interview with Vanessa particularly interesting because it was clear to me that the 'butch lesbian' who pulled a knife on her was sorely provoked. One couldn't simply label Vanessa as a 'victim' of a threatened assault. She was instrumental in creating the situation. Nevertheless, the 'butch lesbian' was armed and ready for a fight, and the fact is that there is a subculture of violent bullying within the gay movement that has many similarities with the sorts of behaviour that I heard about in Britain's roughest council estates.

The links between victimisation and offending are therefore complex. As D.J. Smith's research at Edinburgh University shows, 'young offenders are often also victims of crime', and offenders often seek answers and redress from the people who have bullied them or, in Jamie James's case, people who are rather like them.

The upsurge in violence that Britain has experienced in the last ten years could be explained by the fact that there are many more victims of crime who then go on to become perpetrators. And there are now many more items to steal. Mike Batten pointed out to me that the advent of new technology has meant that there has been a huge increase in street robbery over the last ten years. 'Objects like Gameboys, Playstations, mobile phones, digital cameras, iPods, mini-DVD recorders and so on just didn't exist on the same scale over ten years ago,' he said. 'As a result, no one was being robbed for them. Now we see a very large number of street robberies coming through the courts which are about people having their mobile phones nicked off them.'

If we accept the University of Edinburgh's research as correct, then the vast increase in street robbery might explain why we appear to be seeing an exponential increase in offending: victims are becoming offenders, which in turn leads to more victims, who become offenders, and so on.

'Social deprivation was far worse when I was a child and there was far less offending,' says Batten, who is now 59.

Social deprivation can't explain the explosion in crime we are seeing. What worries me from a judicial point of view is that a society survives by one generation passing codes on to the next. Young people are not getting the right sort of quality contact with adults. They are not learning about the rules that bind society together. They are learning from their own juvenile group, and the older generation is not having an influence upon their development. I grew up on a council estate, in a very poor area of London, much poorer than any area in London now, but I knew if I made a nuisance of myself, the neighbours would notice. There were authority figures around: the bus conductor, the park keeper, the caretaker of the estate. We accepted adult authority. If a neighbour knocked on my parent's door and complained about me, they were listened to, and the situation was sorted out. But now, they are told to fuck off.

There are no collective rules any more. There used to be a joke among magistrates a few years back – we'd talk about some fairly hair-raising characters, and then always finish our conversations by saying, 'They'll grow out of it,' but I am not so sure that this is going to be the case with the youths we are seeing now.

The advent of our brave new world of technology might explain why we are such a troubled society now: it has fuelled a 'grab-what-you-can' culture that has encouraged its traumatised victims into becoming bullies. Our children are learning in the playgrounds and classrooms of our schools, on the streets of our cities and towns, that once you have been beaten up by 'them', it is better to join them and beat up someone else rather than to receive another beating.

Desperate for power

'You will fucking report exactly what I tell you to report; you'll stick to my fucking schedule and nothing else'. Alistair Campbell

'If you can't beat them, join them' is exactly what the Labour Party thought after its bitter election defeat in 1992. One person who took Kinnock's defeat particularly badly was his friend and mentor Alistair Campbell. Later on, while working as Tony Blair's chief spin doctor, he was to become the second most powerful person in Britain.

In 1987, during his spell as a journalist for the *Daily Mirror*, Campbell became very close to the Kinnocks, becoming a 'mixture of adviser, minder, speech-writer, family friend and manservant'.[9] He made no secret of his partisanship, even though nominally he was supposed to be an impartial member of the press. He distorted his press reports so that they were always favourable to the Labour Party, and harangued journalists who were not supportive of the party.

He was also a fan of the *Daily Mirror*'s corrupt proprietor Robert Maxwell. When Maxwell died he got into a fight in the Houses of Parliament with the political editor of the *Guardian*, Michael White, because of something disrespectful White said about Maxwell. Campbell hit White, who then retaliated, and a fight ensued. They received a warning from the Sergeant-at-Arms of the House, instructing them not to fight again.[10] It was this combativeness that Campbell brought to bear against his enemies when he became press spokesman for the new leader of the Labour Party, Tony Blair, in September 1994.

David Cracknell, the political editor of *The Sunday Times* told me:

> The Labour Party changed after 1992. It was then that the aggressive approach to the media came to the fore. A new breed of spin doctors rose to prominence: Alastair Campbell and Peter Mandelson in particular. They took no prisoners. If they didn't like a story you wrote, they would get at reporters by mocking them in front of their peers at lobby briefings or sometimes even phone your editor to complain about you. Campbell once humiliated a journalist by saying his story was 'C.R.A.P' in one briefing, even though the story turned out to be true. Other Labour spin doctors would simply say what you wrote was 'bollocks' – again a non-denial denial. They didn't stop once they had won power either. I myself received such calls, including one from Campbell and another from John Prescott, berating me for stories I have done. These are people with short tempers, and who take pride into bullying people into submission. It is a macho thing, but it all stems back to what they see as the unfair treatment Neil Kinnock received at the hands of the press in 1992. The old joke about it

was 'The Sun Wot Won It' for John Major still stings, that they clutched defeat from the jaws of victory; they still blame the papers for that. Because the top people behave like this, it has infected the whole party. We have even seen brawls in the House of Commons between New Labour MPs and those who dare to speak out.

Like the victims of the gangs we have already looked at, Labour decided to make some alliances with their bullies and, if necessary, adopt their techniques. The BBC in particular was a target for 'day-to-day bullying'[11] about what stories they would run on the Labour Party: Campbell had several subordinates who, infected by his yobbish zeal, would force the cowering corporation to run favourable stories.

Like a true gang leader, Campbell would insist on total obedience. He said to Jeremy Vine, the BBC political correspondent, 'You will fucking report exactly what I tell you to report, you'll stick to my fucking schedule and nothing else'.[12] Other people in the media found his bullying difficult to stomach because it was clear that Labour were going to win the 1997 election without all of this media manipulation. Campbell's riposte to this was, 'I'm preparing to win the election after next, not this one.'

His antipathy towards certain sections of the media, however, has to be understood within the context of the *Sun* headline, which told everyone to switch the lights off when Kinnock came to power. Campbell was giving the media the very same treatment that he felt had been meted out to the Labour Party in 1992. They'd been whacked then, but now it was his turn to do the whacking.

Campbell made a great effort to win over his worst tormentor, the *Sun*, much in the same way the newly initiated bully into a gang knows that he has to curry favour with the leader. Campbell courted the News International Corporation, of which the *Sun* is a part, and urged Tony Blair to meet the owner, the legendary Australian Rupert Murdoch, on Hayman Island in the summer of 1995. After that meeting, the *Sun* became a staunch supporter of New Labour.

Gotcha! - Media yobbery

'It was the most grotesque outburst of a mix of slander and racism that I have ever been subjected to. If it had been in a public place he would have been arrested.'

While Rupert Murdoch himself was far from a victim – his father being a wealthy Australian newspaper owner – his best editors were victims, or at least perceived themselves to be. Having acquired the *Sun* in the late 1960s, Murdoch appointed Larry Lamb to be its editor. It was Lamb's editorship that made the *Sun* the most influential newspaper in the land.

Lamb was a classic victim who channelled all his energy as editor into attacking and defeating what he perceived to be the main source of his pain: the *Daily Mirror*. He had had to work excruciating hours at the *Mirror* for ten years but had only risen to chief sub-editor, a relatively lowly position in the hierarchy. He had then lost his job, and remained bitter towards the *Mirror* for the rest of his career.

It was Lamb's bitterness towards the *Mirror* and certain elitist elements of the British press that fuelled his drive to make the *Sun* so popular. More than anyone, he set up the template for the modern media culture. He made topless girls, sex scandal and celebrity gossip a staple of the breakfast table. His successor as editor of the *Sun*, Kelvin MacKenzie, was from a similar background, and even more outrageous in his approach. MacKenzie passed only one O level before working in newspapers. His general loathing of the liberal elite can probably be explained by his educational failure. Throughout his career, MacKenzie has poured scorn on people who are much more academically successful than him. While he continued with Lamb's innovations like the Page 3 girl, MacKenzie brought a new level of yobbery to the headlines that the *Sun* ran. Most famously, during the Falklands War of 1982, MacKenzie ran headlines like 'STICK THIS UP YOUR JUNTA' in response to the Argentinean dictatorship's invasion of the remote islands in the south Atlantic. Within weeks, the paper was marketing T-shirts with the headline imprinted upon them. Perhaps most disgracefully, MacKenzie ran the headline 'GOTCHA' after the Argentinean battleship the *Belgrano* had been sunk by British torpedoes, drowning 1,200 sailors.

By making the *Sun* such an influential paper, Murdoch bred the conditions that enabled two other victims-cum-bullies to hijack British culture further. After working in advertising, David Sullivan became a pornographer, a sauna and sex shop owner. In 1982 two of his saunas were found to be brothels and were prosecuted.[13] One could speculate that it was this prosecution that really motivated him to get the better of the establishment. He had the last laugh. In 1986 he set up *Sunday Sport*, which continues until this day to publish an unremitting diet of pornography. Its salacious covers nestle beside *The Times* and the *Telegraph* in the newsagents, a reminder that yobbery has become mainstream.

An investigation into the background of another newspaper magnate and pornographer, Richard Desmond, the son of Jewish parents, reveals that he is motivated by combating what he sees as Britain's anti-Semitism. He used the funds from his pornography empire to buy the *Express* newspapers in 2000. Perhaps his anger at British anti-Semitism explains why he wanted to own the rival paper to the *Daily Mail*. Desmond has repeatedly criticised the support shown to Hitler by the *Daily Mail* in the 1930s, which he says 'represents everything I hate'.

Most notably, in April 2004 Desmond launched an astonishing attack on the *Telegraph* bosses at a meeting of their joint venture print works. He called Jeremy Deedes, the *Telegraph* chief executive, a 'miserable piece of shit', and said all Germans were Nazis. He ordered *Express* executives to sing '*Deutschland uber Alles*' and make '*Sieg Heil!*' salutes. Deedes said: 'It was the most grotesque outburst of a mix of slander and racism that I have ever been subjected to. If it had been in a public place he would have been arrested.' Desmond was upset at the *Telegraph* being run by Germans, who included the managing director Hugo Drayton and printing director Bill Ellerd-Styles. He then proceeded to lose his temper and called the *Telegraph* directors 'fucking cunts' and 'fucking wankers'.

This highly aggressive approach is mirrored by the hysterical, hectoring style of all the tabloids. In print, they may swear less than Desmond in full flow, but their tone is identical; the public is to be head-butted by their headlines, whacked across the forehead with their sensational stories and kicked in the crotch by their titillating images.

The *Guardian* columnist and former editor of the *Mirror* Roy Greenslade told me about the influence the tabloids have had upon British culture as a whole.

> On the positive side, the tabloids made a huge contribution towards the democratisation of Britain because they were so influential in breaking down the rigid class structures that existed in the 1950s and 60s. They questioned the old social order, sneered at the worlds of the gentlemen's clubs and the public-school dominated establishment. In my view, this was a good thing.
>
> However, I feel they also threw the baby out with the bathwater. They no longer adhered to the aristocratic, upper

middle-class values of the old-fashioned press, the values of decency, of being polite, of being sensitive to people's privacy. They encouraged a situation where the concept of the individual's rights was paramount, and where it was all right to be disrespectful towards anyone if there was something 'sensational' to be raked up. This has led to a ridiculous situation where the tabloids bemoan the need for ASBOs, and yet at the same time want something done about antisocial behaviour.

Ironically, they have contributed to the yobbish atmosphere of our society by delivering hysterical headlines that have inflamed the minds of their readers. Most of the tabloids fill their pages with semi-naked women and make their money by titillating their readers, and yet also pretend to be outraged by the latest sex scandal they have unearthed. Recently, with the advent of public relations people like Max Clifford, a lot of people have attempted to become famous by doing something outrageous which will catch the media's eye. This has led to a situation where the scandals have had to become progressively worse. So, for example, if someone wants to get some attention, it is no longer good enough for them to sleep with one person, they have to sleep with three – and their dog. This has resulted in newspapers becoming increasingly vulgar in their approach, and has cheapened our culture. It is very worrying that young girls now want to emulate this sort of behaviour. The diet of bad language which streams out of all the media now has undoubtedly meant that swearing has become so commonplace in public that no one bothers to comment upon it. When I was a child in the fifties, you knew that if you said 'fuck' in public you would be scorned.

Perhaps most disturbingly, it is the mixture of this vulgarity with a strong sense of self-righteousness that can lead to the most serious problems. The News of the World's campaign against paedophiles a few years ago led to innocent people such as paediatricians being attacked just because their names had a passing resemblance to the word 'paedophile'. Now I have absolutely no sympathy for paedophiles, but this sort of behaviour by a newspaper is alarming.

In his later years, Larry Lamb, who I knew, bewailed the fact that he hadn't guessed what his editorship of the *Sun* would lead to, and just how influential the paper would be in the wider culture. He hated the way people had become coarser and was disturbed by his own role in contributing towards this. In many ways, though, while he was editor, he was unaware of the influence the *Sun* was having. However, his successor, Kelvin MacKenzie, was quite different; MacKenzie wanted to kick at the establishment. Neither editors were that keen on Page 3 girls. MacKenzie, in particular, was not at all enthusiastic. But they went along with it because they knew it was what the punters wanted. It was under MacKenzie's editorship that the whole Page 3 thing took off. I am not of the view that pornography is a direct cause of sex crimes, but it does create a sleazy mood in society. In my view, it is the seedy combination of self-righteousness and trivial scandals that is the most pernicious aspect of the tabloids.

This hypocrisy was no better exemplified than in the way the Sun and the media generally presented the story of Rebecca Wade, the editor of the *Sun*, being arrested for assaulting her husband, the actor Ross Kemp. According to some reports he received a cut lip. Her own paper made light of the incident saying in a small insert that it was just 'a silly row which got out of hand'. Most of the other papers were positively humorous about the incident, with *The Times* dubbing her 'the Ginger Ninja'. Wade had campaigned against domestic violence in her paper, and had run numerous stories about the foibles of other celebrities, but obviously did not mete out the same treatment to herself. As Mary Riddell said in the *Observer* there is definitely a 'whiff of double-standards' here.[14]

In recent years, the tabloids' influence on popular culture has declined while television's has increased significantly. Since the late 1980s, it is TV personalities – footballers, soap stars, rock singers – who have shaped Britain's cultural attitudes. The theatre director, TV presenter and scientist Jonathan Miller feels that certain TV shows make loutish figures 'acceptably charismatic' and therefore could be encouraging yobbish behaviour.

> If you take characters like the Mitchell brothers in *EastEnders* and examine their representation, you can see that they are deliberately constructed as alluring figures, and their bullying and harassing of other people could be imitated by people who didn't know any better.
>
> I definitely feel that in my own area of Camden Town there has been a marked deterioration in people's behaviour. The people in London seem to be becoming increasingly menacing, and I have great misgivings about living in Britain now because it has changed so much. Unfortunately, politicians and the media don't seem that interested in improving the situation. There was a time in the early 20th century when politicians and other figures of authority viewed the values of decency and sobriety as essential virtues of a civilised society. These values are certainly not celebrated by our politicians or our media now.

While it is very hard to conclusively show that the media has a direct effect upon people's behaviour, there is no doubt that it sets a tone; it provides an atmosphere and backdrop to our lives now because it is all-pervasive. The advent of the Internet, mobile phones and portable video players has resulted in the media being much more pervasive than it used to be, and means that the mainstream media, with its huge financial clout, can dominate. For example, you would have had to be living in a cocoon to avoid knowing something about the reality TV show *Big Brother* in recent years. This show locked the contestants, chosen from the general public, in a house, and gave them various humiliating tasks to complete while filming them 24/7. The public then voted out their least favourite contestant at regular intervals. It has proved to be the most popular TV show in recent years in Britain. This programme, more than any other, has proved to be a barometer of people's yobbery: it has become more and more vulgar with each successive instalment.

The most disturbing element of it is that people seem to have imitated some of the show's attitudes, if not the contestants' behaviour. The most traumatic illustration of this is what happened to the 20-year-old contestant Lesley Saunderson. According to her, the programme's directors deliberately edited the highlighted extracts of the show – which most people watched – so that she was portrayed in a negative light and became the show's 'bitch'. Since appearing on the show, she alleges she has been glassed and kicked by jealous girls in nightclubs, verbally abused by people who think she is evil and constantly hassled by men. She said: 'People ask me how they get on the show . . . I give them one piece of advice: don't do it.'[15]

Sanderson's experiences reveal just how gullible the British public is: people do not see through the very artificial narrative of *Big Brother* and thinks that what they are seeing is 'real people' and their genuine characters when, of course, all they are viewing is a television director's spin on the events that have happened. This example also shows how television can goad the public into yobbish behaviour leaving a young person like Sanderson utterly traumatised.

Bullies and victims in the City

'Virtually every day he would shout at someone by saying that they were "fucking useless, crap at everything, bitches and cunts".'

Yobbery is commonplace in the City of London. Fred grew up in Essex, left school at 16 and worked for a few banks before applying to be a money broker. His interview for the job was unlike any other he had.

> I was down in the pit – this is where all the brokers make their deals – talking to the guys, explaining what experience I had, the stuff I knew about, when I noticed that all the guys seemed to be laughing and pointing at me. I couldn't understand it at first. What the hell was so funny? And then one of the guys told me that it was because I looked like Virgil from *Thunderbirds* – the 1960s children's puppet show. So I got up and did this stupid Virgil walk, just like the puppet does in the show, walking around with jerky arms and feet. As I was doing this, all the brokers were singing the tune and stamping their feet. Everyone was pissing themselves laughing. A few days later, I learned I got the job. Walking around like Virgil definitely helped me get it.

Most importantly, Fred showed the guys in the pit that he was up for a laugh, and was willing to make a fool of himself. But there was a darker side to these sorts of antics.

> As a trainee, you do get a lot of abuse. The brokers would shout at you to get the coffee or their doughnuts or whatever, and if you messed up, you didn't live it down for the rest of the day. You were called a 'cunt' non-stop. 'You fucking cunt, what the fuck do you think you were doing,

cunt?' they would scream at you if you forgot to put the sugar in their coffee. If you didn't laugh it off, you were screwed because the guys would pick on you. If you were someone with a short fuse and lost your temper easily, then you'd find that they'd pick on you, waiting for you to explode, and then fall around laughing, shouting out about what a cunt you were.

I have seen grown men of 25 on the verge of tears because they've had the piss ripped out of them so much they just can't hack it. They've had to leave the office rather than let the others watch them cry. But once you've passed your probationary year as a trainee, there is a brotherly arm around the shoulder, and it is like you are part of the club. Now it's your turn to do it to the next trainee.

The thing is that learning to take this sort of abuse is a really good grounding for what is to come. Customers might not call you a cunt all day but they can be bloody awkward and if you don't keep your calm then you lose important business and money. So, in a way, it's all part of the training.

Fred was very reluctant to condemn this sort of behaviour, which he didn't see as bullying, but just as part of the culture of the City. However, some people I spoke to took a different view.

'The trouble is when you've been the victim of bullying a vicious cycle starts up,' says Jill, who worked for over twenty years in one of the leading investment banks in the City of London. She described to me a world which had changed considerably since the 1980s. Rather like the political scene which New Labour and Campbell so successfully hijacked, there was the remnants of the 'gentleman's club' culture around when she first started working: a world where business was done with 'chaps you trusted', where no-one was pushed too hard, and whether you went to Eton or

Harrow or not was the most important aspect of your character. Black Monday, on 19 October 1987, which was the largest one-day decline in recorded stock market history, smashed that complacent world and heralded in a new 'yobbish' world of market traders whose only interest was making money.

'The worst boss I ever had was someone who could only be described as an adult version of the "playground bully"', says Jill, still shivering at the thought of him.

> He was a very controlling man who demanded that you showed your loyalty to him by trashing other departments. If you didn't you were very 'disloyal'. He was a little man physically and seemed insecure because of this so he was forever trying to intimidate people. Virtually every day he would shout at someone by saying that they were 'fucking useless, crap at everything, bitches and cunts'.
>
> Needless to say, his behaviour infected everyone else. Once someone got a rollicking from him, they would not turn around and shout back at him, but go to their immediate junior colleagues and shout at them. And then that person would then yell at someone else. And so it went on, so that there was a terrible atmosphere of recriminations and hatred in the office. You see, people have to take on a nasty persona in order to survive.

Taj, the member of the Carbrain street gang in Cumbernauld, couldn't agree more. 'It's terrible. There is no getting away from it. I really wish I could be a nice person but I have to be nasty. I know my mother would be horrified to know the things I have done. But I feel like I have to do them in order to survive otherwise I'll become a victim,' he says, adding ruefully, 'I suppose in a way I am a victim.'

The victim who becomes the offender quickly learns who is suitable to form alliances with, and who can be bullied. Campbell is the classic case of this: New Labour's alliance with Rupert Murdoch and his excoriation of the BBC shows a strategic mind at work. The yob divides the world into two: those who are really powerful and who must be befriended, and those who are weak enough to be kicked around.

Throughout all the cases I have examined – from Chris being bullied at school to Jill's experiences with her boss in the City of London – I observed an innate distrust of authority. Chris had been persuaded that the school couldn't stop his bullying, and actually believed that they would make matters worse, while Jill knew that all the codes of practice which insisted upon people being nice to each other were only there for show. She told me: 'The worst bit of the job was the way in which the company preached to us about being ethical, that the customers were us, that we should learn to cooperate with each other, that we should have a work-life balance, that we should look beyond the money and treat each other with civility and respect, and yet, in reality, promoted the people who did the exact opposite.

'The worst people were always promoted. All that mattered was whether you had made a lot of money. People weren't rewarded for doing vital things like encouraging and helping staff to develop their skills. It was the people who specialised in harassing and hectoring others who got promoted.'

Victims, yobs and the law

'The yobs are laughing all the way to their designer clothes' shops.'

Rather like New Labour, which preaches the values of community, civility, probity and respect, but practises the precise opposite of those values, the firms in the City use the 'ethical codes' as a smokescreen for covering up a multitude of sins. As long as the tyrannical bosses are seen to be saying the right things, they can do what they want. In such a way, the modern-day yob learns how to play the system and manipulate codes, regulations and the law to his own ends.

'What I can't understand is why the law always gives the benefit of the doubt to people who are clearly antisocial. The truth of the matter is that the yobs are laughing all the way to their designer clothes' shops,' says Kevin.

The story told to me by him illustrates this point perfectly. Kevin, 48, grew up in Silver Town, in London's Docklands. He was the son of a single mother, and money was tight. Being a bright boy, he passed his 11-plus and attended grammar school during the 1960s in Limehouse.

> I was not a particularly nice person as a youngster. At the time, I was controlled by the society around me. In that London Docklands area, me and my friends didn't form a gang as such, but we did operate as a group, and quite a lot of the time we would come across gangs, and their 'turf'. And sure, we had fights. Lots of them. But once you had a fight, that was that. You didn't come back with a mob, and exact revenge on a totally disproportionate scale. You had a scrap, and honour was settled!
>
> Also, we were very carefully watched. There was a guy on our estate, a caretaker you might call him, but he was much more than that. He was the eyes and ears of the community. He would know exactly what was going on. And he, on more than one occasion, reported me to my mum, who gave me a belt around the ear for being badly behaved. That sort of figure has disappeared now. And parents are not nearly as supportive. You complain about a kid, and you'll be having a fight with the parent next thing you know.

Kevin stops talking here. I am interviewing him in a respectable suburb in north-east London. It is a predominantly working-class area, but relatively wealthy compared with inner London: full employment, only a small proportion living on social security and a high proportion of owner-occupied property. However, like many similar areas in the country, there is a real problem with antisocial behaviour. Kevin points out an ASBO notice in the window of the local estate agent; this forbids groups of youths of larger than three or four to assemble outside the supermarket, or anywhere on this thoroughfare. In the past months, youths have been caught scrawling on the walls, vandalising the shops and bus stop, drinking alcohol, abusing and attacking passers-by, playing loud music and generally making the centre a no-go zone after dark.

'The order ends in June. I wonder what they will do then,' Kevin says. 'Probably business as usual for the yobs.'

We cross the road and come to the place where Kevin's life changed forever.

A few years ago, I was walking along here, past Woolworth's; it was Saturday afternoon, and a dozen 14- or 15-year-olds just started to run. They were running along the pavement and knocking anyone who got in their way to one side. It was a mob, and they were just bowling people over like skittles, and laughing in their faces. It was fun for them. One of them bumped into me and bounced off. Because of the way he had fallen over, he swore at me. So I picked him up by the arm, told him what I thought of him and put him in a puddle by the side of the road. He was about 15. He was really, really angry with me, but he realized that anyone who could put him in a puddle wasn't to be messed around with. So he left me alone. To my old-fashioned way of thinking I hadn't done anything wrong; he bumped into me, he lost out, he should accept it. I go and do my shopping, but what I then realise is that one of these lads is following me.

I realised this, and walked home the long way round, but this guy was persistent and found out where I lived. About a half an hour later, I saw the boy and his dad coming down the street – and about another 20. I was now up against Dad and a whole gang of them. I think this is probably true of most yobs: if one person is attacked the whole lot has got to join in. So up comes Dad ready for a fight. And I'm thinking: 'I've really got to try and defuse this because if this goes badly wrong, there could be a riot.'

Anyway, Dad is very angry with me. He says to me that I've hurt his lad, and I've got to pay the price. It became clear that no amount of apologising and asking for a balanced view of what happened was going to do any good. I said, 'Look, I'm really sorry, but don't you think your lad was doing wrong?' But that kind of reasoning had no effect because a) the chap was very fired up and b) the mob behind him were not going to let him back down.

I was lucky because an old lady came out onto the street at this point, and saw what was going on. She stood on the doorstep watching this, and another chap came out as well.

Dad's daughter came up next and had a right go at me. Her language was absolutely foul: 'You fucking wanker, you cunt . . .' and so on. She really egged the dad on. So by this time, the dad was ready for a fight. I warned the dad at this point, 'If you go for me, I'll really hurt you. If a fight happens, I will have to hurt you because if I go down, this mob here will make mincemeat of me and I can't allow that.'

So he made a mistake and went for me. He threw the first punch. He was digging at me, pushing, shoving, trying to get at me. Goading me into a fight. And I have to say, he got very badly hurt. I beat the shit out of him basically. He didn't have a chance because I am a good fighter. I learnt how to fight in Silver Town, and I haven't forgotten how. He wasn't up to the job. I kept telling him this. He was only interested in fighting me because he had the backing of a huge mob.

The mob was a bit shocked about the mauling he got. After that, I turned to the mob, and I said, totally blazing now, 'Any of you, I'll take you on. Come on, I'll take you on.'

None of them wanted to face me in that mood. Luckily, the neighbours all rushed out and the police were called. When they arrived most of the mob ran off. I was then left standing there with a man on the floor with serious injuries. He gets carted off to hospital. The police initially cautioned me, and warned me that I could be convicted of grievous bodily harm. I was astonished. They were convinced I had hit him with a metal object, but I said it was just my fists. They wouldn't believe me. It was only when they asked the neighbours who had seen the whole thing that they came round to my point of view. They decided that I had been telling the truth.

But the dad wanted to press charges. He had come and instigated the whole thing, and yet he wanted to see me arrested. The only way the police stopped him from doing so was by threatening to charge him with causing an affray, which in legal terms is worse than causing GBH [Grevious Bodily Harm]. So the dad dropped his initial case.

But three days later, I got summonsed for assault and battery of the boy. I had no defence for that. I put him in a puddle, and I got bound over for six months to keep the peace. I had to go to court and pay a solicitor. The solicitor asked, 'Did you do it?' and I replied, 'Yes.' Well, he said, 'You're guilty, then.' So I had to plead that way.

I said to the magistrate at the end of the trial. 'I'd like

to say two things. Firstly, two weeks before this incident, I was commended by a senior police officer for assisting them in arresting a whole gang of youths who were causing trouble, tearing up fences in Romford. Me and an off-duty policeman arrested them, and held them until the police came. The police said that I was a good man and so on.

Secondly, what do I do the next time when I see that mob knocking old ladies down in Collier Row? Because they do it all the time, you know.'

The magistrate said to me, 'You should just cross the road.'

From that day on, I've just thought, 'What is the point?' The magistrate said, 'Cross the road.' Nowadays, the prime minister is saying that we are all supposed to be taking part and making our society better, and yet the law actually punishes people who try and stop antisocial behaviour.

That incident has lived with me ever since because it resulted in me getting a criminal record. I have found it extremely difficult to get jobs because of it. I have had to sweat blood to get jobs because of that. I have to declare it for all my jobs, and if the employers don't like it, then I'm out.

Kevin's mistake was to think that he could act as an authority figure and impose some discipline upon an aberrant child. Rather than being congratulated for encouraging the youth to behave in a civilised fashion, he was punished with a criminal record. Interestingly, in the light of the Edinburgh University research previously discussed, it is highly probable that the youth himself had been the victim of assaults of a far worse nature, but had never pressed charges against his assailants because they were probably people very close to him: his father, the friends in his gang. He knew that he would be beaten very badly if he did 'grass' on them. In fact, the thought probably never crossed his mind. The law in his eyes is only there to defend his right to be a yob, not to protect him as a victim.

Perhaps the most shocking illustration of the law favouring the rights of the perpetrator is the infamous 'Linda Walker' case. This teacher from Umston, Greater Manchester, endured what her friends termed 'three long years of torment' from local youths.[16] On 14 August 2004, her son looked out of his window and saw a broken container dripping liquid on top of his brother's car. Linda went outside to investigate and saw two youths placing a road sign in the middle of the road; they then hid, obviously hoping that a car would hit the sign. Walker removed the sign, and asked one of the youths why he had put it there. The youth then stalked towards her, squaring his shoulders at her in an aggressive fashion. His friends chanted from behind a wall, 'Linda and John, Linda and John!' They knew her, but she didn't know them. She felt frightened.

An argument ensued with one youth because she claimed he had been at her house, but he denied this. She said, 'If you come to my house again, I've got guns.' The youths challenged her to fetch the guns, swearing at her. In a very distressed state, she got her air pistol and broken air rifle from her house. She phoned the police, saying, 'I'm going to shoot the vandals that keep coming around here.' The operator warned her that if she did so, she would be arrested.

Returning outside, Mrs Walker was confronted by Robert McKiernan, who put 'his face to hers, only centimetres away, goading her to shoot him'. She refused, and she shot into the pavement. There were no pellets in the gun, but it made a popping sound because of the gas. Robert McKiernan then said, 'You can't come on to the street and do that, I'm going to call the police,' while waving his phone in her face. A few minutes later, the police arrived and arrested Mrs Walker.[17]

Linda Walker was jailed and, after her release, lost her teaching job because she dared to confront and challenge the yobs in her area. Just as we saw with Kevin's case, the law protected the yobs' right to inflict fear and distress upon their neighbourhood, while punishing in the severest possible sense a reckless, but understandable attempt to eradicate the feeling of menace in the streets of Urmston. 'While I totally condemn what Linda Walker did, I find it painfully comprehensible,' says Bill Pitt, who is the head of the Nuisance Strategy Unit in Manchester. 'The problem is that the law appears to be there to protect the rights of the perpetrator, and does not support the victim. There are thousands of areas like Urmston throughout the country where people are living in fear. The Linda Walker case has sent an important signal to them that they shouldn't try and do anything about it. The only people who benefit from a legal system like this are the lawyers and the yobs themselves.'

Pitt is not the only expert in the field of antisocial behaviour who feels that the legal profession props up our yob culture. 'The current legal system is geared to ensure justice for the suspect, even at the cost of justice in general,' DS Simmons said to me with a real trace of bitterness and disgust in his voice.

> The whole thing is a bit of racket because a lot of middle-class professionals do very nicely out of the system. The Crown Prosecution Service, the CPS, have well-paid jobs in their air-conditioned offices flicking through the cases that the police do all the groundwork for. Now the system has changed so that the police cannot decide whether to prosecute any more. They have to sweat their guts out getting a court-ready package together for the CPS, and the CPS can then decide not to prosecute. That means that lots of cases do not go to court, and are never heard by a jury because the CPS cherry-pick only the cases they think

are winners. So they have pretty easy lives now. The police do all the work for them.

The CPS should let juries decide who is innocent and who is guilty. Twelve good men and true should be listening to the evidence and making up their own minds, not some liberal-minded lawyer who has no idea.

Perhaps most worryingly, clever defence barristers can manipulate the system, and this can lead to some very dangerous criminals getting freed before they should. My colleague and I are currently dealing with a case where a prolific offender, charged with the most serious offences, has a defence team that is, without a doubt, playing the system. Their 'clever-clever' tactics will probably mean he will serve a very reduced sentence. In my view, lawyers employ delaying tactics so that offenders who know that they will be found guilty deliberately put off the trial until the very last moment. You see, serving on remand is worth 'double' that of serving a custodial sentence. In other words, if you have served six months on remand, you will have a year taken off your prison sentence. That can mean that if an offender has spent a year or so in custody, he can effectively walk out of prison a few months after being sentenced to a few years. Which is what is going on in the current case we are prosecuting. This serial offender has served a long time on remand and even if he gets a long custodial sentence, he will probably be walking free after a few months. It is frightening to think of a person like him walking free so soon, but that is what will happen.

The trouble at the moment is that justice is so random. The Lords of Stratford Crew got five years each. Custodial sentences. That judge was 'switched on'. But another judge dealing with very similar offences at Harrow Crown Court – some of them actually worse than the LOS's crimes – gave that gang two years. Simply not enough. That lot is out now, laughing in our faces.

CHAPTER TWO

My Manor

❝ We knew if we approached people in the street they would be scared of us. And we loved it! It was a laugh to watch them cross the road or run away as we approached. ❞

Territory

'Right, that's it! Everyone out! Out now, out of the class! Out! Out!'

Everywhere I travelled to in Britain, observing British yobbery, I came across the issue of territory again and again. The top-dog yob wants the same thing whether it is in the poorest council estate in Glasgow, by the swimming pool on holiday in Cyprus or in the hallowed corridors of power in Whitehall; he wants his 'patch', 'his manor', his 'pitch', his 'ground'.

The yob claims his territory by a number of techniques, many of which I have observed both as a pupil at school, and then as a teacher.

There was a real atmosphere of yobbery in the minor public school I attended in the early 1980s. One of my first memories of the school was sitting at the back of a maths class watching about ten boys rip the plastic tiles from the floor and hurl them at the teacher once his back was turned. As soon as he heard the clunk of a tile hitting the wall beside the blackboard, he whirled around, chalk in hand, and shouted out at the top of his voice, 'Who did that? Who did that?'

There was silence.

He started writing on the board again. Once again, a number of pupils threw the tiles at the teacher. This behaviour puzzled me because in many lessons the pupils worked very hard and in silence, but here, with this teacher, they seemed to be totally different.

Mr Banks whirled around again, and shouted,

'Right, that's it! Everyone out! Out now, out of the class! Out! Out!'

He was subconsciously aware that the class had claimed the territory for its own, and that the only way to reclaim the space was to remove us from it and start again. Of course, he didn't realise that he had now lost the space forever: he had no one in the class that he had formed alliances with; he had only enemies who wanted to remove him from their territory. It was our space now. Not his.

The class burst into laughter, and spontaneously started shouting, 'Out! Out!' We felt so in control that we thought we could order him out of the room. Eventually, he managed to get the class to line up outside the classroom, and then told us to come in again. I remember seeing the sweat drip through his beard. His corduroy jacket was covered in chalk.

Later on, in the changing rooms, a chant began to evolve. Mr Banks was rechristened 'Digger Banks'. In a conscious imitation of the sort of football hooliganism that went on in some football grounds around the country at that time, a lot of the boys started shouting, 'Digger out! Digger out!' with their hands thrust into the air, index fingers jabbing in the direction of the hapless teacher's classroom.

Soon, in lessons, the pupils started shouting the slogan at him. His bluster had gone. He would shout at us, not for shouting at him, but for other more trivial stuff like not looking at the right page in the text book. Once, when he caught a pupil sucking a lollipop behind his briefcase, he dragged the boy over his desk in a fit of rage. The pupil, Derek, was one of his worst tormentors, frequently leading the clarion call of 'Digger out! Digger out!'

The pupils at the school were from wealthy backgrounds. Many of them had working-class parents who ran their own businesses. This type of person was to become more prevalent during the decade as Thatcher's reforms to the economy encouraged more people to be entrepreneurs. In a way, the parents at the school were forerunners of the 'working class' of Britain today, many of whom are much wealthier than their counterparts of 20 years before.

At my school, wealth brought arrogance and the confidence to be outrageous. I think it is no coincidence that it was the children of the wealthiest parents who were the founders of the notorious 'W.C.'. At first, when I saw a sign on the sports noticeboard saying in a red scrawl: 'W.C., Hunter vs Philips, this pm', I didn't know what to make of it.

Digger Banks had left in mysterious circumstances, and our maths teacher was now a tall, elderly man, Mr Withers, with impaired vision and movement. I noticed with a sigh of relief that the lessons were much more orderly than before – there was no more ripping up of tiles and ordering the teacher out of the room – but that didn't mean that some fairly untoward activities weren't going on.

Withers's lessons always followed a set pattern. He would write up the work on the board, and then sit down at his chair for the duration of the lessons, occasionally issuing throaty but loud demands for silence if the class was too noisy. There usually wasn't silence, but he didn't seem to mind unless the noise reached a certain level.

On this afternoon, things were particularly quiet. Everyone had a smile on their faces. Again I was puzzled. What was going on? I got up out of my seat and walked down to the front of the class because I wanted Withers to explain a particular mathematical problem to me. Unlike Banks, he was usually happy to do this.

As I walked past Philips and Hunter, I saw that their flies were undone and that they were pulling hard on their erect penises, while trying their best not to grin inanely. I couldn't understand what I was seeing. Puberty hadn't hit me properly at that point, but clearly it had with Hunter and Philips.

I learnt at the end of the lesson that Hunter had won by 'coming first'. There was much merriment about this. He was slapped on the back, and received huge kudos for his feat. This was the beginning of the 'wanking club' in school. Frequent competitions were held in Mr Withers's class, with bets being placed, and any boy who had the facility seeing whether he could 'come first'.

In a way the whole thing was quite innocent – there was no sense that any of this was connected with sex. It was simply a 'sport', a competition to see who could come first. But it was also consciously 'antisocial'; everyone was aware that it was not the thing that you did. The pupils doing it were trying to prove that they were one of the gang. At a more atavistic level, the pupils were literally leaving their spores on the territory, marking it for their own with semen. Digger Banks had never provoked such a surreptitious usurpation of the territory; we could tell him to his face to go away, but now that some kind of order had been imposed by Withers, we had to be more secretive but no less antisocial in our activities.

The cramped classroom

'66 per cent of frontline teachers feel there is a discipline crisis in our schools.' Teacher TV survey, 2005

Both Withers and Banks were, in their own ways, poor teachers. The content of their lessons did not engage us, and they were not good at keeping an eye on the troublemakers in the class. In our other lessons, my class were generally well behaved: it was silent when a teacher was speaking, took notes, completed its homework and passed the relevant exams. Something quite different is going on in Britain's classrooms today.

Kirsty Smith, a teacher in Dumfries, Scotland, offered me an important insight when she told me that she had been a pupil in the same area where she now teaches. Dumfries is a beautifully situated, prosperous town in Scotland, which would appear, on the surface, to be an idyllic place to teach and go to school. This is what Kirsty told me.

When I was a pupil, there were antisocial incidents but, as I remember it, nothing like compared to now. From what I remember we all had a lot of pressure from our parents to do well and nobody got into any serious trouble, although I remember thinking I was about to be sent to boarding school because I was caught smoking a cigarette, kissing a boy or getting angry at various points during my teenage years. But there was nothing involving the police or anything like that. There were only really one or two people that I vaguely knew who were in a lot of trouble, and in my adult life I've since discovered that they were fairly unhappy people from quite unstable backgrounds.

But now the incidents of antisocial behaviour in school – and the wider society – are definitely on the rise. There seems to be little ambition and drive in the pupils. I'm afraid I blame these low expectations on home and a general lack of good parenting. One frightening fact is that many parents can't say no to their children, and we, as teachers, are then left to deal with the fallout. I think parents depend heavily on schools to not only educate, but also bring up their children. There is a terrible problem in our society in that when children turn into teenagers, parents often think 'That's it, they are grown up, our work here is done. I can now lead my own life.' This is when children need their parents most. I have two nearly teenage girls so I'm coming from some experience.

Swearing is a fairly big problem. I think the root of this is threefold. Firstly, many are allowed to swear at home – maybe just a 'crap' or a 'bloody', but it is not greeted well in school if you then point out it's unacceptable. Parents back the kids up, too. Where does that leave us? The children also watch lots of TV where bad language is normal and frequent. Despite what anyone says, it does affect their idea of what normal is. They all swear together. I think this starts as a bravado thing – as a sorting of the men from the boys – but then becomes ingrained within their social groups.

Fighting is on the rise. I have seen and jumped into many fights – in order to stop them happening, I might add! They usually start in a very immature way: cheeky remarks turn nasty . . . young people unable to control or sort out emotions, not taking a moment to think about consequences. It's almost primitive. There is a lot of 'My dad says if they hit me, I've to hit them back harder'. Explaining that violence doesn't solve or stop anything is an alien concept. That makes things very tough as a teacher.

I know that to be true myself. I have been teaching for nearly 15 years in various comprehensives in London. During that time I have had classes that rioted, pupils smoking in my lessons, missiles thrown at me and ripped cans and spikes left on my chair. I have been verbally abused on numerous occasions, and have had to break up a number of fights occurring in my lessons. I am not an exception – that is normal life for a teacher these days.[18]

I know that even if you are a good teacher, with interesting lessons, and effective discipline, you will have a hard time teaching in many of Britain's schools, whether you are doing so in a deprived area or a middle-class one. I interviewed an American teacher, who had been teaching in both the United States and Britain, and she said that there was a very noticeable difference in the behaviour of British children and American children. 'I know everyone thinks that you are likely to get a lot of bad behaviour in these inner-city American schools. Well, that can be the case, but on the whole American children are not as rowdy or as insolent as British children,' she said.

Anthony de Boers, a fit, personable science and PE teacher, grew up in South Africa and taught there for a few years before coming to work in Britain as a teacher.

The thing is, the classroom in Britain is like a battleground. It's like the children here don't want to accept you as a figure of authority and think that they can do what they want. It's like you are entering their territory. It's very different in South Africa, where schools are very structured and everyone knows their place. I have had some terrible times teaching in England. In many classes I have been in, pupils spend the majority of the time fighting each other, either verbally or physically. In Hackney, Walthamstow and Havering, I have seen the whole gamut of bad behaviour. At one school, a pupil came up to me and took my marker pen as I was about to write something on the board. He went back to his place and started grafitti-ing on the desk. I followed him and told him that it was my marker pen and that I wanted it back. He replied: 'You what, sir? Fuck off to the front. Give us the lesson. That's what you're here for.' I said that it would be difficult to do that without my marker pen. 'You've got another one, haven't you?' he retorted. Rather than demean myself by grabbing it off him, I returned to the front, and reported him when the lesson was finished. Nothing much was done about the incident. Apparently, he was like that in most lessons. I learned that I was lucky that he hadn't tried to assault me.

I think the issue of territory is very important because you have so little space in Britain's schools. There are no playing fields, no racetracks, no sports grounds, only these cramped yards, and squashed up classrooms; it's like the children need more space to run around and be children.

Smith's point is a valid one: an unprecedented number of school playing fields have been sold off since the 1980s, and that has happened at the same time as a rise in bad behaviour in schools. The schools' inspectorate, Ofsted, claimed in a recent report that one in five secondary schools now have pupils with significant behavioural problems.

'Some of the changes that have happened in schools over

the past decades have really affected society for the worse,' says former head teacher Mike Batten, now a fulltime magistrate. 'When I started teaching in the 1960s, I taught in a secondary modern. There was a good youth service attached to the school, with a club for children to go to after school and get involved in playing football, learning music and general socialising. But those youth services have been swept away, and nothing has replaced them.

'Added to this the introduction of the National Curriculum in schools has meant that a lot of pupils have had their interest in learning destroyed. This idiotic curriculum was an imitation of the grammar school curriculum of the 1950s. Once a child starts to fail in this highly pressurised environment, they drop out completely. There is no alternative offered. No wonder so many schools have to deal with such a lot of bad behaviour.'

Pupils and teachers have had their territories stripped away from them both literally and metaphorically: playing spaces have been replaced with buildings, and the teachers' ability to choose their own curriculum has been replaced with a centrally imposed curriculum. The pupils' response has been to claim some space for their own: the classrooms and corridors of the schools, even if that means abusing their teachers in the process.

Unfortunately, schools do not have the power to deal with such pupils. Their only real option is to expel them. This, however, is something that is increasingly difficult to do. In October 2005, Greenwich Council was forced to apologise to a pupil after he had been expelled from school for taking a knife onto the premises. The council was ordered to pay £11,000 in compensation, £5,000 of which was to recompense the 'anxiety and uncertainty' the pupil had endured for being expelled, while £6,000 went to the mother for the home tuition of her son. The pupil had been suspended twice for fighting, and once after he used a knife to rip pages out of a classmate's book.[19]

Such legal cases are not confined to state schools. The father of Rhys Grays, 16, tried to prevent the boarding school

Marlborough College from expelling his son after he had been caught drinking, smoking and bullying other pupils at the school. Marlborough, backed up by some top legal advice and a 50-page witness statement that catalogued Rhys's misdemeanours, won the case, but it had to go to great time and effort to do so.[20]

Thus we can see that parents who aggressively defend their own child's behaviour seem to be creating a climate in which bad behaviour thrives.

It comes as no surprise, then, that classroom backchat and insolence are forcing many teachers to quit the profession. A report commissioned by the National Association of Schoolmasters Union of Women Teachers found that four out of ten newly qualified teachers have to deal with bad behaviour on an hourly basis and eight out of ten say it is a daily occurrence. A 23-year-old female teacher from Stockport told researchers: 'A child decided he did not like me or science, ran around the room verbally abusing me, climbed under the table and ripped his book up, tried to snatch his report and then attempted to escape through the window.' Another teacher explained why they couldn't return to teaching: 'I am unable to return to school because I no longer have the confidence to stand in front of a class. I would love to teach – however, this job is 25 per cent teaching, 75 per cent crowd control.'[21]

Similarly, the education watchdog Ofsted said that many schools were being held back by low-level disruption, and revealed that only one in three secondary schools had acceptable standards of behaviour. Perhaps most revealingly, in an exhaustive survey carried out by the government-sponsored channel Teachers' TV, 66 per cent of teachers felt that there was a discipline crisis in our schools. According to the survey, it was the yobbish behaviour of one or two pupils that caused the most problems for teachers. Clearly, the problems in our schools won't be solved until we stop the yobs from hijacking lessons.

Louts in the lecture theatre

'Too many medical students don't think twice today about cheating, plagiarising, bullying, speaking aggressively, spitting, wearing inappropriate clothes, being disrespectful and generally rude.'

Perhaps not surprisingly given the changes in behaviour in schools, the universities have also seen a cultural change in the way their students behave.

One November morning in 2004, senior medical lecturer Henry Standish showed me round one of the top medical schools in the country, where he lectures. The students were very different from the stereotypes that you find in medic dramas on TV. A large proportion of them were of Asian origin; contrary to the 'Asian doctor' stereotype they seemed streetwise and savvy in their tough-guy tracksuits and hoods, and with their strutting gait. Other students – many with noticeably posh accents – sported multiple rings through their ears, noses, mouths and tongues. Very few fitted the smartly dressed, clean-cut image that is promoted on TV.

Standish guided me into his office, and he had this to say.

The medical profession has always attracted a certain thuggish element. This was certainly true when I started teaching students 27 years ago. The private schools seemed to produce a 'rugby' medical student who liked joking around, getting drunk and playing pranks. These types of student haven't disappeared, but the ranks of 'yobbish' students have been amplified by students from different backgrounds. There are now two other groups, which you may have spotted in the corridor because they are very obvious to see: young British Asian students, usually male, and what might be termed 'grungy' students, who are normally from middle-class backgrounds, though not always.

The Asian students now form nearly 50 per cent of our intake. Because of targets set by the General Medical Council, we are obliged to take students from all ethnic backgrounds so that they can serve the diverse ethnic communities in Britain. The problem is that these boys are often poorly educated and intellectually impoverished. They speak in an 'argot', or vernacular, which can mean that they are incomprehensible to patients, and their manner can be very aggressive and antisocial; their clothes are more reminiscent of gang members with their baggy jeans and baseball caps on the wrong way round.

Perhaps most embarrassingly, a few years ago a lecturer in our department brought in a patient to a lecture in order to show the students the reactions of a patient to various procedures. The patient happened to be an attractive young woman. Unfortunately, the lecture had to be stopped because the woman was wolf-whistled and jeered. Now we don't ask patients into lectures because of the adverse reaction that they receive.

When I first started teaching, lectures were fairly quiet, sedate affairs. At the most, I would lecture to a class of a hundred, and everyone would turn up on time and listen quietly. Now, lectures can be quite rowdy, firstly because our numbers are up to about 350 in an average lecture – we take many more students. Secondly, because the students – the most notable being the rugby crowd, the Asian lads and the body piercers – just don't know how to behave. They often arrive late, and even then will greet their friends with high fives and loud greetings, and then think nothing of gossiping all through the lecture. They like to text each other and read the *Sun*. Some even think that it is OK to speak on their mobile phones.

Now I always spell out a list of rules before I start my lecture series: no latecomers, no phones, no chatting, no eating and so on. This does make some difference, but often less experienced lecturers do flounder, and they can find themselves trying to shout above a chaotic rabble.

Laboratory lessons can be even worse. One lesson I teach concerns the dissection of human brains. For obvious reasons, human brains are treated with extreme caution and respect: these are members of the public who have donated their bodies for the furtherance of science. Recently, I was teaching the basic morphology of the brain to a group of second year undergraduates. I pointed to the brains, and asked, 'Now what can I show you?'

One leader of the group seemed particularly incensed by this question. 'Everything,' he said aggressively. He seemed utterly unaware of the need to treat dead human matter with respect.

I remained calm, and said that I needed some specifics.

'Give me everything, it's your job,' the yob snapped back at me. The implication was that if he failed to pass this topic in the exam, it would be my fault. The trouble is that like so many students I encounter now, he was out of his depth. He was not able to cope with the open question I had posed to the group.

This leads me to my other concern, which is cheating. If you give these students a chance to cheat, they will. We have had to get rid of coursework now because so many dissertations were plagiarised from the Internet, or copied from journals. I even had one student, a very clever student, in fact, who presented a rehashed version of a paper I had written.

Now we run all our tests under exam conditions, but even then we have to be careful. A couple of years ago we found a student had stolen a copy of the paper and was selling it around the university.

While I am aware that what I see is not at the extreme end of yobbery it is, in my view, yobbery. Too many medical students don't think twice today about cheating, plagiarising, bullying, speaking aggressively, spitting, wearing inappropriate clothes, and being disrespectful and generally rude. Things are very different from how they used to be. This is largely due to successive government policies aimed at expanding the numbers of students taking medicine. While this is laudable, unfortunately these students just don't have the education or social skills to make it as doctors. The result is a real dumbing down; we are no longer educating an elite, but desperately trying to socialise a pretty motley bunch of ill-educated thugs.

Observing the students myself, I felt that they were compensating for their lack of knowledge by claiming the territory for their own: the 'gangsta' style dress code and argot was their way of appropriating the university. Rather than adapting to the university's rules, rather than attempting to jump over the relevant academic hurdles, they preferred to bully the institution into accepting their terms of dress, speech and behaviour.

The antisocial behaviour of the students at Queen University and Ulster University in Belfast has got so bad that the authorities have had to introduce wardens on the streets to avoid mass havoc. One resident told me that he'd seen drunken students run over the tops of cars, kick in the windscreens, vomit rivulets in the gutter and abuse the locals on a regular basis. 'Basically, they get very drunk and go mad. There's no end of vomiting, fighting and noise,' he said. In 2004, the university received 240 complaints from local residents about antisocial behaviour. Now they need to be supervised by wardens – day and night.

Street culture

'The whole lot of us would pile into him. A massed ruck of boys piling into one guy. Punching him, kicking him, smacking him around.'

What is fascinating is that the values of street culture have now infiltrated even the august realms of the medical profession – traditionally one of the most conservative professions. The hospitals and surgeries are their 'manor', their territory, to behave in as they please.

Appreciating the concept of the 'manor' is essential if one is to understand fully the implications of this new culture. Devon, a former gang member, explained it to me.

Everything is about your manor. There were a gang of us, and we had our 'manor'. It was our place, and no one else was going to get away with anything on it. This was the area and streets around the George and Dragon pub, in north-east London. We stalked up and down the streets, day after day, night after night, feeling great. There were 20 or so of us you see, and we felt impregnable.

I suppose if I think about it, at the bottom of our hearts we felt it was the only thing we did have: none of us was doing that well at school, and we could hardly hang around in our homes in those numbers where most of us were unwanted, so the streets and the George became our thing. And I'll tell you what, it's a great feeling, walking down the street like you own it. You feel like a millionaire. You feel like you own all the houses and the cars and the street, and it's great. It puts a smile on your face.

We were only teenagers, you see. None of us had that much money. Not much older than 14 years old. And yet the landlord didn't mind us hanging around the George, even though we didn't drink much more than pineapple lemonade. Alcohol wasn't our thing. We smoked spliff. Every Friday night without fail we would go down to the pub so that we could have a fight. It was our pub, you see. And we were untouchable. People were frightened of us. There were so many of us, bigging it in our baggy tracksuit bottoms, our bling-bling jewellery and our hoods. We fitted the absolute cliché of yobs. In truth, the manager Joe liked having us around because it meant that he didn't get the pub trashed. He would give us a drink every now and then. I look back now and realise that he was playing us.

Richard was the gang leader, and he would hype us up. Every week he would tell us something that made us kick off. His common gambits were: 'That guy was looking at me,' 'That guy punched me in the toilet,' 'He was laughing at me,' 'He was looking at my woman.' He'd point them out as we lounged around the pool table, and all of us would lash out.

The whole lot of us would pile into him. A massed ruck of boys piling into one guy, punching him, kicking him, smacking him around. People would get caught in the cross-fire. I remember once seeing bits of glass sticking into the cheek of an innocent passer-by because one of us had chucked a smashed glass across the room.

When the police came, everyone in the pub would be on our side, and there would be no witnesses. It got to be a bit of joke because the police were called so often that they got to know our names, but they never fingered us. Back then, you had to dislike the police. They were the enemy. We despised them. But the trouble was they were quite friendly, and they would call us by our first names, making out that they knew us really well. Things got a bit funny after that because people in the gang would look suspiciously at each other whenever a copper said something friendly to you. It was like you might be an informer or something. The police knew what they were doing. We started bickering amongst ourselves after that.

Devon's experiences in this north-east London suburb are typical of those of many teenagers throughout Britain. In a world where 'ownership' is perceived to be the key to success and happiness – ownership of your house, your car, etc. – the yob's response is to lay claim to ownership of public space. It is not hard to sympathise with this. In Devon's case, not many of his friends had much money, and none of them felt that they had much of a future; a great deal of self-worth was gained by just inhabiting space that felt like theirs.

They quite consciously used bullying tactics to keep the land free of 'intruders'. 'We knew that if we approached people in the street they would be scared of us,' Devon says. 'And we loved it! It was a laugh to watch them cross the road or run away as we approached. It was funny to see the suited businessmen returning home from work scuttling along like frightened mice as we approached. We felt so powerful! It was like we were magicians just clicking our fingers and making people move!'

The Shipley estate

'Razor could have any woman he wants, he doesn't have to rape anyone. I think she strayed onto his manor and 'cos Razor is king of his territory, he feels like he can do what he wants.'

My interview with a close friend and confidante to a number of gang members, whose 'manor' was not far from Stratford in east London, was also revealing about what gang members can and cannot get away with on their manor.

Donna is an articulate, lively 17-year-old who grew up on the Shipley estate, near Manor Park. The Shipley estate was knocked down over ten years ago, and its inhabitants were rehoused in pleasant but small terraced buildings in the same area. The houses are still grouped around a park, which contains a playground, some flowerbeds and a football pitch. Travelling there with her, I was struck by how relatively civilised the area was. The front gardens of the houses were all well tended, there were some expensive cars parked on the roads, and there were no signs of derelict housing or squalid conditions. Yet this area, like many similarly 'respectable' suburbs in the country, is terrorised by gang culture.

At first, I was skeptical about Donna's claim that the 'Shipley' gang 'owned' the 'estate' as she still referred to it, but then she showed me the Shipley park and I could see immediately that there was something wrong. A group of about 20 youths in tracksuits, trainers and the trademark 'hoods' were lounging around the playground. No young children were playing there. The swings were twisted around the top poles. There was broken glass everywhere. The bins had been burnt out, and the climbing frame was covered in graffiti.

'Some people make the mistake of taking a short cut through there,' Donna said, pointing at the playground and chuckling darkly. 'Then they get jacked.'

The word 'jacked' occurs a lot in Donna's conversation: it means to be 'mugged', although interestingly it does not have the same negative connotations of the verb 'mugged'. To be 'jacked' is to have your expensive property removed from your person, and to be 'roughed around' a bit. It does not suggest that such an event is a traumatic experience in the way 'mugged' does. The word trips easily off the tongue with a shrug of the shoulders. Being 'jacked' is just the way things are: being 'jacked' is a condition of life, much in the way having to go to the toilet is.

Donna is in a unique position to talk about the Shipley gang because she is the next-door neighbour and close friend of its leader, Razor.

Razor comes from a good Christian family. I know them well. They are a good, Caribbean family. Strict. There are five children in total, and Razor was the youngest boy. He always looked up to his two older brothers, who were bad for a while. Now they're fine, but they had their moments when they was young. Anyway, Razor was born in 1987, and did OK at primary school. But then something went wrong when he went to secondary. He just dropped out. Started hanging around outside the school. He got permanently excluded for throwing a chair at a teacher, and other stuff like swearing at them.

Although Razor is my friend, he can be really scary. You know I actually didn't think so until I saw this incident with my own eyes. I mean I'd seen him dissing the teachers and everything, but everyone did that. I did that. I was excluded too. That didn't count. No. I only got really scared of Razor when I saw him jack this kid on the high street. In broad daylight, Razor and his gang were walking past the newsagents when they saw Phil, a white kid, coming out of the shop talking into his mobile phone. Razor crossed the road with his posse, and sticks out his hand, and says 'Oi, what you got for me?'

Donna laughed at this point in the interview, and explained that the phrase 'Oi, what you got for me?' could be the catch-phrase of the Shipley estate because it happens so much. It is always said before any 'jacking'.

Anyway, Phil, he's a tiny kid, a little boy. And he is really scared. But he knows a few things. Firstly, he knows who everyone is. And he knows that his older cousin John, a white boy, is in the Shipley gang, and that Razor wouldn't want to piss off John by jacking his little cousin. So he says that he hasn't got nothing. And then, suddenly, Razor goes crazy, pulls out a knife and starts slashing at the boy's coat, ripping it to shreds, saying, 'this is my manor and when you're here, what's yours is mine'. And Phil starts crying. Tears streaming down his face. It was terrible to watch. And the little boy keeps saying that the mobile phone is his mum's and his mum has cancer, and they don't have any money, and please can he keep it? And I know Phil is right. I know Phil's family. But Razor just 'boyed him', and the gang 'boyed him' too.

This phrase is an important concept as well. It means 'to laugh in someone's face'. 'Boying someone' is the privilege of the powerful. If you get 'boyed' by someone of lesser status than you, then you have to retaliate.

Anyway, Phil got jacked, got his coat slashed and was beaten up pretty badly. I saw his big fat, black eyes and his bruises a few days later. They were bad! Not long after that, Phil's big cousin John found out about this, and suddenly there is going to be this big war on the Shipley estate. Some of John's mates from Shipley put on their bullet-proof vests, and get some guns and they say they are going to shoot Razor and his crew. So the gang is at war with itself now, although normally it's properly at war with the gangs from another estate in Manor Park.

Neither Phil nor anyone in his family reported his assault and mugging to the police. 'It's seen as a real dishonour to go to the police,' says Donna. 'No one goes to the police because they know they'll get their houses smashed in if they do.'

As a result of incidents like this, the boy who once was the quiet, sweet younger brother is now both revered and feared. 'Razor likes to see people frightened. I was at a party a few weeks ago, and Razor walked in, and suddenly everyone went silent. I mean the room was noisy and everyone was laughing, and then Razor walked in, and they were quiet. He smiled. He likes it. He likes the feeling of fear he causes in people. You can see this with his gang. They like intimidating people. They find it fun to frighten people. Anyone. People in the street, their families, their friends. That's why they walk around looking so mean. He wants to be like Tupac, the rap star. A bad-ass-muthafucka.'

Girls are not part of Razor's gang, but they hang around the fringes of his entourage. 'Razor could have any woman he wanted,' Donna says. 'But he's suspicious of them 'cos he was put in jail for raping a girl. I knew her. Now I ain't saying Razor is a saint or anything, but I know that girl, and I think she may have been asking for that. She was not a good girl, if you know what I mean. And Razor could have any woman he wants; he doesn't have to rape anyone. I think she strayed onto his manor, and 'cos Razor is king of his territory, he feels like he can do what he wants. No one says no to him on his manor. That's the rules.'

Donna's attitude towards Razor's conviction for rape was instructive in many ways. She did not view him as 'out of order' for committing such a terrible crime: she felt that he might have been wrongfully convicted in the first place. Additionally, even if she felt that he was guilty, she thought that the victim might have 'invited' the attack. I think her attitude towards this, and his other crimes, is important to consider because it is symptomatic of the culture of acceptance that allows characters like Razor to thrive.

Although put in a young offenders' institution for the rape for a few months, Razor has otherwise escaped jail.

'I think Razor got wise after he got out from jail,' Donna says. 'He knew that if he moved around in a pack, then the cops would find it very hard to get him. If there are lots of people saying nothing happened, then the courts are never going to convict. Razor knows his rights now. He won't be going back to jail. He knows what he can and cannot do on his manor.'

Some months after this interview with Donna, I was to learn that Razor had been involved in a serious car accident. He'd been joy-riding around the estate and crashed the car after being pursued by the police. Because he was not wearing a seat belt, he was paralysed from the neck down. However, now that Razor was permanently in a wheelchair, another gang member had taken over and was behaving in much the same way as Razor.

Leaving your spore

Above The gang logo for the Toryglen gang in Scotland. The N stands for Nazi, 1 means number 1, top dog, and TO is short for Toryglen. This symbol is left all over the walls and environs of Toryglen.

Above The insignia for the Brick Lane Massive, the gang that haunts the Bethnal Green neighbourhood.

You can easily tell the space a yob has claimed by the detritus that is left in the area. From London to Manchester, from Glasgow to Belfast, I saw the same phenomenon again and again: spray-painted insignia of varying sizes and complexity, broken glass and bottles, empty beer cans and bottles, ripped up paving and the occasional syringe.

'Unlike real gang members, who are very secretive,' says Jamie James, 'the yob likes to make a mess. He likes to show people he is there. His object is to inspire fear, to deter people from entering his space.'

He needs to leave visible spores in order to prove his worth, and to mark out his territory, to claim ownership of it. Hence the effort that most street gangs will exert in order to make a good logo. In my own area of east London, the Brick Lane Massive – a very large gang of Asians – have a logo of criss-crossing letters which intertwine to form one symbol, while in the Toryglen estate of Glasgow, the gang there showed me their equally carefully designed insignia for the Young Toryglen 1 Gang, which consists of a complicated series of Ys and Ts and Os that are configured to look a little like the swastika. The other name for the gang was the Nazi Circus.

In Belfast, street gang culture of this sort was not so prevalent because the different areas already had their gangs with their own vividly etched spores: fantastic murals depicting the exploits of various terrorist groups, or the deaths of certain terrorist members. Terrorist groups' acronyms were emblazoned on many walls: UDF and UDA in the Protestant areas, and IRA in the Catholic areas.

However, I sensed a real degree of uncertainty on the streets because it was clear that now that these former terrorist groups wanted respectability they had lost their street credibility. People who advocated the armed struggle, like David Ervine on the Protestant side and Gerry Adams on the Catholic side, were now politicians, abstracted from their people. They were rebranding themselves as serious politicians.

They were looking at what New Labour had done for guidance. In much the same way that the street gangs had left their spores on their territory, New Labour aimed to leave its spore upon the people of Britain. Alistair Campbell was instrumental in assisting the Labour Party in this. In the 1997 election, New Labour introduced the concept of pledge cards, which listed the things that the administration would do when in power, while in 2001 young people were texted with messages that exhorted the wonders of New Labour.

However, New Labour's 'spores' are not as influential as gang logos. Unlike the Nazi party, they have never found a symbol which has real 'street cred'. Thank goodness for that.

There are different places that form part of a yob's manor, which I explore in the following section:

- The briefing room – this is where plans are hatched.
- The parade ground – this is where shock, awe, reverence and fear are instilled in the general public.

The army has, of course, formalised these spaces, but the yob has not: a briefing room can easily become a parade ground or battleground if necessary, and vice versa. The modern British yob is not fussed about formal demarcations, which is part of his power: he is flexible, willing to create fear and mayhem wherever it is suitable or convenient to do so.

CHAPTER THREE

Briefing Rooms

❝ Ya see, this is our spot. This is where the cool guys come to discuss the business. The lassies are not allowed here unless it's to get shagged. I'm bringing one here tonight just to do that! ❞

The Toryglen Nazi Circus

'Ya see, we work out how we are going to paste the Rutherglen gang here. We talk about how we pasted them last week, and how we are going to paste them next week.'

I found them behind an abandoned row of shops, lounging around on some stairs. In the distance, fluffy clouds scudded over the skyline of Glasgow's heaps of tower blocks.

'We've got a great view from here, haven't we?' a boy with blue tracksuit bottoms grinned at me. It was true; from here they could see all the major estates of the city: Sighthill, Springburn, Drum Chapel, what remains of the Gorbals, the whole of the city centre and, most importantly for them, Rutherglen.

When I explained that I was a writer interested in hearing about their lives, they welcomed me up onto their elevated platform and let me enjoy the view. I was offered a swig of Buckfast by one youth with pin-hole burns in his trousers. They were all wearing tracksuit bottoms and football jackets of various descriptions.

I could see now that I was in a unique and special place: the elevated platform was not visible from the road, and yet had a wonderful view of the rest of the Toryglen estate. These guys, who formed part of a gang who called themselves the Toryglen Nazi Circus, could see just about everything that was going on in the estate from here. They could also smoke, drink and chat without being seen by anyone as they were tucked away from the shops.

'This is where we have a drink, another drink, and then a smoke, and another smoke, and then another drink, and then another drink,' Sid Hoon told me. He was 13 years old and had been coming to this spot since he was nine to do exactly that. He said proudly: 'Ya see, this is our spot. This is where the cool guys come to discuss the business. The lassies are not allowed here unless it's to get shagged. I'm bringing one here tonight just to do that!'

His mates burst out laughing. He grabbed a spliff off one of them and continued to explain the significance of the spot. 'Ya see, we work out how we are going to paste the Rutherglen gang here. We talk about how we pasted them last week, and how we are going to paste them next week. Ya see, we always beat them. We smash them with bottles, bricks and hockey sticks. Even though there are more of them, we get them. And do ya knae why? 'Cos the lads listen to me. Doncha lads? I tell them who to go for, you see. I've been doing this for years. I knae who is who. I knae what the wee cunts are wearing, and I say, ma lads, you've got to go for that wee wanker and smash his brains out.'

The other boys looked in admiration at him as he said this to me. One of them added, 'Ya knae we would die if it wasnae for Sid 'cos there are more of them. They have about 30 and we only have 20.'

He explained that they usually discussed battle tactics while drinking their Buckfast, and then when that was finished they would have a 'brickie', which was where the boys sucked smouldering dope smoke through a bottle with its end broken off.

Jamie James explained to me that his gang had a similar type of 'briefing room' in Thamesmead, London. 'We used to meet up in a secluded place so that we could plan for our upcoming night,' he said. 'We would sit outside a series of shops: an off-licence, a post office, a café, two grocery stores. We'd all sit outside on the wall talking about what we were going to do, where we were gonna go; we'd drink and laugh about things, and play football. It was our safe ground. We never troubled the shopkeepers 'cos they were good to us. One time, the police came looking for us there. A shopkeeper let me run away through his back door because he was on my side. He knew that we were a form of protection for him. With us outside the shop, he knew that he would never get any trouble from the other kids on the estate.'

After I talked to Jamie James and the boys in the Toryglen Nazi Circus, I reflected upon the similarities and differences of this set-up compared to the briefings that Alistair Campbell would give to his underlings when he was Tony Blair's special advisor. Martin Sixsmith, the former BBC journalist who was appointed as a civil servant in charge of communications in the early years of the New Labour administration, explained to me what happened at these briefings.

> Every morning at 8.30, Campbell would hold a briefing for the communications people. He would have been up very early that morning, deciphering what the papers had said. While pinpointing exactly what needed to be responded to, he would chuck in frequent abuse about the papers. 'Oh, the *Daily Mail*, it's the usual crap ... the *Guardian* have got the usual wankers in today.' His style was yobbish, but authoritative. His manner was domineering, brusque and, at times, menacing, but most of the time it was incredibly jokey. He was forever cracking football jokes. To him, everything was a joke. Human tragedies became a joke and information to be used. I can remember him joking about the British hostage at Guantanomo Bay, treating it as fodder to be manipulated. It was very cynical stuff. He always seemed to be asking the question: 'How can we use this terrible news to our advantage?'
>
> His henchmen, his deputies, would always flank him: Phil Bassett or Godric Smith on the right, and Tom Kelly on the left. Another spin doctor would always be quite near him as well. He was definitely one of the lads. There were endless comments about his favourite football team, Burnley.

Most importantly, at every briefing he would tell us what the politicians were going to say. Remember, this is an unelected official ordering elected officials to say his words.

Campbell's technique was exactly the same as Sid's: to ridicule his enemies, to discuss ways of defeating them. However, it is very important to note that Campbell was very relaxed in this setting, making jokes about football. This is the case with the gangs on the street; the leaders are forever cementing their dominance by cracking jokes. Like Campbell, their favourite topic is usually the ultimate tribal game, football.

The City Yobs

'It was in these sorts of settings that someone would get the nickname 'Stupid' or 'Cunt' – and they'd have to accept it.'

The main topic of conversation in the City yob's briefing room is not football, but money. Jean Herbert has worked as a high-powered trader in many big City institutions and had this to say.

Most big deals in the City are done in very informal settings. The clever thugs always have a coterie of people who they can plot deals and back-stabbings with. The favourite spot at the moment is Itsu, the Japanese sushi bar. These guys – and it usually is guys – perch on their high chairs and watch the sushi and sashimi twirl around and around before them on the conveyor belt, holding their chopsticks up in the air as they cogitate upon who they can shaft. The City is all about who wins the most money on the markets and because that is such an unknowable thing, a lot of City yobs think it is a good idea to destroy their enemies. So they'll sit there in Itsu with a fellow conspirator and discuss how they can get the better of their latest rival. The sorts of people who do this are generally not the working-class trader 'scum' who clog up the trading pits and who live in a simple moral universe of 'cunts' and 'wankers'. No, these are highly educated, usually over-privileged people who love nothing more than wrecking other people's lives. They'll talk about how they need, for the sake of the bank, to expose someone's incompetence. 'He's just not making the grade, is he?' they'll say to each other. 'Now I think it might be best if I brought this to the light of day, otherwise all of us are going to get tarred with the same brush.' Or if they are with a client they will subtly undermine the other people the client might want to do business with. These people might have a colleague or client followed by a private detective in order to find out some dirt about them. Most people have something they want to hide, and once someone knows that information, the subtle thug is in a position to threaten them with exposure unless they agree to the deal that needs to be made. Remember that anything enabling a trader to have some sort of inside information about some deal going on is potentially worth millions.

These sorts of topics are discussed at places like Itsu and if you want to be with the in-crowd at the moment, you need to get out your chopsticks and start swallowing raw fish, munching on the boiled rice and drinking your miso soup. A few years ago, the venues were different; usually in a bar. I remember during my early days as a trader I used to hang out at a bar where all the deals were going down. Standing in a huddle around the head honcho at my bank was the thing to do then. He would puff on his cigar, and get us to buy him drinks as he dispensed his largesse and advice. As we chatted and flirted with him, little titbits of information would come our way about who was for the chop, what deals were the best, who might be good to cultivate next and how we should be going about our jobs. In this sort of mean- dering way, many important decisions were made about what we were going to invest in next, who would definitely have to be frozen out and so on. We would laugh about the pathetic size of someone's bonus – getting anything less than two million was out of the question – and we would belittle that person, perhaps by inventing some humiliating nickname for them, which the poor victim would then have to accept as their name from now on in the office. It was in these sorts of settings that someone would get the nick- name 'Stupid' or 'Cunt' – and they'd have to accept it.

The people in the City are now very careful about what they say in emails because they are aware that they could incrim- inate them.

Ultimately, the cast-iron evidence of the email was to prove Dave Walker's undoing, but not before it had served his purposes very well. Dave Walker was a respectable head of year and history teacher in his thirties, who had an exem- plary record at the Midlands state school where he taught. He also had a secret passion for football hooliganism. Being the savvy person he was, he knew that the old days of foot- ball hooliganism had disappeared; the time when fans from two opposing teams could have a good old ruck on the terraces were long gone because of the tightened security in all foot- ball grounds. In the late 1970s and 80s, football hooliganism was a ramshackle, disorganised affair which relied on often haphazard meetings between football fans in order for real violence to 'kick off'.

The Internet changed all of this. The clever, organised football hooligan could now arrange a precisely timed fight by email or in a specially appointed chat room. The Internet became the forum for the briefing room and allowed the organisers of the violence to be much more specific about where, when and how the fight was to be conducted.

In April 2002 at London's Maze Hill station, Walker and his associates arranged an extremely violent fight between some Charlton and Southampton fans, which left three men in hospital and several others in need of medical attention.

This is what Superintendent Colum Price, the officer in charge of supervising the investigation of the Walker case, told me when I interviewed him.

In recent years we have seen a new phenomenon, which is what I like to call the '40-year-old biker syndrome'. This kind of football hooliganism is committed by middle-aged men who are going through some kind of mid-life crisis and need to prove their masculinity by beating the shit out of each other. The most famous instance of this was a case that I investigated myself, which has become known as the 'Battle of Maze Hill'. My involvement with the case started when the superintendents at BTP were shown some CCTV footage of an incredibly violent fight between two rival groups of football supporters: Charlton and Southampton. These guys were attacking each other with knives, bottles, hammers, chains. This was vicious, vicious stuff.

The images disturbed me enough to want to get the culprits behind bars. They were clearly a menace to society – and quite sinister as well because unlike the football hooligans of yesteryear, they were much more organised, and monied. Unlike in the 1980s, when payphones were used to arrange fights, the advent of mobile phones and email has meant that fights can be orchestrated with the precision of a football match: precise times can be set, lists of 'players' can be written, and flyers can even be printed. Of course, when we were investigating this, we realised that the technology must have left a trail. We got warrants to seize the computers of the main people involved at Maze Hill, and soon found a complicated pathway that led to the Battle of Maze Hill.

In many ways, Dave Walker is typical of the new breed of football hooligan. He held down a respectable job, and yet enjoyed nothing better than organising a violent ruck. But like many of these guys, he would probably be quite happy to sit down and have a pint with someone he has fought when the bundle was over.

All successful male yobs have their briefing rooms, whether in virtual or real space, because it gives them a time and place to get organised, to impose their authority upon their charges, to establish who is top dog and, most importantly, to issue instructions about how the next fight should be conducted.

Female yobs also need their own briefing rooms, but they are not specifically discussing ways of defeating their enemies when they talk among themselves in their kitchens, their bedrooms, over the washbasins in a toilet or in some quiet corner of a bar; they are nearly always preparing for their next big parade.

CHAPTER FOUR

Parades

‘ This place is shag central. The girls think nothing of fucking in the street. ’

Saturday night carnivals

'It's the dressing up. It's the becoming someone else. It's walking up and down and showing everyone what you are made of. It's being proud of who you are. It's not caring at all. It's not giving a fuck any more!'

I was standing in central Cardiff on Saturday night. It was July but the weather was bad: a thin drizzle descended upon the streets, sprinkling all the revellers. Not that this put them off. I marvelled at the scene before me. I remembered this city centre from years ago, in the 1980s. It had been a quiet, depressed place with a number of fusty, smoke-filled pubs, the odd nightclub and people moving morosely around the streets. How different things were now! The city was heaving with party animals. The streets throbbed with the sound of loud music: house music, rock and roll, jazz, reggae. The bars were thronged with people of all descriptions, dressed up to the nines; in designer T-shirts and jeans, in shiny suits and winkle-pickers, in pristine tracksuits and blazing baseball caps. Most outrageously, there were louts with moustaches tarted up as pubescent schoolgirls, all jutting boobs and bums, parping on hooters.

However, the women impressed me the most. How confident and outrageous they were in the Welsh capital! I saw a crowd of women in their twenties who were dressed as Mexicans in sombreros laughing and giggling by the ancient walls of Cardiff Castle; another gaggle of middle-aged women were wearing Playboy bunny basques, stilettos and bunny ears, and another group were sporting cowboy outfits which revealed fishnet thighs. Another group were painted as sexy, busty clowns with purple spangly hats. Others were more quietly shocking – sporting painted moustaches and wearing chic, pinstriped suits with only bras underneath.

'Cardiff is the hen party capital of the world,' said Daphne, a middle-aged woman with a very fake tan and a glittering, silver top. We chatted in the packed out Brewery complex. This yard of bars and clubs used to be where Braines beer was brewed for the cloth-capped miners. Now the brewery has gone and has been replaced with massive watering holes. 'Everyone who is anybody comes here for their hen party. They come from the Welsh valleys, they come from Bristol, they even come from London to have their hen party here. You see, Cardiff is the greatest city in the world now. People have hen parties here even when they are not going to get married. It's got that kind of a reputation.'

I asked her if she had dressed up like any of the troops of women that were parading around the streets.

Daphne nodded her head. 'Many, many times. I've been a Playboy bunny, a schoolgirl and, once, I was a bin man with a Wonderbra!'

She laughed uproariously and slapped her friend Phillis on the wrist (Phillis was clearly a little bit embarrassed by the conversation). Daphne said to Phillis, 'It's all right, he's only a writer, he'll only tell the whole world!'

They were a little bit drunk, but sober enough to explain to me what the appeal of this brave new world was. 'It's the dressing up. It's the becoming someone else. It's walking up and down and showing everyone what you are made of. It's being proud of who you are. It's not caring at all. It's not giving a fuck any more!'

I certainly saw plenty of people who didn't give a fuck on the streets as I wandered around Cardiff that night; girls were swaying around, enjoying being openly drunk, shouting at the tops of their voices. 'Fuck, fuck!' was a frequent invocation, but also I had a few women shout at me, 'You're lovely!'

I am pretty sure that this was not much to do with my personal attractiveness – they always hurried on quickly away from me as they shouted the compliment – but that it was more to do with their general level of intoxication and lack of inhibition. It was as if they weren't hidebound by the old rules of decorum that had constrained women for so many centuries in this country. They were allowed to say what they wanted, to articulate the most hidden taboo of their own desires.

'The women in Cardiff have got a lot of money,' Phil, a bartender at the Holiday Inn told me. 'They are the ones in serious employment around here. And they'll save up their wages just so that they can spend a hundred pounds during a weekend on going to pubs and clubs. It's what they live for. It's great for the guys, too, because if you wander out on the streets at two in the morning, you're bound to find a free shag. The girls are so pissed they'll go with anyone. I've only been in this city for a year and I've had 27 one-night stands. This place is shag central. The girls think nothing of fucking in the street.'

There was also a sense that such showmanship and exhibitionism was a part of a new-found national pride. 'We're Welsh, and we've got our own ways of doing things,' said Ceris, who worked for the Tourist Board. 'We don't need the English to tell us what to do. You won't find a better Saturday night than in Cardiff in the whole of the British Isles because the Welsh do things the right way.'

The dark side of his carnival was high levels of antisocial behaviour. In Cardiff, I saw people vomiting in the street and pissing on cars, and two fights where one guy was glassed in the face. However, I didn't see any sex in public – I had to take Phil's word for that.

A similar carnival was rocking and rolling in other British cities. In Glasgow, two Scottish teachers spoke proudly of the way their city had transformed itself into the nightlife centre of Scotland. Walking down the famous Sauchiehall Street with them at three in the morning on a Saturday night, I found it difficult to disagree: the street was packed with swaying, singing revellers who were making their way out of the clubs, and staggering into the all-night eateries like the Canton Express.

The two teachers guided me into this busy Chinese café, and over cups of green tea and chicken noodle soup explained that everyone from the neighbouring towns descended upon Glasgow on Saturday night to get drunk and have a good time. There wasn't quite the same burlesque atmosphere of Cardiff – I noticed far fewer gangs of women in fancy dress – but there was a definite vibe of jolly drunkenness. It appeared that everyone, from the lads and lasses of the council estates to middle-class professionals, was out for a good time.

'Some women will prepare for the whole week for this night, thinking about what they are going to wear, where they will go, what they will do,' said Sharon, one of the teachers. 'It's quite acceptable for women to go out by themselves without their husbands or even by themselves. The city is so friendly that you always find someone to hook up with.'

In the process of the evening they had befriended a middle-aged woman on her own, a twinkle-faced lawyer with cherry-red lipstick and a low-cut dress. She was a lawyer supervising the legal technicalities of a new transport system in Edinburgh and, like the teachers, was from out of town. 'Everything is changing in Scotland. Women have real power here. There are jobs for us, and we can do what we want. It's like a whole new world has opened up recently. I've got a great job helping Edinburgh built a whole new transport infrastructure. A woman of my age 20 years ago could well have been stuck at home doing nothing. But nowadays, you can have fun!'

Her point is true right across the board in Britain today. A City banker, Jean Herbert, confessed to me that the women in the City could be particularly outrageous on their nights out. 'You know, it really shocks me that some of my female friends get so pissed on their nights out and are so up for having fun that they'll think nothing of giving a guy a blow job in the toilets if they fancy him. They really have no shame.'

I spoke to an architect, George Mulvay, who had moved to Glasgow in the 1960s. 'It is unbelievable, the changes the city has seen in recent years. When I first came to the city, the only thing you could buy for lunch was a mutton pie, instant mash, peas or beans, and a pint of Heavy. Or if you were really pushing the boat, you'd get an "ashit" pie, which was round and had a raised lip of pastry!'

Mulvay and I laughed about this pitiful lack of choice because it seemed so inconceivable now, surrounded as we were by countless bars, restaurants, takeaways and cafés. Mulvay and a number of architects were instrumental in regenerating the city during the 1980s and 90s.

'Our aim was to bring Mediterranean café culture to the city by widening the pavements, developing residential accommodation in the centre, and creating multi-layered living where shops, bars, flats and houses co-existed,' he said. 'We were successful at this, but what we hadn't factored in was the level of antisocial behaviour that has come with it. In France, which I know very well, you don't get noisy, brawling drunks or very loud music, but you do here.'

Having now observed the behaviour of the British in a number of cities, I have to agree that Mulvay is right. The British are an extremely 'loud' race now in certain circumstances; their urban centres throb with noise and raucous shouting every Friday and Saturday night. It is almost as though their subdued, repressed manners during the day – behind supermarket checkouts, in sedate offices, in gigantic call centres – have to find an outlet on the streets at the weekend.

The women in particular like to hold these beauty parades where they show off their bodies, their latest costumes and gear; it is like a cross between a fashion show and a form of theatre. It is as though they have transformed their ordinary mundane, workaday bodies into fabulous, nocturnal sexy beasts.

It is as though they have gone on holiday while still at home. Many of the bars cater for this sensation by draping their walls and windows with pictures of exotic beaches and bikini-clad models, and offering cocktails such as Sex on the Beach at knock-down prices.

The owner of a bar in central Newcastle explained to me the thinking behind this decor and atmosphere. He said: 'In the early nineties, a lot of the publicans got to see what the guys in places like Ibiza and Ayia Napa were doing, and realised that you could recreate the feeling of going on holiday within a bar quite easily by playing the right kind of music, getting the lighting right, having a dance floor and selling the right kinds of drinks. That way you could give the punters the feeling that they were on holiday without them having the bother of paying for expensive flights. I have to say that I think the guys in Newcastle are geniuses to make this rainy, cold, dreary city feel like Cyprus on Saturday night, but they do somehow.'

The yob's holiday parade

'I was at a nightclub and all I did was ask the bouncer for a cigarette and he tried to attack me with a knife. He was going to fucking kill me. He threw me on the floor and started kicking my head in.'

The ripples spread across the pool quietly at first. It was three in the morning. I was sitting with Diane, a girl from Chester-le-Street, sipping a beer and talking about what motivated women to come to a place like Ayia Napa, in Cyprus, for their holidays. Then I noticed out of the corner of my eye that the ripples were inching further and further out in a rhythmical fashion. This was more than someone dangling their feet in the pool.

'Don't look!' Diane said, with her eyes widening. She then added in an astonished whisper, 'They're shagging.'

That certainly made me turn my head. I looked across from the bright lights of the pool bar and into the shadowy area of the pool. There was no one sitting by the edge of the pool, but quite a few lights were on in the rooms above the pool where a few sozzled revellers were lying slouched on their balconies. The light cast from the rooms quite clearly exposed the couple who were in the corner of the pool. It was expressly forbidden to get into the pool after 8 p.m., but these two didn't seem to care.

The plump girl still had her black bikini top on, but her skirt was floating on the water. The blond young man had his T-shirt on but no trousers. She didn't have her arms around him but was clearly attached by other means: she was riding her 'pull', bobbing up and down slowly, as he lunged drunkenly into her.

I couldn't believe that they were doing this in such a public place; everyone in the bar could see them.

'What do they think they are doing?' I asked Diane. 'Even if there is someone in their room, they could go around the corner and shag there without being seen. There are loads of nooks and crannies around here.'

Diane laughed at my unintended double entendre and replied, 'You're missing the point. Those two may look like they are a bit embarrassed, but they're not really. They want to show the world that they're having fun. They want to prove to everyone that they're on holiday. To get tapped while you're on holiday in Ayia Napa is the ultimate in street cred, and it's even better to say that you shagged him in front of everyone in the swimming pool, where you were forbidden to go. That girl – who I don't know by the way – has probably been planning for a moment like this for months. She's been talking with her mates about what kind of guy she wants to shag, how tall he should be, how toned his body should be, what kind of hairstyle he should have, what kind of jeans he should be wearing. She's spent all day from the moment she got up deciding on her costume, and where she'll go with her mates. And then when she's gone out she's felt everyone's eyes on her, and she's loved it. That's the thing about the atmosphere around here; they make you feel and look stunning even when you're not. It's like there's a holiday spirit that has turned you into a model or something. Look at that girl – she's not anything special, she's not that pretty, and yet she's pulled that muscly guy. He's six foot five tall, and he's got a great body, and yet she's quite fat, and not even good-looking. She'd never get a guy like him back home, but she has here. All the normal rules are suspended. And here it's about being in your own little *Big Brother* reality TV show. It's important to have people watching so that you can feel special. Being watched makes you feel like a media star, a celebrity.'

Diane's comments surprised me with their ferocity, their apparent loathing of what was going on. She lit a cigarette and took a swig of WKD.

'You seem a bit angry about it all,' I said.

'I'm sorry, but I'm feeling a bit bitter because the friend I came with left me in the lurch tonight. She's not that good-looking but she pulled this guy. Stunning-looking bloke, and it just made me feel a bit sick, that's all,' she said.

'Is that because you didn't pull?'

Diane shook her head. 'No. The thing about being in Ayia Napa is that any girl knows that she could sleep with a different guy every night if she wanted to. It's not difficult. I thought me and her had come here for more than that.'

'Like what?'

'Like enjoying the whole dressing up part of it more, the

whole tease thing. That's the most enjoyable part of going to a place like this. You put on these clothes and you become somebody else; you become loud and you chat with lots of blokes, and perhaps snog one or two of them, and then you get up on one of the bars and you shake your stuff around, and you feel like a million dollars because you are the centre of attention with all these guys drooling over you, and then you tell them to fuck off, and go home.'

'But I thought the whole point about coming here was to score,' I said.

'It is and it isn't. It's knowing that you could have scored. It is feeling that you are wanted and playing along with it, and kind of flirting and enjoying it, but then knowing when to leave off because any girl with any experience knows that the sex in this place will be absolutely crap. That girl in the pool got lucky in that he looks like one of the more sensitive ones. At least he's taking his time! It's mostly wham-bam-thank-you-mam around here. And there's also the fact that none of the lads know about wearing condoms. That guy in the pool can't be wearing a condom, can he? I mean, when you think about it, what is that girl doing? She's got this huge, victorious grin on her face, but will she have it tomorrow when she finds she's either pregnant or got some vile discharge? Er, I think not.'

Diane swigged her WKD and buried her face in her hands. 'Look, I'm sorry. I've drunk too much. I'm tired, and I've got to wait here until my friend tells me it's all right to sleep in my own bed.'

Ayia Napa truly showed me what a theatrical creature the young British woman has become. Until the late 1970s, this town had been a tiny fishing village, but the enterprising Cypriots, many of whom had fled from the north after the Turks invaded in the 1960s, decided to set up a seaside resort here, replacing the ones they had left behind in the north. Apart from an ancient monastery in the centre of town, they had a blank canvas. So they built a number of clubs and bars above the monastery, and offered cheap package holidays of sea, sun and sex to the Brits. It was a fantastic success. During the 1990s, Ayia Napa acquired a reputation for trendy music and risqué nightlife.

When I was there, nothing appeared to get going properly until 10 p.m., when the revellers, surfacing from the numerous hotels and apartments on the edge of town, would descend upon the bars, and then, lurching out of them at 1 a.m., go onto the clubs.

The whole atmosphere was rather similar to the one I had witnessed in Cardiff, Glasgow and Newcastle, only it was more drunken, more exaggerated, more outrageous. Every night, masses of girls dressed in sexy, skimpy clothes would parade up and down the streets. They would stomp into the bars like gunslingers, climb onto the counters and dance very provocatively to the incessant thudding music. In a few places, the bartenders would pour spirits onto the counters as the girls danced and set the alcohol alight, letting it whoosh in between their legs. They would scream with delight as packs of guys in T-shirts, jeans and topped-up tans would gawp at them. A few bars and clubs had poles; there the girls would leap up and do stripteases, jutting out their breasts and bums at the admiring crowd.

Yet now in 2005 business in Ayia Napa was suffering because it had got a reputation for a being a dangerous place; many girls didn't feel that safe on the big parade.

Claire, an 18-year-old from Guildford in Surrey, told me, 'I just don't feel safe here. Every night I've seen fights outside the clubs. When I was in Faliraki last year, there were no fights. Me and my friends have to hold hands walking around here, because when you go in the bars and on the streets there are all these guys, these dirty pervs, who are just looking at you, not trying to talk to you, but coming up to you and groping you. You've got to always be on your guard.'

Claire had come with 14 other friends from Surrey. There were nine girls and five guys. All of them had been to college together, and now were going their separate ways: some into jobs but quite a few to university. Having a holiday in Ayia Napa was their way of saying goodbye to each other. Unfortunately, though, the holiday had turned sour because many of the girls didn't feel safe in the resort, and because squabbles which would have remained buried at home now surfaced under the pressure of having to be with each other day and night.

The following night, two of the girls in the group became embroiled in a vicious fight by the pool. I was to learn later that the fight's origins were complicated; one girl in the gang, Celia, had abandoned her boyfriend – who was also on the trip – in order to sleep with a guy she had pulled in a club. He was upset, but not as upset as her female friends, who were incensed on his behalf. They all got talking in the bar on the night Celia was 'shagging her pull' from the club, and worked out that the girl had been slagging them off behind their backs. 'She'd been bad-mouthing us to each other and we didn't know until it all came out that night,' Alison, a well-spoken girl with a fabulous hairdo, told me. 'We even found out that she'd called the only black girl in the group a nigger behind her back. She is a bossy girl, and was always ordering us around. We'd all decided we'd had enough.'

So the night after Celia's 'pull', they all confronted her, and one of the girls, Jane, fuelled by alcohol and self-righteousness, attacked Celia, ripping at her hair and clothes. The new boyfriend, who had hitherto been keeping his distance from the group, tried to break up the fight, but was then attacked by the former boyfriend, and a great ruckus ensued; fists flew, hair was pulled, blows were inflicted and the air was blue with swearing. The fight only stopped when the bartender, Spiros, threatened to call the police.

All the fights between women I came across as I travelled around Britain and in Cyprus were at root about men. The ultimate betrayal in a girlfriend's eyes was for their friend to walk off with a man who had not in some way got their blessing. All the women I observed tried their best to co-operate with each other. I eavesdropped upon conversations between women in Cardiff, Glasgow, Newcastle, London and Ayia Napa, which were largely about the group deciding collectively what they were going to do, what they should wear the next night and what they should do in the day. The conversations meandered in a way that many men would have found frustrating because they never seemed to actually decide upon anything; the mere fact of discussing these issues was the point. This emphasis upon cooperation might explain why groups of women felt betrayed when men were pulled without their say-so. It was as if the collective group's intentions were often at cross-purposes to the individual woman's desires. For the group, it was the parade, the prancing up and down in the streets, in the bars, in the clubs, which was the whole point of an evening out, or even a whole holiday, whereas for the individual woman 'scoring' with a man was the ultimate proof of sexiness. This in-built tension between the group's wishes and intentions and the individual's desire caused grief.

Most nightclubs and bars seemed designed to exacerbate this tension: they were designed so that the women could flaunt their bodies, and yet offered hidey-holes for them 'to cop off'. The only activities on offer were drinking and dancing. Conversation was out of the question because the noise was so loud. However, there was one bar, Linekers, which was by far the girls' favourite because it supervised games which were basically variations on trivial pursuit and bingo with names like 'Shag the Sheep' and 'Bonk the Donkey'. The success of Linekers made me think that bars and nightclubs were so intent upon selling drink and sex that they had ignored the key ingredient of the reason why most girls go out: to have fun. However, in most places, instead of having the fun that they had been promised or they had promised themselves, the girls became tangled with fighting with each other over who was allowed to 'pull'. For all their increased spending power and superficial power over men at the bar, they were still victims of male desire. Most women simply wanted to 'tease' the men, to have their 'attractiveness' confirmed and validated, and that was all. Instead, however, they often found themselves dragooned into unpleasant shags in toilets. This was the very reverse of women's liberation; they were the playthings of men.

'The women here think that they are so powerful,' Diane told me the night after I met her in the swimming pool bar. 'But they're not. They are only kidding themselves that they are. In fact, I think it might even be worse than it used to be. In the olden days, women were taken out by men: wined, dined and possibly shagged. Now the women pay for everything, don't even get chatted up, do all the sexy dancing and then give the bloke a shag for free in order to feel like they're having a good time. At least in the olden days, a bloke had to spend a bit of effort and money on getting a shag.'

'Yes, but that was a form of prostitution, wasn't it?' I asked her.

'Now they are prostitutes without charging,' Diane said bitterly. 'The bloke is paying them by giving them some sort of cock-eyed emotional reassurance that they are attractive.'

Diane's extreme distaste for these new sexual mores made me ask her why she was in Ayia Napa. Here she was, an intelligent, middle-class girl with all A grades at A level, about to go to university to study social work, and yet she had come to this place. 'You don't understand, do you? This is what everyone my age does. Whether it's in Ibiza, or Faliraki, or Newcastle, it's the same old shit. There's no getting away from it. It's everywhere.'

The women I interviewed were concerned above all about their safety. This could have explained why Ayia Napa was losing popularity as a holiday resort; many women felt that it was not as well policed as the other popular resorts, and that a different type of guy went to Ayia Napa.

'This is much more your Burberry and baseball cap kind of place,' Claire said to me. 'You don't get your sweet-faced, cute guys here. These guys are rough, and they like being rough.'

I spoke to an owner of a nightclub, Anthony, who had been running bars and clubs here since the 1980s. He puffed on his cigar outside as we watched the phalanxes of revellers troop up and down the main drag where most of the night-clubs were. Great gouts of dry ice gusted out of the clubs, and the crazed thud of music crashed all around us, as he explained that things had quietened down a lot. 'We peaked from about 2000 to 2002. There was a Channel 4 documentary about Ayia Napa around that time, and also we got the top DJs from around the world coming here. Radio One staged a massive rave here, and I have to say that at about that time, this was the trendiest place on earth. But we paid dearly for that Channel 4 documentary. It made out the place to be very violent when it wasn't really. They filmed us at a club I was working for, and got loads of footage, but they edited it all down so that it made out that I was a really nasty boss, and I was basically brutal to my employees. Nothing could have been further from the truth; it was clever editing, that was all. That sort of thing happened time and again.

'The documentary did increase the popularity of the resort, but it brought with it everyone who was looking for a fight. That has had a big long-term effect on us; families and women don't think this is a safe place to come to. And so, since 2002, we've had declining attendances.'

Anthony didn't say that there were more and more fights, but I felt that this was the implication of what he was saying. Things had been further complicated by the fact that the mayor of Ayia Napa had been trying to re-brand the town as a family holiday destination. Apart from the few nutty families who wheeled their toddlers around the bars and clubs at midnight, I couldn't think of a place less suited to a family holiday. I saw a couple of kids, who were being dragged around by their tarted-up mothers, actually howling with pain as they were pushed along the main drag; they were covering their ears and screaming tears because the noise was so great. Their mothers had fixed smiles on their faces and beer bottles in their hands. I think they were too drunk to notice the agony they were putting their children through.

The men were much more aggressive in their day-to-day routines than the women. There was a permanent competition going on between the men. Whereas the girls were performing for an audience of men – many of whom they did not know – the boys were exclusively performing for each other, or perhaps more accurately trying to outperform each other. Most visibly, this took the form of trying to out-drink each other.

I watched in awe as Jason, a 19-year-old trainee plasterer from Croydon, lined up 15 shots of vodka on the bar and then downed each one. He proceeded to ask for a pint of vodka, gin and tequila, which Spiros, the bartender, had dubbed as 'Headfuck' in a scruffy handwritten sign by the bar. Jason swigged it down as though it was a pint of beer, and swayed towards me saying he was having a great holiday. 'This is what it's all about, getting lashed,' he said. 'Getting so lashed, that you're too drunk to think.'

He was worryingly coherent for someone who had imbibed so much alcohol. By my estimation, he had probably drunk enough alcohol to kill some other people. But he seemed to be OK, and he was keen to prove this to his mates. He lurched back to them, exhorting them to drink some more. They moved half-heartedly to the bar, but it was clear that he had won the competition hands down, and they seemed reluctant to keep up. However, now that Headfuck had won the drinking contest – as I had christened Jason in my head – the competition moved to other grounds.

'I bet Gary turns up in a minute.'

'No, he won't.'

'Yes, he will. He's not going to stay in that club forever.'

'You don't know him.'

'He'll be here.'

After a drunken contest about who knew where Gary was, one of the lads, Roy, told Joe to get the bartender to turn up the music. Joe then ordered the boy sitting next to him to do the same, and a general argument ensued about who would approach the barman. Again, it was another contest about who was the one to be ordered to do something. When stalemate happened, the conversation twisted into a dare about who would go behind the bar and turn up the music without the barman's permission.

Headfuck won by lurching up out of his seat. He swaggered up to the bar and half-heartedly tried to turn up the music. Spiros, who had been listening to the conversation anyway, turned up the music before Headfuck could reach it.

Headfuck had a swagger and panache and daring about him that made him stand out amidst his 15-strong group. The following night, he appeared in the hotel bar looking reasonably sober but livid with anger. I asked him what was the matter. 'I was at a nightclub and all I did was ask the bouncer for a cigarette and he tried to attack me with a knife. He was going to fucking kill me. He threw me on the floor and started kicking my head in. And do you know what? My friends, my fucking so-called friends, left me there. They saw me getting a kicking and they abandoned me. All I did was ask the guy for a cigarette.'

He sat down with me and ordered an alcopop, downing it in one. Shortly after this, a few of his friends appeared and demanded to know what he was up to. In particular, Danielle, perhaps the most articulate and together of the group, was furious with him. 'What were you doing Jason? What were you up to? You nutter, you were threatening those guys. You can't do that.'

'You fucking abandoned me, you bastards! You fucking left me there to be battered, you cunts!' Jason shouted.

Later on, Danielle came over to me and explained to me her version of events. 'He was refused entry into a club, and he threatened to kill the bouncers with a knife,' she said. 'He could have got himself killed if we hadn't stopped him from being beaten in. It was his mates who managed to get the bouncers to stop hitting him.'

Danielle was very disillusioned with the trip because of Jason's crazy behaviour and because the whole group had fallen out so badly with Celia. 'If we hadn't come we would still be friends. This whole place is like a nightmare. Still, I am pleased I am still with my boyfriend. Everyone told us that we shouldn't go to Ayia Napa as a couple, but we went – and we're still together! Mind you, there was a narrow squeak the other night because my boyfriend nearly hit a guy over the head with a bar stool. There was this really creepy man who criticised my dancing, and my boyfriend just went for him. Luckily, one of the bouncers here caught him and stopped the bar stool just as it was about to hit the guy's head. Then we got kicked out.'

Later on, Jason swayed over to me. He'd had a few alcoholic jellies to fortify him. He said, 'You know, the guys in my gang don't know what it is really like.' I asked him to explain what he meant and he leant more closely to me and said in a low voice, 'None of them have a crack addict for a mother.' He shook his head violently. 'They don't. They don't. They come from good homes. They are pussies compared with me. They are out here for the laugh. Then to get lashed. I'm only here to get lashed.'

He repeated that the gang knew nothing, and then explained, 'You see, I lived with my mum until I was five years old. And it was chaos. There were no guidelines. She was always sitting on the sofa getting high. Smoking crack. And there were guys coming around all the time. In the end, I went to live with my nan. But the damage was done. I had no sense of doing things in a regular way. I had a good job a while back, but I just smoked dope all the time. I didn't get up in the morning, and then they sacked me. It was after that my nan's husband took me on as a plasterer. I am lucky I have got her. I think I would be dead without her.

'But my mum will die soon. And I won't care. I won't give a shit. I have told her that she is drinking herself to death. She is an alcoholic now. She's off the crack, but she is killing herself with drink. I told her I wouldn't care if she went ahead and killed herself. I go around there and she's half out of it with drink.'

'But what about you, Jason? It looks like you're drinking a lot too,' I said.

He lit a cigarette and said that he was really pleased with himself. 'I haven't smoked any dope since the trip began. That's seven days without dope. That's a miracle for me. I've been really good on this trip. Sure, I've got lashed, but everyone gets lashed on holiday.'

Jason's alcoholic exhibitionism was partly due to his family background, but it was also to prove that the others were 'pussies' compared with him. He was locked in a competition with the others to show that he was 'harder' than everyone else by publicly consuming vast quantities of alcohol. In a way, it was the opposite of being a secretive alcoholic. He was celebrated for his drinking. He gained a real sense of self-worth by drinking more than the others.

The presence of the girls meant that the competitiveness never got out of hand. Danielle in particular stopped Jason from drinking to the point of extinction: I saw her take drinks away from him on a number of occasions, warning him of the consequences.

However, with the all-male groups, the competitive exhibitionism was not held in check. Perhaps most disturbingly, I saw a group of students from Wales bully one member of their group mercilessly. Nick Shoehorn's jutting teeth, inch-thick spectacles and hunched, intense manner made him a perfect target for a couple of dominant males in the group. I saw them bully him again and again: they would snatch his cap off him, punch him in the stomach under the guise of playing with him, call him a 'four-eyed fucker', tell him he had a one-inch dick, and shout out that he was a virgin in front of groups of girls. He frequently tried to protest, but his yelps of distress were drowned out by the group's laughter.

As I left Ayia Napa, I reflected that the girls' parading was causing multiple problems in these resorts: their garish flaunting of their bodies created an atmosphere of 'licentiousness', where people felt entitled to do what they wanted and didn't make the girls happy in the long run either. On the surface, their showmanship was a manifestation of their growing economic power and status, but a close examination of the issue revealed that they were being exploited. They were being suckered into pleasing men. For all their talk about being tough, the girls were still the playthings of the men and, in many cases, no better off than unpaid prostitutes.

Meanwhile, the men's competitive parading led inevitably to ridiculous drinking contests, chronic bullying and fights. I have already mentioned Jamie James, 29, the former yob from the Thamesmead area in London – he explained to me the nature of male parading on his 'manor'.

The Thamesmead boys loved the glory of being known as 'harder than hard'. I wasn't part of their gang, but instead was part of a smaller gang, which was more secretive really.

The Thamesmead boys were proper yobs because they liked the whole public nature of prancing around acting like real hard men. The Thamesmead boys loved to bump into people and watch the fear in people's faces. They actually much preferred this than actually doing any fighting. The best example of this was an incident that involved my sister. I had heard from my sister about a geezer who was suspected by her and her mates of raping a friend of theirs. I decided to deal with this and so sought him out with my sister and a group of my mates. We found him walking down the street, totally oblivious to what we were going to do. I smacked him in the face. He fell to the floor. He was very shocked. I didn't ask him whether he raped the girl – I just assumed he was guilty. Then my sister told my mates why I had hit him, as he was lying there on the floor. They all piled in, kicking him in the head, whacking him across the chest. Mashing him up pretty bad. Somehow he managed to get up and run off into a garage. We had given him a pretty good hiding so we just left it at that.

Then a group of mechanics came out of the garage, having heard from the kid about how we had beaten him up. They saw a gang of the Thamesmead (TM) boys passing by and assumed that the TM boys had beaten him up. When they saw so many of the TM boys – there was a group of about 15 of them – they decided to leave them alone. The TM boys then learned that they were famous for beating up a rapist. They had had nothing to do with it, but they took the glory. That story gave them a real boost. It made them seem like Robin Hood in the area. Fighting the bad guy. After that they walked around Bexley Heath like they owned the place. They'd go around in really big groups and strut around with their shoulders held high. Everyone knew who they were, but no one dared confront them. Even the security guards wouldn't confront them. The Thamesmead boys loved it. The ideal situation for a yob to be in is where he doesn't need to be violent because of a previous reputation. That allows him to parade around like he is a king.

The Bullingdon Society – the network of the parade

'It was an absolutely horrible experience with all the blue fluid from the loo slopping around and me slopping around too.'

B ut do parades of the sort seen in Cardiff and Ayia Napa occur in our more upper-crust environments?

My research revealed that yobbish parades are endemic in all social classes, from the 'NEDs' [Non-educated delinquents] on the estates of Glasgow to the upper-class toffs who have gone to Britain's top public schools and universities. It is a trait that is part and parcel of the British character – almost inexplicable to other nations – but so natural to the British that they rarely, if ever, feel the need to justify their actions; the drunken parade is one of those essential British rituals that enable the British to express the more outrageous aspects of their characters.

'I think that the people at the Bullingdon Society [the notorious Oxford Society], who have now all become journalists, lawyers, academics and MPs, were not naturally violent,' says Harry Mount, a journalist who attended one of Britain's top public schools and Oxford University. He is a diffident, mild-mannered chap who is anxious to put you at ease – the very antithesis of the snorting, boorish aristocrat who dismisses most of the British population with an airy wave of the hand. 'They weren't constantly straining at the leash to beat each other up. The Bullingdon Society was composed entirely of upper-class students at Oxford University; you were invited to join because you had gone to the right public school and you were going to be a successful person, who it was important to know later on in life.

'The Bullingdon's drunken antics were an entirely ritualised affair. It was an occasion when one was allowed to beat up others, drink too much, sing songs very loudly, be sick, tease each other and, I am afraid, shamingly, take one's clothes off.

'But the next day, these very same people would be studying very hard for their exams. On the whole, with the odd exception, they have all ended up doing quite well. In fact, I think that these two things go together. The same people who want to get on, want to get elected into these societies where one is very antisocial. Boris Johnson, the Conservative MP and editor of the *Spectator*, David Cameron, leader of the opposition and George Osborne, shadow chancellor in the Conservative Party, were all members of the Bullingdon Society.'

Just exactly what Cameron and Osborne got up to at the Bullingdon is to a degree a mystery because the society is very secretive about its habits. While it may be clandestine to the outside world, clearly the Bullingdon is about theatricality; it is about toffs showing off to other toffs. This was no more clearly shown than in a photograph of the 22-year-old Osborne published in the *News of the World* in October 2005. In this photo, Osborne is pictured ostentatiously smoking with a self-confessed prostitute who sold her services to a friend of his. It's a 'look-at-me-what-a-bad-boy-I-am' kind of picture.

Osborne's close friend David Cameron is famously coy about revealing his drug-taking habits to the general public. Clearly, he knows a thing or two about upper-crust yobbery.

Mount spends a moment to think why such privileged, and supposedly cultured, civilised people, would do a thing like this. 'They were members of the Bullingdon Society not because they are savages,' says Mount. 'It is because they are deeply ambitious and want to be in the club of popular people. Wearing 19th-century tailcoats, and conspicuously consuming money, drink and expensive food, indicates an aspiration to be grand and superior.'

> The incident that happened to me was actually deeply shaming. After dressing up in your tailcoats, you get in a mini-bus to go near Oxford town centre because historically the Bullingdon had been banned for doing all sorts of disgusting things, including smashing all 500 windows in Christ Church's Quad. As a result, there is a tradition of going to a place outside Oxford. We went to a summer house in a big place outside Oxford, where we had a huge, elaborate three-course meal including lobster, with lots of champagne and wine. There were also lots of drinking games that make you get drunker and drunker.
>
> After that, this very shaming episode happened to me. I went to the loo, one of these modern Portaloos, a portable box in a field. It was at the top of a hill. While I was relieving myself I suddenly I felt it rocking around, and before I knew it, I was being rolled down the hill. It was an absolutely horrible experience with all the blue fluid from the loo slopping around and me slopping around too.
>
> But this was part of the ritualised aspect of it. I knew that it was all part of the game. So even while I was rolling around in the miserable, humiliating blue toilet fluid, I knew that when the Portaloo came to a halt on its side – thank God the door was sky-side up – there would be lots of laughing and teasing, but that I would have to go along with it.

Mount was now properly one of the club; he had suffered his ritualised humiliation. Unlike many members of it, he decided not to exploit this incident and shied away from the people at the Bullingdon Society, but he could no doubt have

called in many favours at a later date because of his member-
ship. At a London club such as the Garrick he might have
chortled about the incident over a glass of port and then
mentioned in passing that he was looking for a position in
such and such a company, and he would have received a
helping hand. As he pointed out, the whole society was more
than aristocrats flaunting their outrageous behaviour; it was
a form of networking.

Perhaps the worst instance of Bullingdon Society yobbery
was committed by Princess Diana's nephew and his friends
on 1 December 2004. The landlord of the White Hart Inn,
Ian Rogers, said: 'The group was impeccably dressed in jackets
and ties, tweeds and dinner suits, and was very polite. After
filing into the beautiful setting of the underground cellar that
had been booked exclusively for their use, the group immediately became boisterous and began to bang their fists on
the tables.'

After about five minutes, Rogers went into the beer cellar
after hearing two glasses smash. He found one member of
the club with 'a deep cut on his cheek; he was bleeding a lot
onto his shirt'.

The injured man refused all offers of help and two other
members intervened to reiterate that he did not want a plaster
or any assistance. In addition to noting this odd behaviour,
Rogers commented that despite being extremely polite to
him and his staff, the men's language when addressing each
other contained 'graphic swear words' and was 'very antag-
onistic'.

Soon after he and his waitresses had delivered the main
courses to the men, Rogers said he heard 'an eruption of
noise'. After running into the cellar he encountered a
shocking scene: 'All the food and plates had been thrown
everywhere and they were jumping on top of each other on
the table like kids in a playground.'

The experience took on a surreal nature as each time

Rogers confronted a member 'they apologised profusely but offered no explanation. The Club also continued its violence; only two wine bottles out of 20 remained intact as the rest were smashed on the walls and thrown across the room.'[22]

In much the same way that the hoodie on the council estate parades his power by beating up his rivals, the people in the Bullingdon Society were parading their power by smashing up the pub and beating each other up.

The fires in Belfast

'I'd get my whole shop torched if I went to the police.'

Just off the Falls' Road in Belfast, I found about 30 children standing on top of a huge mound of broken wood. They were Catholic children who were going to light the wood that night. It was one of the last remnants of the Catholic parades that used to occur at this time of the year, on 8 August. The fire was built high enough against a lamp post so that the Protestant area opposite the Falls' Road could see them burning the Union Jack. Earlier in the summer the Protestant children had built their own bonfires where the Irish Tricolour and effigies of the Pope were burnt within sight of the Catholic area.

I talked to a number of the boys who were building the bonfire and asked them about the gang culture in the city. Unlike in Glasgow, Manchester and London, these children had not formed their own gangs with their own names because they had their own ready-formed one: the Irish Republican Army. Whether or not they were junior members of it, they certainly felt part of it. In the Protestant areas, in the run-down estates behind the Shankill Road, I found a similar situation: the children felt part of the Loyalist paramilitaries, the Ulster

Defence Force and the Ulster Defence Alliance.

Unlike the gangs in other areas in Britain, they had ready-made outlets for their aggression. They didn't have to have to invent their own 'parades' where they displayed their strength and might to the neighbourhood; they had parades of their own that were centuries old.

I spoke to a number of shop owners near these areas and they said that in the build-up to these bonfires and parades, they had experienced some very serious disorder. 'You see the teenagers strutting around collecting wood for their fires, and acting in a very cocky fashion before the parades,' Mr White, a harassed shopkeeper in the university area of the city, told me. 'I had a kid just this week walking into the shop and threatening to punch me in the face if I didn't give him 20 boxes of matches. He was only ten years old. I felt that it would have taught him a lesson to punch him, but I knew I would get into trouble if I did. He took the matches and walked out very cocky.'

I asked him why he didn't go to the police and he raised his arms up to the air. 'No one ever, ever goes to the police here. They are not trusted. Since the Troubles began in the 1960s, the police have been viewed as the enemy. I'd get my whole shop torched if I went to the police.'

Later on into my trip I spoke to a few policemen from the newly formed Northern Irish Police Force. 'A lot of people think that there are three religions in Northern Ireland: the Catholics, the Protestants and the Police. And the one religion which is hated by everyone is the police,' a middle-aged, kindly faced man with white hair said to me. 'People call us up so that they can stone us, throw petrol bombs at us, glass us, shoot at us. Calling the police is like having a turkey shoot: the kids are the shooters and we're the turkeys. And I have to say, this sort of attitude is causing real problems for the communities. There was a time when the two communities were self-policing. They kept the kids in order by knee-capping the drug dealers and threatening joy riders with knee-capping. But now the paramilitaries want to be respectable politicians and councillors, they can't rule like that any more. They actually need the police to arrest some of these hood-lums, but they are still very suspicious of us.'

So the IRA ceasefire and the Good Friday Agreement of 1998 had brought mixed fortunes to the city. There was a clear sense of optimism and wealth in the area: all of the checkpoints were being taken down. You could now walk into the city centre without passing through barricades with police and army carrying machine guns, and you passed police stations that were no longer protected by vast concrete blocks. All the watchtowers appeared to have gone.

Now that the conflict seems to have ended, however, Northern Ireland's real problems appeared to be beginning. During the Troubles the estates had ironically been very peace-able because the paramilitaries had policed them so strictly: no youths dared step out of line for fear of getting a severe beating. Now, this iron grip was in the process of relaxing and all the certainties of a nation at war were slipping away. 'The trouble is there is nothing for the kids to do in Belfast,' said Steve Mahon, a community youth in the city. 'The Catholic areas are actually a bit better than the Protestant ones. The Catholic side has always been quite good about things like community art projects and artsy things in general. But the Protestant areas have nothing. The Protestant council estates are very under-resourced areas where drugs, drink and antisocial behaviour are really beginning to emerge. Young guys used to have a very important role in these places as soldiers in the war against the other community. Now they don't, and they're very confused, bored, envious and angry. The suicide rates among young men in both areas have skyrocketed. The parades are the only things left now that give them a sense of meaning.'

Political parades

'Behind these violent and ugly displays of rank bullying lies a profound irony which exposes the true pusillanimous nature of New Labour.'
Bob Marshall Andrews, Labour MP

No politician better understood the importance of the political parade than Tony Blair. At the height of his power, he knew the importance of appearing top dog. He rarely missed an opportunity to be paraded in a positive and powerful light. However, behind his glossy parade, there lurked a whole world of yobbery. This shadowy world has only been exposed on a few occasions. One striking example was the furore caused by Black Rod, the royal official who was in charge of making the arrangements for the Queen Mother's funeral. Michael Willcocks, traditionally known as Black Rod, is Queen Elizabeth's emissary to the House of Commons. In a memo that was leaked to the British press, Black Rod said that he and his staff had been placed under 'sustained and constant pressure' by Downing Street to give Blair a more prominent role in the Queen Mother's funeral. The memo claimed that during the eight-day mourning period before the royal funeral, Blair's office suggested to Black Rod that the prime minister should walk from Downing Street to Westminster Abbey, meet the Queen Mother's coffin and enter through the main entrance in front of television cameras.[23]

When he was most influential, Tony Blair was very keyed into the thinking of the British. He knew that they invest status and authority in people who are at the front of an important parade. While there was obviously nothing particularly yobbish about Blair walking to meet the Queen Mother's coffin, the desperate instinct to do this is the yob's instinct for parading his power. Moreover, the tactics by which Blair tried to muscle in on the funeral certainly were yobbish.

Most infamously, the 2005 Labour Party Conference was marred by the way a frail 82-year-old accountant was bundled out of the conference hall just because he shouted out that the foreign secretary, Jack Straw, was speaking 'nonsense' during a 'debate' about Iraq. A nightclub bouncer grabbed the elderly Walter Wolfgang by the scruff of the neck and bundled him out of the conference hall because he was criticising Jack Straw's remarks about the Iraq war. The nightclub bouncer, Joe Ifill, had been hired by the Labour Party to ensure that they could parade their power without being embarrassed. Ifill said: 'Our team leader went through with us exactly what to do if there were hecklers or other troublemakers.'[24] This policy was applied across the board so that even a Holocaust survivor and long-time supporter of the Labour Party like Wolfgang was manhandled by the party's hired yobs, even though he was clearly no threat to anyone. Steve Forrest, the chairman of Erith and Thamesmead Labour Party, was also ejected after complaining about Mr Wolfgang's treatment. He had protested: 'Leave him alone, he's an old man.' At that point, he was yanked out of the hall himself. He said: 'Where is the democracy in this party? It seems that the leadership is full of paranoia.' A Labour Party official said at the time: 'A few years ago nobody would have objected to anyone heckling like that.'[25]

Bob Marshall Andrews, Labour MP for Medway, noted in the *Daily Telegraph*: 'This event is not isolated. On the same day, Austin Mitchell, the venerable, clever and wholly amiable MP for Grimsby, has his camera snatched and the contents sanitised in order to eradicate pictures of a queue . . . Behind these violent and ugly displays of rank bullying lies a profound irony which exposes the true pusillanimous nature of New Labour . . . The cheerful indiscipline of conferences past may have cost Labour votes but those losses will be nothing compared with the seismic effect of the bullying of Walter Wolfgang.'[26]

Ironically, this attempt at creating a successful political parade totally backfired because the bouncer was caught on camera abusing the frail Wolfgang. The negative publicity in the media was so overwhelming that it resulted in a mealy mouthed apology from the prime minister. More successfully for the Labour Party, during that same conference, 600 innocent people were detained under the Terrorism Act because they wanted to protest about the government's policies. Little or nothing was heard about the way their legitimate complaints about the government's policies were muzzled.[27]

While the yobbish antics of Tony Blair's closest advisor Alistair Campbell have been well documented, it was rarely the case that the prime minister's own yobbish tendencies were exposed. However, the publication of an ex-spin doctor's diary gave a fleeting glimpse of the real man who has so successfully maintained his grip on power for so many years. Lance Price's memoirs detailed how Blair repeatedly shouted out in rage 'fucking Welsh, fucking Welsh, fucking Welsh' when an election in the principality was going against Labour. The prime minister also appeared to 'relish' sending British troops to war in Iraq as his 'first blooding', while publicly claiming he did it 'with a heavy heart'.[28] In other words, the concerned, caring image that Tony Blair presented to the public was a sham.

The City yob's parade

'He stripped off naked, poured a green alcoholic drink around his nuts, set fire to his bollocks and then jumped ten feet from the balcony.' City broker

City insider and trader Jean Herbert explained to me the different ways in which City yobs parade their wealth.

There are three distinct types of people in the City: the chavs, the chippy but brainy working-class northerners and the over-privileged brats who love to play mind games. All of them, in their own ways, like to parade their status and wealth.

The trader who's come from nothing, and has worked like the proverbial dog, and made a lot of money, is a vulgar creature. This guy is like someone who has won the lottery and, as a result, all the clichéd things that are associated with wealth suddenly appear: the top-of-the-range Ferrari, the rocks for the wife and the mistresses, the massive mansion with the swimming pool, and so on. The stereotype is very much alive and kicking in places like Chigwell and other areas in Essex, and the home counties generally. I'll give you an anecdote of the sorts of behaviour these characters indulge in.

I have an old friend from school who is a money broker who fits this category. He is called Richard, but is known as Big Dick. Everyone gets a nickname like that in the City. And they are called by that name wherever they go. I know someone who is known as 'Moron' because he isn't fantastically bright. Everywhere he goes, whether it's to a restaurant or a wedding, he's called 'Moron'.

Anyway, a group of my girlfriends and I went to meet up with Big Dick at a nightclub he goes to called Thrills on the A127, a typical Essex nightclub full of escorts and sleaze bags. We went to be voyeurs and we weren't disappointed. I introduced BD to my girlfriends on the dance floor, and we exchanged pleasantries. BD then disappeared for a while, and I told my friends what a nice guy he was. They'd never met him before. Anyway, it was a bit embarrassing because BD had picked up a girl and had had sex with her in the corridor of the nightclub while we were talking. He then nicked her knickers and came rushing onto the dance floor, twirling the knickers around his head. A gaggle of the girl's friends then rushed onto the floor and jumped on him, shouting at the tops of their voices, 'Give us our mate's fucking knickers, you wanker. We'll fucking kill you.'

He got savaged. But he was laughing his head off. He loved it.

My friends turned to me, and said, 'Hmm, yes, nice friend you've got there.'

On reflection, I realise now that the whole thing was an act. BD was playing to his image: the sexually voracious, well-hung, macho city trader who can shag any woman he wants. Nightclubs like Thrills are perfect venues for people like that to parade their wealth and power.

Money brokers – who are a more cut-throat breed of trader in the City – are generally very extravagant and outrageous in the way they parade their power and status. This is what I learned from Fred, who has been a money broker for 20 years.

Money brokers like to work hard and to play hard. Keeping the customer happy is a vital part of the broker's job. A broker, you see, is the middle man between two banks. Banks are always lending and borrowing money, but they need to get that money with the best deal possible, the best rate of interest and so on. The money broker sorts that out for the bank, which is his customer: he matches a bank to another bank that is offering the best deal at that moment. The broker therefore needs to keep his customers very, very happy so that they go to him for the next deal and stay happy with the current deal. This is a very basic explanation of what brokers do, and when you go into it, it can be much more complex.

As a result, brokers are always entertaining their customers in new and special ways. They put on a show for them. So, for example, they might take them out on the piss in the City, and then to a strip club, where the customer can have a good time watching naked girls lap dance. Sometimes, the broker might even have to arrange a little bit more than a lap dance for the client, and pay some dancer to really entertain him!

There was a small guy called Parrot. He was reading the *Sun* with Boris, who was a big broker on the desk. They were reading the sport pages when Parrot said to Boris while they were looking at Paul Gasgoine's latest short, blond haircut, 'I wouldn't look that much of a cunt for at least 300 quid.' Boris put 300 quid on the desk, and said 'Off you go!' Having to save his own face, Parrot had to get his hair done. When he came back he looked as gay as Jean-Paul Gaultier. The black guy on the back of the desk shouted out, 'You should have at least asked for 500 quid, you mug!' Everyone in the room looked at each other and said, 'Let's have a whip round!' The black guy, who thought of himself as really macho, squirmed, but he had to accept his fate, and went off to get his hair done. When he came back, his new nickname was 'Guinness' because he looked like a pint of Guinness. Everyone was rolling up with laughter. Guinness's wife took the cash and didn't give him a penny!

One of the most outlandish and dangerous things I ever saw was carried out by this nutter called the Big Fiddler – no broker is called by their real name; we all have nick-names. He got into this thing we called 'bar diving', where the idea was you jumped off the bar and got caught by your mates, who had their arms interlinked to stop you from breaking your neck. The bravest divers would belly flop into the guys' interlocked hands. Anyway, the Big Fiddler's bar diving got progressively more dangerous and outrageous, until one day, in one of the most famous bars in the City, he stripped off naked, poured some kind of green alcoholic drink around his nuts, set fire to his bollocks and then jumped ten feet from the balcony into our arms. We caught him and he was fine – except he did complain that he had a blister on his nuts.

CHAPTER FIVE

Battlefields

You can tell the real Daddies by a look in their eyes. These are the guys who really don't give a fuck. These are the guys who will take you out and they won't think twice. They don't care about dying, and they don't care about killing you.

Kicking off - fighting for your territory

'And there was I, kicking over a table in a pub, brandishing a smashed glass, ready to fight, a middle-aged father with a good job, a nice wife and kids, just about to throw everything away.'

So much of what was learnt on the football terraces in the 1970s and 80s has now been adopted by the yobs on our streets, and in the boardrooms of our companies and institutions. Football has given the people of Britain a language, a code, a series of metaphors in which violence is inherent. Football is a form of sublimated war. More than any other game, it is about invading territory, about dominance and about intimidation.

It is no coincidence that the decline of football hooliganism has happened at a time when Britain has seen a huge rise in antisocial behaviour. Everywhere I have travelled to in Britain, I have seen the pervasive influence of the football hooligan upon the street thug, the city banker and the politician.

Perhaps most importantly, football gives the yob a language that automatically justifies and explains what he is doing. Every man – yes, it is always men – I have talked to has referred to the beginning of a major confrontation as 'kicking off'. The gangs I spoke to in Glasgow, the street robbers I interviewed in London and perhaps most pertinently, characters like Alistair Campbell, refer to their fights as 'kicking off' because they view them like football matches. It is an intriguing and instructive phrase because it initially sounds so innocent. When I have heard the phrase, 'Yeah, and it was kicking off . . .' I have initially assumed that this was a metaphor for a beginning: that people were shouting at each other, that a confrontation was *about* to begin. It can mean this, but in nine times out of ten when I have heard the phrase it has both a literal and a metaphorical meaning: people are literally 'kicking' or hitting each other. 'Yeah, it was kicking off . . .' is code for 'people were beating the shit out of each other'. Its derivation is from the argot of football hooligans who, of course, had taken it from the game itself: for the football hooligan, getting things 'kicking off' was a result. Violence was happening; this was the be all and end all of their existence.

Most informative in this regard was my interview with a former football hooligan who told me about the days that used to be.

Don still looks pretty tough. Now in his mid-thirties, he has a shaven head and gym-trimmed arms. As he tells me his story, he becomes more and more animated, starting to pace the room and sweat as he recalls the day of fear and exhilaration.

I grew up in the 1970s and 80s always moving around. My family mostly lived in London but we were always moving around: Leyton, Southgate, Essex Road in Islington, Forest Gate, Bow. We moved to Norfolk for a while, but it was back to London after that. Looking back now, I can see that I was rootless. My dad was a harsh man. He beat me regularly. I didn't really feel like I had a family except with the Arsenal.

No matter where I was living, I always made sure that I was watching Arsenal on Saturday afternoon from about the age of 16. About this time, the Arsenal 'firm' [gang] were just about getting organised. I suppose the catalyst for the firm getting serious was 1985, when West Ham came and took the North Bank [terraces] from us. We were outnumbered then, and we took a beating. That defeat really hurt. We were total victims. Completely pulverised by those bastards. Hit over the head with broken bottles, stabbed with knives, kicked to shit. Left bleeding and gasping on the concrete.

After that, we made up our minds that we would never be victims again and decided to run a tight ship like the West Ham lot. You see, West Ham were the first lot to get really organised. This was before the days of mobile phones and email, but their firm, from the very early 1980s, knew how to kick things off. And they mashed a lot of other teams.

But in 1986 we fought back properly. I'll never forget that day. It was probably our greatest moment, the day when we defeated the mighty West Ham firm. You see, the thing is with football hooligans, everything is about the honour of taking over someone else's territory. It's a bit like the knights of old riding into battle. West Ham had humiliated us by storming us on our own territory in '85, but now we were determined to get them.

I look back at myself then with horror. I lived for the violence. All week, I would be working at some crap job, and thinking, dreaming about the beating I would give some cunt in another firm. I would imagine the punches I might throw. Think about the tools I would need: usually I carried a Stanley knife, sometimes ammonia in a lemonade bottle, perhaps a hammer. And I would also be pretty bothered about the types of clothes I wore. I was a casual. And the guys in the Arsenal had style. We were quite mixed racially – there were a lot of black guys in the firm – but we weren't like the scruffy northern bastards, we had style and panache. Or we thought we did with our Pringle sweaters, our golfing shirts, Lois jeans, our brogues. We were the Gooners, and we were proud. The Gooners, by the way, was the nickname given to us after we went up north, and smacked the Geordies around: the way they pronounced the Gunners made us sound like the Gooners – and the name stuck with us.

The fight I was most anticipating was the return match with West Ham. All of us had been dreaming about this for a year. Psyching ourselves up for it. And finally the day came. About 250 of us got onto the Tube. There was about a train and a half of us. It was about eleven in the morning. A clear, crisp day of blue sky and hate. We got off at Plaistow, and there they were, all waiting for us, at the top of the stairs, at the very entrance to the Tube.

They were expecting us to run. To bottle it. I remember looking up at the leader of our firm, known to us as our proper daddy. He was our top guy. The toughest hardnut we had. There was a moment of silence as he stood at the head of pack and stared into the eyes of the West Ham daddy. Both guys staring at each other. Fronting it. Trying to see who would bottle out first.

I could see that the West Ham daddy felt sure we would bottle it. But we didn't 'cos our daddy was a bigger psycho than him. When he lunged into that lot with his knife, he couldn't have been thinking straight because West Ham held the advantage. They controlled the entrance to the station. They could just wait there and clobber us as we passed.

The thing was we were so psyched up, and we were so determined to get our revenge, that we didn't care. The adrenalin kicked in, and you get a high like nothing else. I remember just plunging into the fight lashing out at anyone who came at me. I was like an animal literally foaming at the mouth. Rabid. Uncontrollable. Totally out of control.

It was amazing, but we beat them. We sent them running. It was definitely our greatest hour. The odds were so against us then, but we won.

Like I said, I lived for the fights. We went all around the country, handing out beatings to whoever would take us on. The Millwall, Leeds and Birmingham firms were the worst, the most violent, but some of the little-known teams like Bristol were mean too. One of the most surprisingly violent firms was the Carlisle one. That town is in the middle of Cumbria, in the middle of absolutely nowhere, but bloody hell, they were fucking nutters. I guess there is nothing else to do there except fight.

It got to the point, though, that we became so well known that the police would divert the trains, and make us walk three or four miles to the grounds so that we avoided the city centres. A lot of paranoia started to enter the firms in the late 1980s because the police seemed to know all of our moves. They had us on CCTV, and a lot of people began to think that there were informers. They were suspicious of everyone they knew. Although there were no initiation ceremonies as such, you had to prove yourself if you were a new guy. You had to prove you weren't a fake. So that usually meant that the daddy would test your bottle by throwing you into a fight, and watching carefully how you did.

I had my own special type of initiation; it was very like an incident that happens in *The Football Factory*, a film about football hooligans. I was in a pub, a young rookie, and I didn't know what was what because the daddy, who I didn't know at the time was the daddy, asked me to get him a pint, and I responded, 'Get one yourself, you tight cunt.' It was only when I looked at him properly that I realised that he was *the* daddy. You can tell the real daddies by a look in their eyes. These are the guys who really don't give a fuck. These are the guys who will take you out and they won't think twice. They don't care about dying, and they don't care about killing you.

In a split second, I realised all of this. And I also realised that if I looked like I was frightened I would get done. So I fronted it, masked my fear and kept on, like I was joking, 'Get your own, you tight cunt.'

He smiled. He could have gone either way. Either I would get a very severe beating, or he could admire my front. I was lucky he chose to admire my front.

In my experience, the Old Bill loved all the violence. I remember coming home after a game against Tottenham, and things were kicking off behind me, but I actually hadn't had much to do with anything this time. But anyway, a cop came after me with a great big truncheon in his hand, on a horse, and cracked me unconscious. The Old Bill had all the advantages back then. They were often on horses, and had truncheons, and they got paid overtime. I suppose I am bitter because they said I was at a riot, when I wasn't, and that meant I got sent to Feltham Young Offenders' Institution for a few months. And God, was that place terrible.

There was no sense it was about rehabilitation. I came out of there more violent than when I went in. When I first got there, I was told by a prison officer to run across to the gate if I wanted my food, like this was the done thing. But as soon as I got to the gate, I was smashed around the face, the hardest I've ever been, by a prison officer because there was no running in the yard. That place was a total waste of time. Twenty-four hours banged up. Then my conviction was quashed because it there was no evidence. And so I don't have a criminal record.

I began to lose interest in the whole thing after a particularly scary incident in London. It was the Liverpool versus Everton FA Cup Final, and our little firm, which was an established smaller firm that often joined the bigger ones when something big was kicking off, decided to give the Scousers a slap. So we followed a firm of Liverpool supporters to a pub in Bond Street, and did a recce in the pub to see that they were really a genuine firm. They were. You can tell the firms by the clothes they wear – which are often not the team colours – and a look in their eyes. So we smashed the windows of the pub, and stormed in with our fists. I punched a few of them, and then I got cornered. I was surrounded by five Scousers. I realised that it was either me or them.

So I pulled out my Stanley knife, and came out slashing, catching a couple of them as I did. They backed off, but after that incident I realised that I wasn't that hard. I realised that I was scared. That I didn't want to die. And so I began to bottle out. You get a lot agro, if you bottle out. You can get beaten up, but you also suffer the humiliation of being a bottler.

Soon after me, though, a lot of the other guys began to give it up. The police were more on top of things, and by then it was the early 1990s, and the whole acid house thing was taking off, and everyone was getting 'E'd' up by taking Ecstasy. The firms were moving on to other stuff like arranging the security for the raves, or selling drugs. And some people I know were making very good money. Some are even millionaires running their own security firms, or selling drugs or doing semi-legit stuff. A lot, like me, are family men – they have a lot more to lose.

I can't believe half the things I did then. I was such an idiot. But I think I know now why I did it. I was hit around at home, and I did the same in the firms to other people. It all comes down to what happened to you as a kid. Now that I have children, I have been determined not to do that stuff to them. Not to rule by fear. By violence. I don't want them growing up like I did.

But this said, every now and then the urge hits me. It's like I can't help myself. There was an Arsenal versus Blackburn match recently, and we were drinking in the pub after the match when five Mancs guys came in. Now we could tell immediately that they were part of an old firm. It was their clothes. The designer-label clothes – the Hackett shirts and the Stone Ireland gear – gave them away. There were eight of them and they were pissed, and taking the piss, saying what a bunch of cunts we were. So we fronted them, shouting, 'Well, come on then!' And there was I, kicking over a table in a pub, brandishing a smashed glass, ready to fight, a middle-aged father with a good job, a nice wife and kids, just about to throw everything away. I remember thinking, 'I'm a dad. I could lose my job.' But the buzz hit me. The adrenalin hit me. It was like I was 16 again. So I lashed out at them, and luckily they backed down and nothing really happened.

There are still some old members involved in the scene. Sometimes, they'll get organised for a really big match. But things have calmed down a lot. Football is so much more about the money now. There are mega-bucks in it. Some of the old hooligans have got into the security guard racket, or catering side of things, and they are making serious cash out of it.

Perhaps most interestingly, some of the most violent hooligans now are very middle class. I know a couple of solicitors who use the Internet to arrange some pretty bad punch-ups. These are respectable characters with big houses, kids and two cars. But they need something more.

During the time that Don was a football hooligan, the commercial environment in which football clubs operated underwent huge cultural changes. The Thatcherite revolution brought unprecedented wealth into the hands of private entrepreneurs who recognised the potential for football clubs to become 'brands' in themselves, with their own clothes and merchandise being sold around the world. The spread of satellite TV resulted in teams like Arsenal and Manchester United becoming global products whose potential to make profits from the world's six billion people was unique; no other products, save Coca-Cola and the odd pop and movie star, had such appeal. Football became truly commercialised. As a result, it was imperative that the problem of hooliganism be eradicated so that it could be a truly family, cross-cultural and cross-class product. Terraces were replaced with seats, stadiums were upgraded, CCTV was installed everywhere. The government and police were shamed internationally. In particular, MPs had to face their angry constituents, who demanded to know why the yobs had been allowed a free reign in the football grounds. This led to effective law-enforcement policies that isolated trouble-makers and punished the miscreants.

Colum Price, a policeman for British Transport Police (BTP), explained to me how things used to be on the receiving end of football hooligans and how the police managed to stop the problem. He is a big, burly man, with red hair and a very jovial manner. He is a superintendent, and therefore an important manager in the BTP, and it is immediately clear that he has the fluent manner of someone who is used to dealing with the press.

I have been 23 years in the BTP, and I have done absolutely everything. I cut my teeth as a police officer in the late 1970s and 80s, which was the height of the football hooligans, their great heyday, as it were. I was match commander at Chelsea and Fulham then, so I encountered quite a bit of hooliganism.

The scariest moment I ever had to deal with was at Earl's Court. It's the early 1980s, and some of the hooligans I had to deal with were very vicious indeed. Anyway, we were escorting a group of Chelsea fans to an Arsenal match, and we changed trains at Earl's Court, when suddenly we saw that there were a whole gang of Arsenal fans at the other end of the station. There was just me and two other POs, and we were in the middle of these two groups of fans who basically wanted to kill each other. The thing about a situation like that is that the adrenalin really hits you. You know that you could get killed if the two gangs go for you. We were the meat in the sandwich.

What we did was get our batons out, and stalk around trying our best to look aggressive and mean. That is the only thing you can do in a situation like that. We were woefully understaffed in those days. We still hadn't worked out the best ways to stop the hooligans. We radioed through for urgent assistance, and then as the gangs approached us, we charged. Luckily, most of the mob backed off, but I remember a knife coming out. It was at this point that I found myself being shoved onto the train. The mob came with me, and the doors to the train shut behind me. I was trapped by myself on the train with the fans. I was shitting myself. I tapped furiously on the window, indicating that my colleagues needed to do something. But what, I didn't know, because the train was pulling away.

It was at that point I realised my mortality because I was faced with the hardcore Chelsea and Arsenal fans who wanted to take me out. I turned around to face them, and somehow managed to hold them off with my baton. The thing is if you are dealing with a mob, you have to go for the leader, and keep him down with your aggression. Generally, crowds only follow the leader, the head psycho, and so if you keep him down, you can actually hold a big crowd at bay even if you are only one person. Well, that's the theory. It worked for me that time. Mind you, that train ride to the next station was the longest ride I ever took in my life, even though it was only a few minutes.

Added to which, in the early eighties, although there was much more violence on the terraces, overall people had more respect for the police. It was very rare for a policeman to get attacked, whereas now it is such a common occurrence that it doesn't get reported any more.

The police managed to stop the football hooliganism of the 1980s through a combination of deploying CCTV footage and the introduction of new laws that enable the police to ban people from going to football grounds. Alcohol bans at football grounds helped a lot as well.

If you can't play the ball, go for the man – playing football with the truth

'We're fucked. I'm fucked, it's the biggest cock-up ever, and we're all completely fucked.'
Richard Mottram, senior civil servant

An understanding of the fundamental principles of football is essential if one is to fully comprehend New Labour's motivations, philosophy and modus operandi. The truth for New Labour is rather like a football: it is the person who has the ball, the upper hand, who is telling the truth. Hence, truth is not something to be established by reasoned, considered argument, but by battling for it in the same way that the most dogged football teams battle for the ball. Few stories better illustrate this than Martin Sixsmith's – one of the few people to score a goal against the New Labour machine.

'I find it very ironic that the New Labour government are cracking down on yobs, when they are the biggest bunch of yobs themselves. For them, the truth is a tradable commodity that they can kick around. The truth is that there are no gentlemen in politics any more,' says Sixsmith, as he shows me where he used to work, pointing to Richmond House, opposite Downing Street. We are at the centre of power in Britain. Having worked here for over six years, Sixsmith is in a unique position to offer me an insight into it.

Sixsmith worked as a BBC news correspondent for many years and became a famous face in the 1990s with his frequent appearances on BBC news as a foreign correspondent. He was educated at Manchester Grammar, Oxford University, Harvard, the Sorbonne and Leningrad. He joined the BBC in 1980 and reported from Moscow during the end of the Cold War. In 1997 he left the BBC to become director of communications at the Department of Social Security, working for Harriet Harman and Alistair Darling. He hoped to play a role in assisting the newly elected government in their management of the media.

> In 1997 the government had a clear-out of the civil service who dealt with the media. What I didn't realise at the time when I joined the civil service was that they wanted to put their own men into the civil service. It was, in reality, an underhand way of subverting the whole ethos of impartiality that the civil service was built on. They made civil servants the adjuncts to 'spin doctors'. They were expected to twist the truth to suit the purposes of New Labour and not the interests of the British public.
>
> By appointing Alistair Campbell as a special advisor, they entirely dispensed with the values of impartiality. Campbell's way of running things was totally different from what had gone on before. He promulgated throughout government the widespread use of bullying tactics.
>
> My main tangle with Campbell and the thugs in government came when I was assigned to supervise the communications strategy for Stephen Byers, who was transport secretary at the time. Byers had worked his way up the greasy pole by being the New Labour man par excellence: always on message and dapper-suited.
>
> I was asked to be part of some pretty unsavoury smear campaigns. Byers, and the government generally, didn't like the new London mayor, Ken Livingstone, or his transport commissioner, Bob Kylie. My predecessor was asked to spread a smear campaign against Kylie and was moved out when he wouldn't do it. Shortly after this, the woman who had been injured very badly – she had to wear a face mask – in the Paddington rail crash had a meeting with Byers, during which he agreed to install a new safety system on the railways. He told her to keep quiet about this, but when it became clear to her weeks later that he was going

to do nothing about it, she went to the press and pointed out yet another of Byer's promises. Shortly after this, an email was circulated around Labour PR headquarters at Millbank asking whether they had any dirt on this woman.

Added to this, Byers and Moore tried to bully me into appointing a New Labour 'place woman' as a communications civil servant. When I refused to have this obvious political appointee in the department, because another candidate was far better based on merit and experience, Byers threatened to slash my budget, and said darkly to me, 'I hope you know what you are doing.'

In the end my chosen person was appointed, but only after much bitterness.

Things really came to a head on the day when Princess Margaret died. It was announced that she was to be buried the next Friday. Byers and Moore felt that this would be a good time to publish rail statistics that were particularly embarrassing to the government. I warned them that this was not a good idea at all. The newspapers then published this email, which was a corrupted version of mine, 'There is no way I will allow any substantive announcement next Friday. Princess Margaret is being buried on that day. I will absolutely not allow anything else to be.'

Within half an hour, two newspapers had the email. I didn't leak the email. Despite this, I was called by some No. 10 officials to explain myself. I told them that I had sent such an email but that the wording was different. They then issued a statement saying, 'There is no such email.' You have to understand that the government think like lawyers. The word 'such' justified this comment because the *Express* had got a couple of words wrong.

But there was an email. I was contacted by two press officers, Alistair Campbell's two deputies Godric Smith and Tom Kelly, in a joint phone call asking me to say that there was no such email. I refused to do so.

At this point, the government had been conclusively proved to be lying because the very person who had sent the email was refusing to say that it was a fabrication. Jo Moore was forced to resign. Byers was so pissed off at losing his best girl, he demanded that I resign too.

Campbell took over at this juncture, and announced that I had resigned – even though I had said that I wouldn't. He was the government's hatchet man. And he was feared. When he demanded that politicians resign, they resigned. When I told him that I was not going to resign, he was not happy.

When Richard Mottram, the permanent secretary to the Department for Transport, Local Government and the Regions, heard what had happened, he wrote the immortal words, which he will be forever remembered for, 'We're fucked. I'm fucked, it's the biggest cock-up ever and we're all completely fucked.'

You see, I didn't do the usual disappearing routine and I paid for it. I became the victim of a smear campaign. The newspapers were fed some totally false information about some supposedly dodgy property deals I had done.

In the end, though, because I had told the truth throughout, and I didn't buckle under pressure, the government issued me an apology, acknowledging I hadn't resigned, and paid me a lot of money. However, when they realised I hadn't signed a confidentiality agreement, they sent me a very heavy legal letter, saying that if I wrote a book about it, they would sue me. I got around this by writing a novel called *Spin*, a political satire set in the future, which encapsulates the atmosphere of bullying, subversion and strong-arm tactics that characterise this government.

Sixsmith pauses for a moment, collecting his thoughts. He is a very mild-mannered person who you sense does not become angry very often but clearly he is still upset by what happened to him, years later.

What happened to David Kelly, happened to me on a much smaller scale. David Kelly, being an expert on the weapons' capability in Iraq, was a very important civil servant. Despite what the government said about him, he was an authority on Saddam's armoury, and a very brave man who had risked his life in order to discover what was going on in Iraq. He was no junior official as the New Labour smears claimed. When he tipped off the press that Campbell and the government had been lying about Saddam's weapons' capability so that they could justify going to war, he was mercilessly hung out to dry. When the government found out that it was he who had given the journalist Andrew Gilligan the information about the claim that Saddam could launch weapons of mass destruction within 45 minutes, they pursued him like a pack of hounds. They put him in front a parliamentary committee, where he was basically publicly humiliated, they removed his pension, they suggested he was a fantasist and a minor official – which he certainly wasn't.

You see, the government knew that they were caught. It was at this point that Campbell's maxim, 'If you are in trouble, and you can't play the ball, go for the man', came into play. He wrote in his diary that he was going to 'fuck' Gilligan. The whole thing was a very successful sideshow that distracted the public's attention away from the fact that Blair had made a disastrous error in going to war with Iraq. Campbell spotted a way out. He knew the dossier was full of lies. He knew he was banged to rights, so he created a diversion. He accused the BBC of being biased, and attacked both Gilligan and Kelly. The result was that David Kelly, who was obviously a fragile man in certain ways, couldn't take the pressure and killed himself. As a result of the ridiculous whitewash of the Hutton report, which exonerated the government and blamed the BBC, Gilligan was sacked, and the top people at the BBC were removed. The BBC was cowed for some time by the government. Hutton changed forever the way political parties – any political party – will treat the media. Now the media will always be bullied because New Labour showed how the yobbish technique of the football hooligan works.

This highly confrontational style of politics, of bad mouthing any sort of criticism or ridiculing public figures, has resulted in New Labour politicians being so wound up, so highly aggressive, that they can lose it entirely. Most famously, in May 2001, during the election campaign, John Prescott punched a protestor at an election rally. Protesters had gathered outside the Little Theatre, in the North Wales seaside resort of Rhyl, where Prescott arrived to attend a Labour rally. A protestor threw an egg at Prescott and he totally lost his cool, smashing the protestor in the face with his fist.

Prescott's violent outburst is not the only one. Much more seriously, Labour peer Mike Watson was sentenced to 16 months in prison for drunkenly setting fire to a curtain in an Edinburgh hotel and putting the lives of the guests and staff at risk. Lord Watson of Invergowrie had got very drunk at a ceremony, and then demanded more drink from the hotel staff when the bar was closed, before attempting to set the hotel on fire. He admitted a charge of 'wilful fire-raising' and received a custodial sentence.

More illustrative of the aggression that permeates New Labour is the altercation between the backbench 'rebellious' MP Bob Marshall-Andrews and the 'on-message' Labour MPs Barry Sherman and Jim Dowd. Just before the crucial vote on the terrorism bill that Blair was trying to push through parliament in November 2005, one MP witnessed the following extraordinary row: 'Barry Sherman saw Bob talking to some Tory MPs, and very aggressively accused him of plotting with the Opposition. Bob was just having an amiable chat with the Tories, asking what was likely to happen over the terror vote. All the aggression came from Mr Sherman, Bob was very calm and relaxed. He responded by telling Mr Sherman to go and sober up – at which Mr Sherman said he didn't drink. Then Jim Dowd passed by, and also started berating him. Bob told Jim to clear off, at which point Jim lunged at him.' Afterwards, Mr Dowd did not deny claims of a punch-up.[29]

It isn't only the Labour Party that is guilty of such yobbery. As we have seen, some very high-ranking Tories were members of the notorious Bullingdon Club. In this new 'yobbish' climate created by New Labour, they too are being drawn away from aristocratic yobbery. The Labour MP for Ealing, Stephen Pound, claims that the Conservative MP Philip Davies 'completely lost the plot' after an acrimonious argument on a radio show. Pound had read out an email on the radio show that alleged that one of Mr Davies's staff had asked local Tories to ring in to the show to support him. Pound said: 'As soon as the programme finished, we went into the control room and he completely lost the plot. He was trying to grab the email and wrestling me around the room, grabbing me and grappling, crashing around the place . . . He has got a bit of a temper and needs to calm down a bit.' Ian Collins, the talk-show host, saw the incident, and said: 'It was an absolutely ridiculous sight. Two grown men in their Saville Row suits brawling as if they were in a playground. They were in a bear hug and were really going for it. They were serious. We broke it up, but as they were leaving, one taunted the other and it broke out all over again.'[30]

MPs are not the only political figures guilty of such aggression, however. Martin Samways, president of the train drivers' union, was said to have hit a woman in the face before getting into a brawl with Shaun Brady, the union's Blairite general secretary. Brady told an employment tribunal he had met Samways at a barbecue: 'Mr Samways was very drunk and, after he sat down at the table, he started calling the other guests "fucking traitors". I told him to stop and to come under the umbrella because he was getting wet, to which he said "Fuck off".' As other guests tried to calm Samways down, he lashed out, hitting Julie Atkinson, the union administration manager. Brady then tried to restrain Samways, but failed to do so. Samways stalked off and then returned, trying to punch Brady again. Brady said: 'I ran into the garden. He was chasing after me and I was pushing him away. The third time I pushed he . . . ended up on the lawn.' Brady also faced disciplinary charges for the incident.[31]

Peter Riddell, who is the author of a number of important books about politics as well as a political correspondent for *The Times*, observes in a detached way that the political culture has changed incredibly in the last 20 years. 'Football culture has infected this government, and many of the people who surround the government – the advisors, the union members and the political journalists. It is an anti-intellectual, winner-takes-all culture, which means that rules are bent, and is characterised by high levels of aggression. It isn't just Campbell who is like this, it is a lot of people both in government and the opposition. What's happened, you see, is that the rise of the Nick Hornby generation, middle-class men who profess to love football, has coincided with New Labour getting into power.'

Riddell is a cultured man in his late fifties with a love of reading, opera and theatre. He represents a disappearing species: a dispassionate, balanced, analytical observer of the political scene. While Sixsmith's condemnation of New Labour is quite extreme, Riddell, who arrives at many similar conclusions, is more interested in the nuances of the 'yob' phenomenon at the heart of government. 'Gordon Brown is a devotee of football, and surrounds himself with people like Ed Balls and Charlie Whelan, who are football fanatics. Blair professes a love of football because he has to, and has teenage sons. Charles Clarke, the home secretary, also fits into this category. Add Campbell and his coterie into this, and you have, for the first time ever, a "football" culture in the corridors of power. Machismo rules the roost.'

Francis Beckett, who is the co-author, with David Hencke, of *The Blairs and Their Court*, is even more critical of New Labour, and Tony Blair in particular.

Many people think that the whole yobbery of New Labour has always come from a level below Tony Blair. Everyone in the know acknowledges that Alistair Campbell is a yob and a thug, but they have always believed that Blair is a 'pretty straight sort of guy' – as he once described himself. But one of the most revealing things that Campbell ever said was this: 'Everything I do, I do because the prime minister wants me to.' In other words, all of Campbell's thuggery happened because he was instructed to behave that way by Blair. You see, Tony Blair is the most skilled politician of his generation and has always managed to avoid being tarred with the brush of being a bully, but the truth is that Blair is at the heart of all of the yobbery. Tony Blair said that what happened to the poor, elderly Wolfgang was merely the result of an 'over-zealous steward', when in truth the manhandling of Wolfgang at the conference was indicative of how New Labour operates. New Labour has a real Stalinist streak that will not tolerate dissension. Unfortunately, Blair has been ably supported in his bullying by a supine parliamentary lobby who are only too willing to print or say on TV what he wants them to say.

Most crucially Blair and his inner circle set up the template upon which all British politicians will now model themselves. All leaders who succeed him – whether from New Labour or the opposition – will employ very aggressive henchmen who will bully their party, the media and anyone else who gets in their way because they now know that these techniques work and that if they don't behave like this, their opponents will.

Down in the pits

'You wouldn't have spoken to your dog in the way that he spoke to me. It was worse than any hoodie in the street yelling at you because it felt such a betrayal.'

While it is the battle for the truth that is at the heart of New Labour's fights with its opponents, it is the battle for money that motivates some of the most aggressive behaviour in the City of London. Peter Riddell felt that while New Labour politicians liked to twist the truth in order to put their party in a positive light, there was very little financial corruption in British politics. 'No one goes into politics for the money,' Riddell told me. 'They are motivated by a desire for power, to serve their party, to aggrandise themselves, but there are very, very few characters who are trying to squeeze money out of people. And the few financial sleaze stories that have happened – such as the Neil Hamilton case – have been about relatively small amounts of money. British politics is not like the US, where money rules the roost and there are some very questionable conflicts of interest.'

'If a yob wants to make a lot of money, he doesn't join a political party like he might in the States or many other countries around the world. No, he gets a job in a City bank,' says Jean Herbert, who is now a consultant to many of the top banks in the City. She worked for ten years as a derivatives trader, in one of the most intellectually demanding and nail-biting aspects of trading.

The thing about working in the City is that the money is so good. Once you get in there, you are playing for millions. When Goldman Sachs, the merchant bank, was floated on the stock market, even the doorman got eight million dollars. And when that kind of money is at stake, it can bring out the worst in people. It is a fight to be the best, to get the most dosh. It's a war.

London has become the financial centre of the world now. After 9/11, and the crisis with Enron, which exposed insider dealing in America, Wall Street, the financial capital of America, has become over-regulated, and a lot of banks have moved their main business to London as a result.

They love London because the City is ring-fenced. We are allowed to do what we want. Gordon Brown doesn't dare touch us. If he phoned up Goldman Sachs to help him out, he'd be told to piss off. They hate him in the City. He's seen as a commie.

Because the top banks in the City can do whatever they want, this has led to a kind of mass yobbery. The top banks, like Goldman Sachs, J.P. Morgan, and CSFB, are more powerful than governments, and have the power to destroy countries overnight if they chose to.

There is a very animalistic, aggressive culture in the City. The worst people for out-and-out yobbery are the pit traders. On the trading floor there are these pits where the traders buy and sell stocks and shares directly off each other. It is like a horrible, twisted version of *Gladiators* down there. These massive, burly men dressed in their red jackets – which indicate that they are trading on their own accounts, with their own money – snort, stamp and step from side to side as they do their deals. It is cut-throat. They are trading millions of their own money with nods of their heads, blinks of their eyes, punches with their fists. They are desperate to screw the best deal out of their opponent, and vice versa. Everyone is trying to trick them into selling or buying at a bad price, and they are going to be fucked if they are going to be fooled. And they use physical intimidation to make it clear that they will kill someone who fucks them over. This is a mean, mean world because there is so much money at stake.

Hanging over the pits are these tarts, who are unbelievably attractive, taking messages for the boys in the pit, and absolutely desperate to grab themselves a trader, and live the billionaire's life.

Next to the Liffe traders are the ICAP and Tullet boys, the money brokers, who are in everyone's estimation the scum of the City. My friend went to work for Tullets, and every morning she would pass the money brokers. Each one would hold up a card, which was a rating out of ten for how sexy she looked that day. She'd often get low scores, until one day she went out with one of the boys and the next morning got rated ten out of ten. It was a completely soul-destroying experience and, in the end, she found it so distressing that she had to leave her job.

The constant bullying in the City nearly killed me.

I studied Japanese at university and joined Solomon's as a graduate trainee. I was put on the Japanese trading desk because of my language skills. It was a gruelling schedule. You had to start early and work to very late. Within a year I was headhunted by J.P. Morgan, who were looking to recruit bright graduates. My boss there was a scary-looking psycho who knew nothing. He would strut around in his designer suits, never smiling, and staring menacingly at people. He had a goatee beard, and a thin, quietly snarling face. We nicknamed him Ming the Merciless because he looked like that evil character from *Flash Gordon*. He carried around with him a real aura of fear, and he loved that. His favourite thing to do was blame everyone else for any cock-up – even if it was his fault, which it usually was. I can remember him waltzing into a meeting after we'd lost some money on a trade and saying that it was all the idiot's fault who wrote the report on the deal we were negotiating. 'He's fired,' he said. And with a click of his fingers that poor sap was out of a job. He did this to numerous people. Now what's important to realise here is that he wasn't like the guys in the Liffe pit, but it was exactly the same effect: he wanted to induce fear. He attacked anyone he could so long as he wasn't in the firing line.

It was a wretched, miserable job, but the money was unbelievable. It was almost like all the screaming and abuse we absorbed every day was our punishment for getting paid so well. I was looking after the New York and Tokyo side of things, which again meant staying up very late because of the markets opening at different times from British time. I can remember the way we used to handle billions of pounds with lots of people shouting at us. Our boss shouted about everything. He was a yob par excellence. We were always fucking cunts. Bastards. And every day we would get the blame for some sort of cock-up that usually wasn't our fault.

I worked with this guy called Andy who was devastated one year because he only got a 15 million dollar bonus. Now I know that most people will find this completely unbelievable, but it's true! The thing is that people at the top in the City make obscene amounts of money. Ming the Merciless, for example, was rumoured to be making in the region of $50 million in bonuses every year. Andy knew that his bonus didn't come near this. I remember him talking so hopefully about how in January he would be so happy if he got a massive bonus; how he would see life anew and afresh. He was building himself up so that getting a big bonus was the be all and end all of existence. Nothing else mattered to him but getting a whacking great bonus.

He tried so hard in the job. He wanted so badly to do well. And you see, when you enter that atmosphere, that nest of back-stabbers, you don't think about what everyone else is earning, you only compare yourself with everyone else. I remember very vividly how he began to act increasingly strangely. He felt so crushed by getting such a low bonus that he began to lose his mind. I found him once hiding underneath his desk, sharpening pencils.

The memory that saddens me the most is leaving work with him at 3 a.m. on Christmas Eve and looking down at Victoria Embankment in the street-lit gloom. We shook hands before heading home.

He was dead within two weeks. He died suddenly of leukaemia, which I am certain was caused by the stress of not getting the bonus he wanted.

Another friend set up a new trading desk with me, and again felt very humiliated by the size of his bonus. He went on holiday, but never returned. Eventually, his flat was broken into. He had committed suicide because his bonus wasn't big enough.

I myself nearly died from the stress of the job. I had internal haemorrhaging, which was caused by my stomach being gnawed away with nerves day in, day out. The doctor ordered me to give up my job otherwise I would die. When I told my boss, he tried to do everything to get me to stay. He promised a sabbatical of a year and so forth. But I had to tell him that this was it. I couldn't go on. When he eventually realised I was going, he got nasty and said that he had deliberately 'burned' me. He wanted to brainwash me so that he would see whether I was any good or not. 'But you're fucking not up to it, love, are you?'

I don't do that really high-pressure job any more. I work

as a consultant training people for the banks, and strictly control the way I work. I order the people I train to leave at 6 p.m. and get a life.

But things haven't changed much. There's still the same macho bullshit about working long hours, and getting massive bonuses, that there was when I was a trader.

Jill's story is no less horrific.

'I worked in the City for 20 years with all the different types of traders: currency, futures, stock market, and commodities traders,' she says. 'All of them buying and selling various things which could potentially make them huge amounts of money.'

One of the worst places I worked was a major City bank, where the trading floor was laid out in concentric circles so that everyone could see everyone else. The open-plan accentuates an atmosphere; if there is a noise from one area, then very quickly the noise infects everyone else, and everyone is shouting. Like a bullring.

I had a boss who was a complete nightmare. His favourite threat, which is a favourite threat of all bosses in the City, is that he would slash your bonus. The bonus is everything in the City. It can be a huge amount of money. Often 200 per cent of your salary.

This boss tended to leave me alone, but once he did lean over my desk, with his face only about an inch away from me, and say, 'You fucking bitch, you bitch, how could you have fucked me over like that?'

What had happened was that I had tried to assist him with a problem. He hadn't been able to sort this complex financial problem out, but I managed to with help from an ex-boss in another department. When my boss found out, he went mad. This meant, in my boss's mind, that I was trying to humiliate him. That I was being disloyal. Instead of saying to me that I had fielded the problem well, instead of praising me, as he should have done if he was following the company's policies, he chose to hurl abuse at me. I can still hear the stream of abuse coming out of his mouth. It was terrible. You wouldn't have spoken to your dog in the way that he spoke to me. It worse than any hoodie in the street yelling at you because it felt such a betrayal. I felt betrayed because I had worked so hard for him. I had tried to sort out his problem, and been repaid with this hatred.

He was a married man with children but that they didn't stop him sleeping with three of the women in the office who worked for him. And no one complained about any of his behaviour because everyone was frightened of him, except for one other person in the office, who was ten times worse!

The only thing that kept me going was the money, and the knowledge that I could leave anytime. Because this is another very important point about working in the City, all jobs are very short-term. So many people get made redundant at least three or four times in their working lives. There is no sense of job satisfaction, of completing a job well done, of feeling part of a good institution.

Getting sacked or made redundant is always a humiliating experience. It used to be that people were sacked over the Tannoy, or would find a black bin liner on their desk, or sometimes be escorted off the premises by a security guard. The methods may have improved now but the impact on your life is the same.

I was sacked because I had a child. The firm had been looking for ways of getting rid of me since I announced that I was pregnant although I carried on working hard. I dropped my child off one day at nursery, was called in to be told I was being made redundant and by lunchtime I was at home watching daytime TV and wondering what to do with the rest of my life. It was over. I still haven't gone back. Even though the money is amazing, I am not sure that I can face it anymore.

The world of the money broker can be particularly brutal. Fred Troy has worked for over 20 years as a broker and has seen every sort of animal behaviour you can imagine.

The pit where the brokers work can be a lot like a zoo. It's 90 per cent men, and the testosterone really flows when there are big deals going down. You see, when you are dealing with such large sums of money, emotions run high. I remember once I saw this guy fuck up big time on a deal: basically he lost the firm 30 grand in the space of a few minutes because of his incompetence. The senior broker was furious when he learnt about it. Completely livid. This was really bad news. And the senior broker just went berserk.

Now you have to understand that if anyone is caught punching an employee they will be sacked because that's employment law, but what goes on behind closed doors is a different matter. If no one's looking, it is fair game for someone to put the boot in – particularly if it is justified. And this is what happened in this case; the senior broker couldn't control his fury. He grabbed the broker's telephone and started whacking him around the body with it, telling him that he was a stupid cunt, a fucking cunt who wasn't fit to pick the shit out of his arsehole. And this grown man was just being beaten like a dog, whimpering with fright. Seeing it made me think, 'Fuck, I don't want to be the next guy receiving that treatment.'

However, a weird thing is that there is a bit of code. If you take your punishment and keep quiet, then you're still a mate. So later in the evening of that day, senior trader bought the drinks for broker, and said, 'Sorry I lost my temper today. But sorry you were a cunt today.' A laugh will be had by both, and it will be fine again afterwards.

That was a serious incident that I witnessed but there have been others that have been a lot funnier.

The smaller battles are usually verbal jousts that go on constantly in the office. We had one trader who was called E9 because that is Hackney's postcode, and this guy had particularly bad acne. Once E9 tried to have a dig at a fat trainee by saying, 'Oi, Fatty, why are you so fat?'

Fatty wasn't going to let this one ride. He retorted immediately, 'That's because every time I shag your mum, she gives me a cream cake!'

The guys in the office really admired Fatty for fighting back against a senior broker like that. He had the balls and the wit to get his own back. He was much more respected afterwards.

Once we had a senior broker who demanded that one of his underlings went and got him some tooth floss just at a particularly busy moment of the day. Everyone in the office groaned. Did he really need to have some tooth floss right now? But the senior broker insisted and sure enough one of his subordinates went out and got the tooth floss. However, the junior got his own back a few days later because he took the guy's tooth floss and wiped it around his 'old chap' and his arse, and then put the floss back onto the reel. We pissed ourselves laughing when we watched that guy floss his teeth, I can tell you! And he had no idea except the sense of a bad smell being around in the office!

This guy bought a large bottle of Listerine. He was gargling every day and he was an irritating cunt who we nicknamed Thrush. The guy sitting next to him was really irritated by Thrush's constant gargling as he was eating his breakfast. So when Thrush went to lunch, the other guy would take Thrush's mouthwash to the bogs and top it up with piss.

Another time, there was a guy in the office, called Cheesey because he had these disgusting cheesey feet that stank whenever he took off his shoes. He was pissed off with someone called Vomit – the guy was famous for chucking up after a few rounds. Anyway, Cheesey got hold of Vomit's jacket and filled it with all sorts of crap, litter and general detritus from the rubbish bin, as well as the cheesey flaky bits from his feet. Vomit was totally pissed off about this but couldn't figure out what to do about it. Anyway, that evening, Cheesey left work before Vomit, leaving only a couple of other blokes in the office. One of these other guys said he needed to take a dump and was about to go to the toilet when Vomit suddenly came up with this great idea. He pulled out Cheesey's drawer at his desk and told his mate to go down to the toilet and take a dump in Cheesey's drawer – which is what he did. The drawer was left over the weekend. When Cheesey opened it the next Monday, he actually vomited, he was so disgusted. After that, everyone called him Cheesey Vomit in memory of his infamous comeuppance!

The thing is if someone picks on you, you need to nip it in the bud before you get it in the neck again. You're showing that there is no end to what you do to get them back, and so you scare them off. And unless you are a complete nutter, you won't do it again.

The alcoholic battlefield – Britain in the 21st century

'There were boys and girls just covered in blood. They were laughing about it! Yo-ho-ho-boyo! Look at me! Look what I got. It was almost as if it was a badge of courage to be covered in blood.'

In Newport, Wales, I spoke to some exhausted ambulance paramedics about the drinking problems in this town.

'We have about 30 to 40 casualties coming in every Friday and Saturday night in here,' said one of them with a weary smile, which seemed to indicate that he was simply stating the obvious.

It's always the same old story: people get drunk, smash a glass and poke it in someone's face. The majority of serious injuries we get in here are from fights. It has been like this since I can remember. Newport is famous for its rowdy behaviour. Mind you, one thing that is getting worse is the girls.

Last night, we had a call from a pub where a girl had flung another girl onto the floor, and stabbed her stiletto heel through her cheek. She'd then lost her shoe and trodden on some broken glass. So we had to deal with someone with a hole in her cheek, and another girl hobbling around with glass in her foot.

We find that the bouncers can be a particular problem as well. They are not doing that job because they want to be nice to people. They love the thrill of pushing people around. I had a friend last week who was told to drink up, and when she took a little longer than usual, the bouncer attacked her and twisted her arm behind her back, marching her out of the pub. She had to go to casualty. Her arm still hurts now.

Both paramedics reflected upon the cost all of this.

We were estimating the other day that every call-out on a Friday and Saturday night costs about £1,000 because there are so many professional people being paid to mop up other people's mess: ambulance paramedics, reception-ists, nurses, doctors, consultants. There's also the cost incurred by manning the hospital with so many people at that time of night, the cost of the specialist equipment in the ambulance and the hospital. But mainly, it is the wages you have to pay to so many people working at such unsociable hours. It's a lot of money. Every Friday and Saturday night is costing taxpayers in this hospital about £30,000. Now this stuff is happening all across the country, everywhere. The drinks industry is making billions out of causing chaos; meanwhile the public has to foot the bill. It is shocking.

The official statistics are even more shocking than this. Alcohol-related harm, according to a report produced for the prime minister in 2004, was costed by the NHS at £1.7 billion. A *Guardian* investigation noted, however: 'Add to this the £95 million invested in specialist NHS alcohol treatment programmes, plus £7.3 billion to combat crime and antisocial behaviour, plus £6.4 billion incurred by loss of productivity, plus £4.7 billion human and emotional costs to the family, reaching a total of £21.05 billion. However, income from the drinks industry is more than £30 billion a year, incorporating £7 billion in excise duties paid to the government, plus one million jobs created. So subtracting one from the other leaves £8.9 billion reasons why Britain is likely to remain drunk.'[32] While some of the *Guardian*'s figures may be questionable – most experts put the turnover of the drinks industry at £23 billion – the overall point is a strong one: both the government and the drinks industry are profiting from the business; it is only the poor, law-abiding public who is suffering.

Inside the Accident and Emergency waiting room at Newport, I saw youths with bandages on their foreheads and plasters on their faces, and one with his arm in a sling. The mood was very quiet and subdued: hung-over. I met a large, white-haired man coming out of the hospital, who volunteered, 'I came in there early this morning. I had difficulty breathing. I've got something wrong with my chest. And there were boys and girls just covered in blood. They were laughing about it! Yo-ho-ho-boyo! Look at me! Look what I got. It was almost as if it was a badge of courage to be covered in blood.'

We stopped by the railings that overlooked the car park, and he told me about his life. John Graves had grown up in a small village in the valleys, and worked for seven years as a miner at Oakdale colliery; he'd then become a swimming instructor before joining the forces and working for many years as an engineer. He was now retired and, at 62, seemed in poor health. He could barely walk 5 yards without pausing for breath. 'When I was 15 you thought you were wonderful if you drank a half of shandy in a pub,' he said. 'Now all of that is completely different. I worked underground through my late teens, and would sing in the chapel choir. Now all the chapels are empty. You wouldn't find a teenager in them for love nor money.'

I walked into town reflecting upon what he had told me. Hard drinking had always been the province of the Welsh miners, but now that the industry had gone, the drinking had continued, and spread: teenagers who never used to drink were now part of the scene. The old communal cultural pursuits like the chapel choir were totally defunct and had been replaced by listening to tinned music blaring out at top volume from some tacky pub's groaning sound system. Where was the fulfilment in that? Where was the creativity?

In town, I found the usual suspects: the Walkabout Bar, the Reflex Bar – both national chains – and lots of adverts in the bars offering cut-price drinks if you bought two bottles of alcopops. I reflected upon the proudly proclaimed obscenity of some of the adverts. A large picture of a semi-naked Abi Titmus was plastered across the front of one bar, with 'Pick up your Celebrity Love Island Mask and join in the fun'. I knew far too much about Abi Titmus: the fact that she used to be the girlfriend of an ex-presenter of *Blue Peter*, John Leslie, and a nurse, and that they had made a porn video which had been leaked on the Internet. A tabloid scandal has ensued, and she had decided to use the notoriety of those pictures to launch a media career: she now adorned the pages of numerous 'lads' magazines', had appeared in a crap reality TV programme called *Celebrity Love Island* and made lots of money appearing in bars like this one in Newport.

From being a nurse who tried to cure the sick, she now appeared to be encouraging being sick by promoting bars such as this. Her tale was emblematic of our times: she was the reverse of the Victorian stereotype of Florence Nightingale. Abi Titmus was celebrated for her sexual attractiveness, not for the traditional feminine role of 'caregiver to the ill'. When Abi Titmus dressed up in a nurse's uniform now it was for some provocative pose in a soft-porn magazine.

In a way, her meteoric rise to fame reflected a growing unease about the role of women. They were no longer there to care for men; they were there to tease them, and to entice them into drinking more.

The drinks industry

'Don't give a XXXX for last orders? Vote Labour.'

A bi Titmus and other sex symbols were used by an unscrupulous drinks industry in glossy adverts to give the drinkers in towns like Newport the feeling that they were sexy, healthy and successful. The advertising campaigns for the new alcopops were as subtle as the ones for cigarettes; they fed upon the insecurities of the British, presenting sleek, impossibly beautiful people playing with bottles of alcohol as though they were sex toys.

The Institute of Alcohol Studies concluded after rigorous surveys that the drinks industry was attempting to 'expand their market share' and was specifically targeting the young with adverts that appealed to alcohol's 'street cred'.[33] A recent study in the *Observer* revealed that bar managers are being offered big bonuses the more drink they serve: one journalist found that she was served enough drink to kill her in one evening.[34]

Perhaps most disturbingly, the IAS survey found that young people themselves felt that alcohol advertising suggested drinking's 'therapeutic' value, and that it was a 'gateway to social and sexual success'.

In most European countries, alcohol adverts are banned in a variety of media – from TV to billboards – in a way that they are not in the United Kingdom. Indeed, the British government seems to be in the pockets of the drinks industry. In the 2001 general election, New Labour sent a text message to voters: 'Don't give a XXXX for last orders? Vote Labour'. The subsequent Licensing Act of 2003 has resulted in pubs being able to serve drinks around the clock, and it is, for all the government's rhetoric about closing down troublesome pubs, very difficult for local residents to stop 24-hour drinking licences from being granted.[35]

Most symptomatic of the present malaise, where politicians appear to be in cahoots with the drinks industry, is the tale of the company Urbium. This company, whose directors once included the current opposition leader David Cameron, has mounted a legal challenge to Westminster City Council, who want to stop children from entering bars. Urbium has quoted the new Licensing Act in defence of letting children into its bars. The company is the owner of the Tiger Tiger chain of late-night 'super-bars' and has been at the forefront of the massive expansion of the drinks industry.[36]

Perhaps it is the enormous size of this industry – which could fund the economies of nearly half of Africa – that explains why politicians of both left and right are so keen to keep Britain drinking. The Tory administration of the late 1980s realised that one way of regenerating town centres was by encouraging bars and nightclubs to be built there. In the early 1990s, the Conservative government did little to curtail the rise of new products like alcopops – which have contributed towards millions more young people drinking. New Labour with its Licensing Act of 2003 has accelerated the massive expansion of the industry with its round-the-clock opening hours for pubs.

Most strikingly, in the 1980s and 90s, the City of London became heavily involved in financing pubs and bars. The City financiers had only one interest in the industry: to get people to spend as much money as possible on buying drink. As Peter Haydon points out in *An Inebriated History of Britain*, the small pub landlords and even mighty breweries like Bass were swept aside as the merchant banks moved in to finance operations which were run more like McDonald's than the pubs of yesteryear. Haydon highlights the role of the Japanese bank Nomura, who bankrolled a massive expansion of bars, which encouraged the 'factory-style' drinking that we see in so many places in Britain today. Haydon writes that Nomura are 'interested in maximising returns from a raft of investments. They care little if in order to get them pubs are induced to sell alcoholic fruit juice to teenagers.'[37]

In fact, Haydon is being rather kind on the company here. Nomura, and banks like it, fund bars that actively want teenagers to drink expensive alcoholic fruit juice because it greatly boosts profits.

As we saw in the first part of the book, one of the most powerful forms of indoctrination into yobbish behaviour is being the victim of it; quite clearly a significant proportion of children who are accompanying adults into bars will be victims of drunken antics. As the IAS research shows, children entering these bars will also become the unwitting victims of pernicious advertising campaigns where the message is that drinking is cool and full of street cred. Studies suggest that nearly eight million children are living in families adversely affected by alcohol. In other words, these children were living in hell, being brought up by parents who are drunk, and possibly being encouraged to drink themselves.[38]

Perhaps most crucially, alcohol is much cheaper than it used to be, which has led to a sharp rise in its consumption; it is, in relative terms, half as cheap as it was in 1965.[39] This is another huge contributing factor towards the vast rise in the number of people binge drinking in the UK.

What we have, then, is a new, aggressive cultural promotion of alcohol, which is spearheaded by the drinks industry but ably assisted by politicians who see the value in the tax revenue to be gained from such a massively expanding industry.

Dig the new breed: the hard-drinking, middle-class ladette

'My favourite slob moment is you sicking up at the top of the ramp, which was right next to the uni bar, and then letting it all run down to the path like a river of vom, while you sat at the top and pointed.'

So what is the net result of all these behind-the-scenes changes in the law and marketing techniques for the average British citizen?

Many of us are both victims and perpetrators. There has been a seismic shift in attitudes towards drink in Britain. Most revealing of this new state of mind was my interview with Sarah, 29, who is a sales manager in London. She is the very reverse of the stereotype of the hard-drinking, working-class football hooligan, which was, let's face it, the national stereotype for Britain during the 1970s and 80s. She is an air force officer's daughter who went to a convent boarding school and then to a top university to study English.

Fascinatingly, the antics of women like her are breeding a new stereotype for the nation: the drunk British woman having sex with a stranger in the toilets of a club. As described in Cardiff and Ayia Napa, the increased earning power of women has changed the face of our town and city centres on Friday and Saturday nights.

These are the highlights of her drinking career so far in her own words, with email additions from her friends.

1. Being impaled on a park railing

At university I funded my incessant drinking activity by working at a local nightclub. On a night off I was drinking excessively elsewhere with my bar manager and other friends. Shots, shooters, slammers, you name it.

A few hours later, around the middle of the night, I found myself lying on the grass of a park, snogging my bar manager. In a rare moment of clarity I apparently thought, 'Hang on, this isn't perhaps the best idea. He's my boss and I don't fancy him,' so I made my excuses and legged it. In my haste to vacate the park I seem to have decided to shun the wide-open gateway and opt for clambering over some tall park railings (the kind with sharp spikes at the top). It wasn't until I got to my home to be greeted with screams of horror from my housemates that I realised my jeans were drenched in blood and there was a gaping 4-inch hole in my inner left thigh.

A friend drove me to the nearest casualty ward where an extremely attractive Dutch doctor stitched my wound. I have a very fond memory of lying on my back with a sexy Dutch man between my legs, asking him if he was married and would like to go for a drink sometime. (Sadly, he was married.)

2. Cracked ribs

I cracked some ribs on my last (28th) birthday by launching into a handstand that I expected a big strong man to support by catching my legs. Unfortunately, he was long gone from the spot he had been standing in when I decided to perform my act of grace and agility and I just crashed to the ground. Ouch.

3. Kissing the wrong boy

I actually can't even remember this story – a friend recounted it to me recently. I thought it was hilarious. Apparently, at a university rag ball, I was (very drunk) kissing a young man. Went to the toilet, came back and promptly started kissing a completely different chap, with the first one looking on in bewilderment. Well, they all start to look the same after a few drinks!

4. Naked photography in passport photo booth with (ex) boyfriend at Croydon station

Speaks for itself really!

5. Falling into bins

In 2000 a big group of my friends had a weekend in Madrid to explore its culture, architecture and fine cuisine. Yeah, right. Twenty hardened drinking graduates in a city where a double measure fills the glass = carnage.

As well as spectacularly knocking over a table with about 40 glasses on it (we were asked to leave that particular bar quite shortly afterwards), I earned the temporary nickname 'Dustbin Bag Sarah' (incidentally, I didn't know about that nickname until today; a friend just told me when I asked for reminders!). I'm still not entirely sure why, but it involved collapsing into a stack of dustbins down some alley next to a club. Aha, just got another email from the friend: 'There was the miraculous, smooth, almost singular move through a table full of drinks, several chairs, several people, through the open door, over the street and into the assembled bin bags. Then the rather less smooth move of being dragged by your feet by those of us who carried you back to the hotel and to bed.'

Her friend comments that 'It was all brilliant'. Sarah's exploits have become legendary; they are still talked about with wonder and amazement. Her friend adds the following notes.

My favourite slob moment is you sicking up at the top of the ramp, which was right next to the Uni bar, and then letting it all run down to the path like a river of vom, while you sat at the top and pointed.

There's also pulling a man and bringing him back to your room, telling him that you were 'right behind him' so he went to your room, while you went back to the bar to find out if you could pull the other man you'd been talking to, just in case he put out and then you wouldn't have to shag the first guy. Only to realise you didn't actually like the second guy after all, calling him a cunt and going back to your room – about three hours after your pull had arrived.

When I spoke to Sarah, the thing that struck me the most was the pride that she and her friends had in these exploits. It was almost as though she felt she had really achieved something, as though she deserved a medal for being so outrageous, so outspoken, so boldly sexual, so paralytically drunk. She explained to me that there was a real code of honour among her friends that they should *never, ever* criticise each other for their drunken antics the night before.

It's the hangover code. 'You don't ever suggest that someone was out of order for doing something stupid while they were pissed. For me, Zoe Ball and Sara Cox were the pioneers of the ladette culture during the 1990s, and I think they unconsciously influenced me. I used to look at them with admiration in the tabloids with their bottles of JD in one hand and a fag in the other. With hindsight, they seemed to make ladette behaviour acceptable. If Johnny Ball's daughter was like that, then that gave licence for a lot of girls to do the same. There she was, a very attractive blonde – always looking stunning – and always on the piss. I must have thought, if she can do that, then it's OK. Binge drinking is a bit like a form of extreme theatre – you're living a play that can be talked about afterwards. Normally the main actor can't remember what they've done.

My first realisation of this was when I was at university and I got drunk for the first time. I got horrifically drunk and woke up the next morning feeling very embarrassed about all the stupid things I had said, but then I found that everyone appeared to be slapping me on the back for them. I was celebrated! The alcohol had given me the chance to override all the normal rules of decorum: I could swear like a trooper, scream at people, be rude when I liked and vomit in public, and I was praised for it! These sorts of things are just not allowed in Britain when you don't have a glass of alcohol in your hand. You'd be viewed as psychotic if you did these things sober. But it's like the alcohol gives you a passport into another land, a place where it's OK to be violently stupid.

What is most important to consider here are the cultural attitudes towards alcohol, which have changed in the last 20 years ago. There was a time when getting drunk and doing embarrassing things was frowned upon by the tight-lipped, buttoned-up British middle class. In fact, there is a sort of reverse 'puritanism' at work here: it is now almost not acceptable for people to condemn drunken misbehaviour. You are viewed as stuffy, out of touch and prudish if you do.

Chaos on the streets

'These types of intensely violent assault, fuelled by alcohol, are happening every weekend in every town and city in the country. This is an epidemic.'
Superintendent David Baines

Sarah didn't consider her behaviour – her coarseness, her vandalism, her ubiquitous bad language – as particularly yobbish. Compared with some of the worst behaviour described in this book it wasn't, but at the root of her antics was the same attitude of mind that has caused some very serious crimes indeed. In particular, her implicit notion that drinking gives someone the right to behave in an 'extraordinary' fashion is very similar to the state of mind of the most violent offenders.

At Swinton police station, Superintendent David Baines switched on the television and showed me some CCTV footage of a typical Sunday night in Greater Manchester. In it I saw three men kicking the head of a man lying prostrate next to a bus shelter. They were savaging him with their kicks; he was barely moving. Then from the corner of the frame, another bloke came rushing in and whacked the poor man in the head with his boot. He was soon joined by two girls, who also kicked the man's head brutally. Away from the bus stop, another fight developed between two men headbutting each other. The girls also joined in with this fight, although interestingly they were waved away by the brawling men.

Baines switched off the TV and explained that nine arrests resulted from the incident and that the man being kicked at the bus stop had to have very serious reconstructive surgery around his jaw, which was broken in several places.

'This sort of incident is not unique. These types of intensely violent assault, fuelled by alcohol, are happening every weekend in every town and city in the country. This is an epidemic,' he said.

My interviews with people throughout Britain confirm his observation. It is a cross-cultural phenomenon. Groups that are not stereotypically associated with drunken violence can be just as vituperative when they drink.

Blood on my shoes

'Mohammed picked up a glass and smashed it over Anish's face, and he fell to the floor covered in blood.'

A 17-year-old student of mine, Matthew Exley, told me about the situation in his area, Ilford, which is a relatively affluent suburb in north-east London. In stark contradiction to the stereotype that it is white men that are the main perpetrators of alcohol-fuelled violence, he told a tale that illustrates that different ethnic groups are just as likely to fight after they have been drinking. He explained to me that it was alcohol that seemed to exacerbate pre-existing inter-ethnic feuds in the area. This is what he had to say.

> In Ilford, there are three groups of people. You've got the black people, Africans and West Indians, the Asians, Indians and Pakistanis, and the white people. As far as I can see, the black people hate each other almost as much as they hate the Asians. The white people are hated by both groups, as are black people. There is real ethnic tension. The Indians and the Pakistanis hate each other. This means that there are constant fights and aggravation in the area.

Take the music. If you go to a bar, the Asians refuse to dance to anything except Bhangra music. The black and white people refuse to dance Bhangra, and so the whole evening can be spent with the three different races segregated, and squabbling over the music.

Recently, I was sitting in Shout bar in Ilford late on Saturday night. I had just finished dancing to 'Dirty' by Christina Aguilera. I sat down and I saw that an Asian man, Mohammed, probably about 23, dressed in tightish dark jeans and a black T-shirt, was having a row with another Asian man, Anish, who was wearing jeans and a white T-shirt and a red jumper. I couldn't hear what it was about but both of them were clearly drunk. One of the bouncers separated them. Mohammed threw his glass with his drink in it at Anish and then walked over to him. Covered in beer, Anish punched Mohammed in the face. Mohammed picked up a glass and smashed it over Anish's face, and he fell to the floor covered in blood. I was about seven feet away from it. Then Mohammed and his friend started kicking Anish when he was on the floor.

Suddenly, five or six of a gang appeared, all dressed in jeans, and started kicking him. Mohammed kicked Anish square in the face, and broke his nose. There was blood all over the floor as the gang began to pick up bar stools and hit Anish with them.

By the time the bar's bouncers had separated them, the police were there with an ambulance. Anish was semi-conscious, groaning in a pool of blood with pieces of glass embedded in his face. I was wearing new shoes and a new shirt and they all got splattered with blood. That was the last time I went to that bar.

Saturday afternoons – a barmaid's story

'Then suddenly I felt his glass whistling past my ears. It sailed over the counter and smashed against the mirror. All hell broke loose then.'

W hite men in London tend to be more clannish, attacking obvious targets rather than fighting among themselves. Bronwen, who works part-time in a pub in the outskirts of London, recounted a chilling incident she observed first hand.

There were three of them. They all looked respectable enough. It was a hot summer's day, a Saturday afternoon just after a rugby match, so they were dressed in shorts and T-shirts. One of them drove one of those Chelsea tractors – an expensive 4x4 – so we weren't expecting any trouble from them, but I could see as they swayed towards us that they were quite drunk. (Technically it is illegal to serve people if they are already drunk, but sometimes a blind eye is turned if it means we get another sale.) They bought a pitcher of lager from my colleague, and stood at the bar, and started laughing and joking very loudly. 'You fucking bastard, no, you didn't, you fucking tosser,' one of them kept shouting at the top of his voice.

Now, we're the kind of pub where you don't expect to get much trouble, situated in a quiet suburb. So I went over and asked them to quieten down a little. This was a mistake because immediately they got lairy. One of them stood up and brandished his pint glass in his hand like a baseball player holding a ball. I got really scared because he started saying that I was a fucking cunt, a fucking bitch. All this filth was coming out of his mouth. And the thing was he was quite well spoken – clearly, a middle-class guy in his early thirties with a good job. But pissed. Very pissed.

Then suddenly I felt his glass whistling past my ears. It sailed over the bar and smashed against the mirror, and shattered it as well as some of the products we had arranged in a display. All hell broke loose then. Two of the blokes staggered towards me, I dodged out of the way, and Hal, the pub owner, approached them, telling them to get out. The smallest man of the three started getting violent and pushing some of the tables out of the way, while one of the others tried to escape out of the main door, sending fragments of glass everywhere as he ran into it. We didn't even realise until afterwards, but he'd punched a woman who had the misfortune to be entering the pub just as he was trying to get out; luckily she wasn't badly hurt. In the end, we had to call the police, which was enough to scare them away. They had good jobs, you see. They didn't want to get arrested.

One of the most unusual incidents at the bar was when a bloke in his late thirties came into the pub and asked to speak to the boss, so I called Hal. I didn't notice at the time, but the man had a table leg in the sleeve of his jacket which he used as a weapon to repeatedly thump Hal over the head while calling him a 'fat fucker'. It turned out that Hal had refused entry to his under-age daughter on karaoke night (the most popular night of the week) and the man had come to give Hal a 'seeing to'. Not many people try to pick a fight with Hal unless they are armed because he is known as a bit of a hard nut in the local area.

Bronwen feels that the way that drinks are advertised in pubs now is partly to blame, and the whole credit card culture. She notes that lots of drinks often come with special deals in pubs so that people opt for 'special offers' like three drinks for the price of two, or go for happy hour drinks where they are cut price. So there is an incentive to get drunk very quickly. She says: 'But that isn't the main problem, the main thing is that credit cards are often handed over at the bar, and people carry on drinking as long as they want because they don't run out of cash.'

The bar manager's story

'I can't drink in any of the bars around here, because there's always some idiot who wants to have a pop at me because I've kicked him out of the pub'.

Sabbs Henchard runs 'The Jolly Giant' in east London and perhaps more than anyone I have met knows the truth about what goes on in Britain's pubs. He is massive. He stalks out of the bar like a great, grizzled bear. His hair is grey, peppered with white, his muscular arms are covered in faded tattoos and a big belly protrudes out of a long shirt. A gold bracelet jangles against an expensive watch as he sits down beside me.

'Without doubt, things are getting worse around here,' he says, pointing at the window, which reveals a nicely tended row of shops, a busy roundabout and a dazzling blue sky over the polite rooftops of the suburban houses.

A lot of kids around here just aren't frightened of authority any more. Before I cleaned up the pub, kids used to come in here and openly smoke spliffs. When I challenged them, they would say, 'Come on, it's only a bit of blow, what are getting so upset about?' They were a bit shocked when I dragged them out, I can tell you. Back then, a couple of years ago, before I sorted things out, there was a lot of bad stuff going on: kids shooting up wherever and when-ever they could, fights breaking out, snorting cocaine in the toilets, good customers being shouted at and abused, girls' arses being pinched, and all these kids giving it the 'large', general lairiness.

Once, I had a gang of men come in here and try to sell drugs. They were about 40 years old. When I told them to hop it, they started battering me with the chairs. They shouldn't have done that because one of them ended up in intensive care. One of them had an iron bar, and really tried to kill me. But I wasn't frightened. I can look after myself. On a couple of occasions, I've had some guys try to run me over in the car park. I've had kids smashing my windows because I've kicked them out on their arses, and then when I prosecuted them – I knew exactly who they were – they threatened to kill me if I stood up in court and testified against them.

I can't drink in any of the bars around here, because there's always some idiot who wants to have a pop at me because I've kicked him out of the pub. But I've sorted things out, and now the pub is very popular because it is one of the few places where you don't get molested. The nice people can have a drink in peace here.

The thing is there are a lot of graduates going into pub management now, and they don't realise that niceness is seen as a weakness by these guys. I grew up in working-class Middlesbrough. That was a bloody hard place. I was always getting into fights. But even though we were hard, we didn't large it like these fuckers. We had respect for authority, and we knew how to earn it. The graduate bar managers have not a clue. All they want to do is hear the cash tills ringing and watch the punters getting pissed out of their heads. They've one thing on their mind: money, and nothing else.

I found my interview with Sabs particularly interesting because he represented the 'old breed' of pub landlord: the tough authoritarian who wasn't going to accept any drunken violence on or near his premises. His primary motive was not profit, but maintaining order. He knew that if he did this, his profits would take care of themselves. However, he was quite different from what he termed the graduate bar managers, whose sole motive, having been specially trained by the multi-national breweries, was profit. They had neither the 'nouse' nor the interest in maintaining order; their primary concern was to turn the old-fashioned pubs into 'drinking factories' where all the furniture and booths were swept away and replaced by benches, stripped pine floors, a long bar where drinks could be rapidly served and thumping loud music to give the feeling everything was cool and hip.

Drunk Bristol - a sour, drink-sodden city

'Snob yobs are the university types who are always trying to get the better of you. They are often obnoxious and rude, and can be extremely drunk. I hate their patronising manner.'

I f any city puts paid to the myth that drinking gives people high spirits and makes them cheery it is Bristol.

Bristol is one of the richest cities in England, with unemployment being well below the national average, and social deprivation being relatively low. It is booming, with Lloyds TSB, Sun Life Assurance and Nat West Life all relocating their headquarters there in the 1990s. It is choc-a-bloc with hi-tech and telecoms businesses such as Telewest Communications, Orange, British Telecom and Hewlett Packard.

Yet this hasn't enabled them to have a good time. Perhaps the reverse; the groups I saw and heard about – from successful businessmen, middle-class students and working-class 'chavs' – seemed very defensive, guarded and suspicious. The crime rate in Bristol is roughly twice the national average, with violence against people affecting 33 out of every 1,000 people.[40]

But why is this? Why has this successful, thriving city been so afflicted by antisocial behaviour?

I travelled to the city to find some answers.

Dusk was beginning to fall over Bristol's waterfront; this is where over 200 years ago ships loaded with booty would sail off in order to buy slaves on the West African coast. Bristol's heyday died when the slave trade was abolished in the early 19th century, but now the waterfront has been revived by its nightlife and the spending habits of Bristol's wealthy citizens. It is heavy with bars and clubs, throbbing with music and thronging with people of all ages.

I spotted a little boy pushing his baby sister in a battered pushchair into a water fountain. His dad didn't stop him from mucking around, but once he slipped off the fountain, just preventing the pushchair from tipping over, the dad yelled with his can of Red Stripe waving in the air: 'What are you fucking doing, you idiot?'

The dad's earrings glinted in the street light. The boy ignored his father and continued to race ahead of his parents. His mum shouted very loudly at him to come back, and reluctantly the boy returned.

The waterfront felt claustrophobic because it overlooked a relatively narrow strip of water, and was covered in scaffolding. Out on the covered pedestrian walkway, where once the ships must have taken on their cargo, there were wealthy, suntanned, middle-aged couples slowly sipping their lagers.

Outside Philips, a big bar that felt more like a nightclub with its large dance floor, I talked to Bob, who had worked as a security guard in Bristol for over 14 years. He was a very well-built man in his forties – handsome and calm, with a fatherly, authoritative manner. He brimmed with stories about drunks in Bristol, explaining that alcohol-fuelled violence afflicted all the social classes.

It was Christmas Eve, and we'd been having trouble with some businessmen, who while they had been well-behaved all year, suddenly decided to take on the whole world. They'd got drunk, and started hurling abuse at the customers. I can understand this. They've been cooped up all year in the office being good boys, but a time like Christmas Eve is when they can let it all hang out. It's quite a common phenomenon, wealthy guys just drinking too much, and 'bigging it up', as they say. Anyway, we'd managed to sort them out, and get them out of the bar, when I heard on the radio that some scaffolders were doing the rounds around town. Most bouncers now have these police radios that they can speak on, and hear what's going on around town, and so other bouncers at other nightclubs can tell everyone who is trouble.

Scaffolders are a breed to be respected. Because of their work, they are very strong and they have no fear. I'd got the nod on the radio that we shouldn't allow all 11 of them into the bar. They came around the corner, and I could tell immediately that they were going to be difficult. They were dressed in Adidas white T-shirts and jeans, and their boots were dusty. Anyway, this guy just walks at me, with a determined stride, like he was not going to let me stop him from going into the bar. I approached him, put my hand on his chest and said, 'Hang on a minute.' Suddenly I was surrounded. All 11 of the guys had enclosed us and were flinging bottles at us. Glass was shattered everywhere; it was like standing in the middle of a thunderstorm, only the rain was glass. They were only five of us against those huge guys. Luckily, I managed to beat up two of them very quickly, but then a massive brawl ensued, and those guys got badly hurt.

I have this strange thing happen to me when something like this kicks off. I get a huge adrenalin surge, and lose my memory completely. I can only remember being pulled off one guy, and being told that it was all right. The police had arrived and the scaffolders were taken away.

There are a number of known troublemakers in Bristol. The scaffolders that time were visitors from Liverpool, I think, but the yobs in Bristol are very distinctive. The main ones are the chavs who wear Burberry, white trainers and baseball caps; sometimes they wear blue tops with 'Old Glory' on the back. They've been brought up in very hard, working-class areas in Bristol: Hartcliff, Noel West and South Mead. They are extremely easy to spot, and essentially, give or take a bit of violence, easy to handle. At most clubs and bars now, there is a no white baseball cap rule, and a no white trainers rule. You see, the baseball cap is a mask, and when you've got that mask on, lots of these kids take on the persona of a hard guy. We've also found the same thing happens with white trainers: it's like it's a green light for them to misbehave. Their personalities change. It's all linked with football hooliganism. Chav culture with the Burberry started to happen when kids wore the uniform of the hooligans: the Burberry, the trainers, the Hackett T-shirts, the Stone Ireland gear.

Once you've established that they can't go in in this gear, you can also sort out the aggressive ones by slipping a snide joke at them, and seeing how they respond. So I might say to someone who looks like they are rooting to beat people up, 'What's the matter, didn't you clean your shoes this morning?' Normally, if they are trouble, the chest comes out, and they stiffen, and challenge you. Then you've got them and say, 'Sorry mate, you better go elsewhere.' If they laugh it off, you know they are all right.

Some of the girls from these areas can be fun too. I remember one night in particular when a whole gang of girls from Hartcliff dressed to the nines in wads of make-up, and tiny dresses, loads of gold rings and ridiculous permed hair, were going around pissed out of their heads, snogging as many guys as possible. Anyway, one poor chap refused to snog one of the girls, and the furious girl swung her handbag at him, and smashed a bottle over his head right in front of me. I restrained her, holding her back from completely mangling this guy, and marched her out of the club. When I returned I saw that the girls had got their phones out. I thought: 'Uh-oh, here come their blokes to really give me one.' A Red Cavalier pulled up outside the club, and I braced myself to fight the blokes. But the doors swung open, and a great gaggle of middle-aged mums, with ridiculous perms too, trundled out, screaming at me, 'You picked on my daughter! You fucking cunt, we'll have you for that, you bastard pervert fucker!' I just laughed at them. They didn't touch me, but clearly they thought they could intimidate me.

Leaving Bob, I walked around the town, moving in and out of the bars, feeling the mood on the streets. It felt tense. As Bob said, there were gangs of drunk working-class kids roaming around, swaying, swearing loudly and chucking pizza boxes into the flower beds, but there were also middle-aged men with beer bellies poorly hidden behind designer shirts lurching around, as well as women of all ages – ranging from late middle age to teenagers – tottering around in their armour: stiletto heels, tight, revealing tops and short skirts.

I spoke to a friend of Bob's, Alex, a strikingly handsome South African in his twenties, who is a security guard at Fez's, a nightclub tucked away in a side street behind the waterfront. He explained the source of the tension that is often felt in Bristol: the age-old conflict between the 'townies' and the 'students'. As a young person, he has a different perspective from Bob. While Bob felt rather affectionate but disinterested towards the 'chavs', Alex seemed to have sided with them. He had most contempt for what he called the 'snob yobs'.

> Snob yobs are the university types who are always trying to get the better of you. They are often obnoxious and rude, and can be extremely drunk. I hate their patronising manner. They think because I am working here that I am not educated, so they shout at me in a slow, mocking tone of voice, as though I am deaf or simple. And while they rarely get into fights, they can do something worse: waste your time. You find yourself engaged in an argument with one of them for 15 minutes to half an hour, if you won't let one of them in. It's quite different with the Burberry brigade. If you refuse one of them entry, they go quickly. They may try and fight you, or call you a fucking cunt, and so on, but they disappear pretty sharpish once you've made it clear who is the boss. But these students, they won't let go! Added to which, they are the most dishonest. They'll try and lift things: candles, glasses and any other fixtures from the club they can get hold of.

Once he had finished talking to me about his contempt for students, Alex also explained to me the etiquette of drunken nights out in Bristol.

> There usually five guys in a gang going on the piss. And they nearly always follow this pattern, I find: there's a good-looking one, the joker, the hard one, the guy who think he's hard by being mouthy and the quiet one. It is nearly always the mouthy ones that trigger the fights. They fire off by cussing you for something or other – usually because

you haven't let them into the club. And then the hard guy steps forward to take you on. And you have to fight who you have to fight, using reasonable force. Nowadays, bouncers have to be very careful, because we are all licensed by the Security Industry Association, the SIA. You'll be in court before you know it if you have done something you shouldn't have. They want you to talk till you are blue in the face, rather than fight. But sometimes, you have to fight. It is the only way.

The younger generation are a problem because they are more tooled up. I routinely confiscate Stanley knives, knuckle-dusters and CS gas. Usually kids are carrying this stuff around more as a threat than because they are going to use it.

Drinking is a real problem here. Well, it is good for the clubs, but bad for just about everyone else. Certain vodka bars say things like they will write your name on the ceiling if you have 20 vodkas in a row. The Aussie chain Walkabout offers oceans of drink at cheap prices once you have paid to go in. I would say that some kids can spend at least £120 a night on drink. These are kids who work in call centres, hairdressers, office jobs and the hi-tech business parks that dominate the city outskirts. They live with their parents, and they save to go out on Saturday night. Some go on the piss with their parents.

I left Alex and wandered around the town, sitting in the bars, and waiting until closing time at 1 a.m. to see what was happening. A bleak, sour mood descended with the seagulls at 'chucking out and chucking up' time. Several students jumped in the river, and then one, dripping wet, lay down on the deck below the bars, sobbing in the arms of a girl. The seagulls swooped and picked at the chip wrappers, the half-eaten kebabs, the pizza boxes. A drunken, middle-class man, with a T-shirt that read 'Amateur gynaecologist at your cervix', lunged around, shouting at his friend, 'Sorry to change the subject, but follow that arse!'

A girl in a tiny, spangly dress leered at me, shouting, 'I love you, you fucking pervert!' and disappeared giggling around the corner with her friends.

There were several knots of people who were bleary-eyed and bad tempered, cursing at each other. 'Why don't you fuck off, you cunt! Go on, fuck off!'

Two boys, brandishing tins of lager like revolvers, who had spotted me taking notes on the bench, then approached me. 'What the fuck are you doing, you cunt? Are you a spy, or what?'

I moved away from them quickly, but they followed me. 'You fucking cunt, you deserve your head kicked in! Come on, let's get him!'

I ran at this point, listening to curses of the city rise around me. All the swearing seemed to merge into a general clarion call: 'Fucking cunts! Fucking cunts! Everyone is a fucking cunt!'

At that moment, I hated the city with every fibre of my being because I felt there was no reason for this. This place had every social advantage compared with most areas on the planet, and yet it seemed to be one of the most aggressive, most unpleasant and most out of control at this moment in time.

As Superintendent David Baines said to me, 'It is a battlefield out there every Friday and Saturday night. People of all social backgrounds, some from the politest middle-class homes, are out of control.'

Ideological drunkenness

'I've seen such a deterioration in private and public behaviour in the last ten years or so that I do not feel comfortable in my own country any more.'
Theodore Dalrymple

Alcoholic Britain is a sickening creature. Drinking too much alcohol has led to an increase in cancers, brain damage, blackouts, strokes, paralysis, dementia, loss of libido and other sexual difficulties, foetal abnormalities, liver cirrhosis, essential hypertension, chronic stomach complaints and injuries caused by violence. It can also cause depression, suicide, manic-depressive illness, obsessive-compulsive disorders and schizophrenia.

Most visibly, though, before Britain's chronic drinkers are tucked away safely in hospital having dialysis, they are causing problems on Britain's streets. A huge number of British people become dangerously drunk in public.

A close analysis of the numbers being admitted to hospital because of the effects of alcohol gives a rough picture of just how much binge drinking is going on. During 2003–4, those admissions rose by 15 per cent, from 35,740 to 41,122.[41] A Liberal Democrat spokesman, Paul Burston, said these figures show that 'binge drinking is completely out of control'. Most worryingly, the figures for young people are staggering. As many as 13 children a day are admitted to hospital suffering from the effects of alcohol. Admissions to hospital have increased 11 per cent since the mid-1990s. In 2003–4, some 4,647 children were admitted to hospital suffering from mental and behavioural disorders caused by alcohol, liver disease or the toxic effects of bingeing.[42]

Even more disturbingly, the number of under-age drinkers who were prosecuted for being drunk and disorderly rose above a whopping 31,000 in 2003. Since Labour has come to power, the figures have leapt by nearly 15 per cent, while in Cambridgeshire, Lincolnshire and Surrey prosecutions among 10- to 17-year-olds rose by over 200 per cent.[43]

Twenty-three per cent of 11- to 15-year-olds say that they drink, and for the first time girls are drinking as often as boys, according to an NHS survey that questioned 10,000 children. Almost half the girls said that they had become inebriated, and a tenth said that they had vomited because of drink.[44] 'The courts are seeing increasing numbers of girls coming before us because they have committed violent offences, usually under the influence of alcohol,' magistrate Mike Batten told me.

British teenagers are the heaviest drinkers in Europe, 29 per cent of girls and 25 per cent of boys aged 15–16 admitting to binge drinking in the previous month.[45] In some parts of Britain, such as Plymouth, field hospitals have been opened on Friday and Saturday nights in order to cope with the number of casualties that are caused by binge drinking. Remember that the vast majority of casualties are not caused by alcohol poisoning but by the violence fuelled by the alcohol.

It is very difficult to estimate the crimes committed by drunks. Less than a quarter of violent offences that result in treatment at Accident and Emergency departments are known to the police.[46] Police figures therefore radically underestimate the problem. We do know, however, that in the areas where there are concentrations of pubs and nightclubs, the crime rates are highest. As an example, in 2001 in the city of Bath, levels of crime and disorder were far higher in Abbey Ward, which contains the nightclub zone, than in any other ward of Bath and north-east Somerset.[47]

Professor Richard Hobbs, who holds a chair in sociology at Durham University, and has studied the night-time economies of British towns and cities in depth, points out that while the opening of bars and pubs has boosted the economies of many parts of Britain, it has also brought with it a 'rise in violence and disorder'. His figures reveal that the industry is growing by 10 per cent, accounting for 3 per cent of UK Gross Domestic Product. He says: 'In every research site across the country analysed by Durham researchers, it was found that violence and disorder were exacerbated in direct proportion to the number of drinkers coming into the town or city. Further, we were able to trace the spread of violence and disorder that accompanied the development of new drinking circuits adjacent to established drinking routes.'[48] When you put his findings together, a very bleak picture emerges. Since the industry is growing at a very rapid rate, and since it is incontrovertible that crime grows in direct proportion to the numbers drinking, it appears inevitable that antisocial behaviour is going to get a lot worse in the coming years, perhaps exponentially when round-the-clock drinking is introduced.

Katie Fox in her anthropological guide *Watching the English* accuses us of having a 'dis-ease' at the centre of our psyche as a result of which we become violently aggressive when we are drunk and which leads us to drink more. She points out that numerous studies have shown that it isn't the alcohol which makes people violent, but cultural attitudes about alcohol.

'I've seen such a deterioration in private and public behaviour in the last ten years or so that I do not feel comfortable in my own country any more,' the journalist and doctor Theodore Darymple told me. 'It is as though we are now afflicted with an ideological drunkenness in this country. Many people feel that it is more than a right to get drunk and hurl abuse at all and sundry; it is almost a duty, a categorical imperative, an indicator that they are living their lives to the full. It has become the cool thing to do.'

We are now an image-obsessed nation yearning to escape from the mundanity of our lives. Unlike other people living in Europe, we are not happy with our lot. We do not want the sedate contentment of sipping wine with a nicely prepared, home-cooked meal; we want the ecstasy of getting off our faces and feeling as though we have taken a rocket out of a place called normality. Our obsession with discovering extremes of happiness has ironically caused us the most unhappiness.

Moreover, if the research of experts like Professor Richard Hobbs is to be believed, we ain't seen nothing yet. With round-the-clock drinking and the continuing expansion of the industry, with no curbs on the advertising of alcohol, with the introduction of children being allowed in bars, we will almost certainly see an even bigger increase in alcohol-fuelled crime in the coming years.

The street robber's battlefield

'First of all I was hit in the mouth and my tooth came out, and the next two blows hit me on the side and the back of the head. They said: "What are you doing walking down our street?"'[49]

It was a hot August Bank Holiday Monday as I took my five-year-old son out for a bicycle ride in our local park, Ravenscroft Park. The sun shone brightly through a piercing blue sky, illuminating the broken glass on the playground's floor. My son, Theo, wobbled on his bike, pushing hard with his legs. The bicycle was too small for him, but he didn't moan; he wanted a good old race-around and nothing was going to stop him. Nothing, that is, except for a pack of dogs – two pit bull terriers, an Alsatian, a Jack Russell and slavering Labrador – which were milling around the fringes of the playground, exactly where Theo wanted to ride his bike.

The owners of the dogs were sitting down by some burnt-out bins, and twirling their leads around their fingers. They were white men in their late teens and early twenties. Each one of them was drinking a can of Red Stripe and they were laughing loudly. I was surrounded by signs saying that dogs should not be let off their leads, but I knew that these signs are never, ever adhered to. The whole of Ravenscroft Park is a dog's playground.

I stopped Theo for a moment, much to his chagrin, and scanned the dogs. Some of the lads, in their white Adidas tops, had now approached the swings and were inviting their pit bulls to jump up and bite the seats of the swings, which they did with ever-increasing enthusiasm. Soon all the dogs had joined in, each one jumping up madly and biting the swings.

Theo didn't understand what was going on, and wanted to cycle over to have a look. I had to explain to him that it was not safe to go near the dogs. Obviously, I wanted to approach the dog owners and tell them to put their dogs on leads. However, I knew that the exercise would be pointless at best and, at worst, highly dangerous. They'd almost certainly laugh at me and ignore my request, and could quite possibly set the dogs on me.

They were grinning in a predatory fashion, enjoying the feeling of fear that they were creating in the people around them. 'This is what respect means to a lot of people,' Donna, a friend of the gang members on the Shipley estate, told me. 'It means that you are frightened of people. Gangs use dogs to create that feeling of fear.'

Theo nearly cried when I insisted that we left the park and went to the other recreation area, but he recognised that the dogs didn't look too safe and cycled with me around the back of the park to Jesus Green, a little park in the centre of an Edwardian estate of workmen's cottages. It is one of the few picturesque areas in Bethnal Green. The majority of houses are now owned by professional, middle-class couples that work in the City. This is not the case with the street where I live, which consists mainly of council tenants. The area has recently been in the headlines of the local paper, the *East London Advertiser*, because a gang of Asian youths from the nearby council estate has been attacking white residents.

At the beginning of August the residents from the estate called for the police to take action against the youths because of a spate of attacks. A barman who worked in the local pub, the Royal Oak Bar on Columbia Road, reported how he was attacked. 'I was walking down the road, I turned around the corner and I walked into a large group of 15- and 16-year-olds. First of all I was hit in the mouth and my tooth came out, and the next two blows hit me on the side and the back of the head. They said: "What are you doing walking down our street?"'[50]

Linda Wilkinson of the area's Jesus Hospital Estate Residents Association said that a gang had been attacking white people for over a year. 'It's absolutely appalling; people have been hospitalised; it's a gang of Asian youths and it's a turf war,' she said. A local shop owner told me about how he was now frightened to walk out at night in a way he has never been before after his friend was brutally set upon and beaten with chains and bits of wood.

A Jewish teenager who lives in the area had this to say.

At half-term the kids have nothing to do, and so they like to hang around at the bottom of our road with a lot of sticks. One afternoon, my dad drove his Morris Minor van back to our house, and unloaded some wood from the roof of the van. As he was doing this, the boys – Bengali boys from the local school – gathered around him and abused him. 'We're gonna smash your crappy van up! What's that doing on the road?'

As he was going into the house, two of them cycled

past on their little BMX bikes and threw eggs into the house, laughing hysterically as they raced away. The whole street got egged after that. Later on, my dad's wing mirrors got smashed.

I was walking up the road the other day and I got called a 'white pig' and had apples thrown at me.

Knowing this, I was wary about letting Theo bicycle around the park when I saw a number of Asian youths sitting on benches in the Green and smoking. I knew he would be fine because it was daylight and there were other people around, but I was tired and just didn't want the slightest hint of aggravation. Just the mere fact of having teenagers around looking menacing can be enough to put people off from entering an area in case it becomes a battlefield.

In the end, I took Theo to Shoreditch Park where there were no gangs of youths hanging around, only innocent sunbathers reading books and having picnics. I felt lucky in that my area has enough places to go that you don't feel hemmed in by gangs of youths looking menacing.

In 2005, a United Nations report revealed that Britain is actually one of the most violent places in the world. Scotland was named as the most violent. People there are almost three times more likely to be assaulted than in America. England and Wales had a similarly high percentage of people who had been assaulted.[51]

Superintendent David Baines confessed to me that violent gang culture was rife in Greater Manchester, while in Glasgow and Belfast nearly everyone I spoke to felt that that 'NED' culture was on the rise.

On the Sighthill estate in Glasgow, a middle-aged mother of three told me about how she had been mugged the week before and that all of her friends had been attacked within the last year. 'It is absolutely terrible. The gangs are hanging around the streets and fighting each other, and then bashing anyone they think they can take money from, or who looks like they might be weak,' she said, trembling by the bus stop and looking anxiously around.

The Sighthill estate was quite similar to the set-up at Ravenscroft Park; there was a stretch of open ground with a playground, some shops and a library, surrounded by tower blocks. As in the case of the Ravenscroft, the Shipley estate, even the genteel Jesus Green estate and so many other estates I saw, it was configured with a piece of land in the middle of a built-up residential area. Houses and residential accommodation looked down upon what was essentially a perfect layout for a battlefield.

Two opposing teams could enter from different directions, and had the luxury of being watched by all and sundry. One thing I found to be very important for the yob was that he was watched while he was fighting. Most yobs of this sort who were involved in turf wars had no fear of being caught by the police.

Rambo, a 15-year-old boy who I interviewed in the deprived Carbrain estate in Cumbernauld, laughed when I mentioned the police. 'Listen, I've been arrested by the police sae many times that I dunnae give a fook mate,' he said. 'The only thing that counts is winning, and making sure that everybody sees ya winning. Like last week, I got this guy and I punched him in the face, and I kept punching, and I mashed up his nose so that he was all covered in blood. Blood streaming down his face.'

Taj, a gang member in Carbrain, told me that it was creating a fear factor that was the all-important thing when it came to fighting. 'The ideal situation is when you get your opponent so frightened of you that you don't even have to fight, so that they have given up even before you have fought. That way, if you do get into a fight you know you will win,' he said.

Another gang member told me about how enjoyable it

was to create such a feeling of fear in the public. Jefferson grew up in east London, like the members of the Lords of Stratford Cru, and went on mugging sprees as a teenager.

We were into street robbery. We would travel up and down on the trains in east London, looking for people to rob. We would travel in a pack, and attack when the target looked easy to rob. We were cocky. We loved the feeling of frightening everyone.

When we saw a target, we would go straight for the kill. It was funny because we didn't need to speak to each other about who we would mug. We had got to know each other so well that all it would take was a few glances, lasting maybe a second or two, and we all knew who was going to be attacked. We got so good at it that after a while we didn't even need to look at each other. It was like telepathy. It was like we knew automatically.

We'd see someone who had a nice watch, or mobile, or hat, and just go up to him and, pow!, we'd snatch the thing off him. Pow! Your hat has gone. We wouldn't talk. We would just look at each other and just know that we had our target. We didn't say nothing to each other. Perhaps, if we were feeling in the mood, we would slap someone around a bit. But mostly, we would just grab whatever we wanted off whoever.

It took the incident with the Indian in the park to make us realise that our leader, Green, was a psycho. He came back to our manor in Stoke Newington one day, screaming that some Indian had ripped him off in a park near Shoreditch. And all of us thought: fucking hell, we've gotta sort this Indian out. So we all piled down there, and being led by Green, found an Indian, and kicked his head really badly. And the thing was, he probably wasn't the guy. Maybe there was no guy. It was just Green. So we just kicked someone to shit for nothing.

And when we got together at our manor later, we talked about this. Green wasn't there. We avoided him after that.

But that didn't stop me getting a criminal record. I had done a lot that could have got me in real trouble. I thought I would never get caught. But I did. Me and a couple of mates turned over an off-licence. I wanted to be tough so when we asked the old geezer behind the till for his cash, I also elbowed him in the face. I really regret that now. He was an old geezer. And his boy was there. His son. And he saw his old man get beaten.

There was CCTV footage, and I was wearing purple trousers. So when the police came around and searched my house, they found the purple trousers, and I was nicked. I got convicted, and sentenced to community service. My parents were good people, quite strict but good to me. I can't blame them for what I did. I did it for the buzz, and because I was easily led. Very easily led.

What is important to consider in Jefferson's story are some factors that he left out: his educational attainment was low – he achieved only a couple of GCSEs at low grades – and he was unaware that his actions had consequences. There was a childish selfishness about what he and his friends did: they were utterly unconcerned about the effect that they were having upon their victims. They hadn't considered the pain that they would go through after they had been assaulted. All they were aware of was that they were, in all likelihood, not going to get caught. In the same way that soldiers in a war are trained to think of the enemy not as people but as obstacles to a goal – obstacles which must be obliterated – the prevalent culture around Jefferson taught him that the people involved were simply obstacles preventing him and his gang achieving his goal of having some new trainers, or a mobile phone, and so on.

In a multiplicity of ways, modern British culture creates

the atmosphere in which our streets are turning into battle-fields. It is highly materialistic, with every type of media from TV to the Internet celebrating the acquisition of costly goods – such as jewellery, trainers and designer clothes – and it is also individualistic, with its emphasis upon the individual achieving what he wants no matter what the consequences upon other people. All-pervasive advertising suggests that success can be achieved instantaneously by buying the right kind of drink, item of clothing or lottery ticket. When children like Jefferson see that they are not going to achieve academic success in our moribund, boring schools, they search for instantaneous success on the streets. The culture has already trained them to think of people as little more than skittles that need to be knocked over in order to achieve that success. Fuelled by alcohol, greed, hatred, bullying or a persuasive leader, they go in search of a fight. Once they have tasted combat, most people don't want to give it up. Even policemen have told me about the thrill of whacking people, of going to war. 'The adrenalin high is addictive,' one policeman told me.

Gang members are the same. 'It is like nothing else on earth. It's like taking drugs, only better. You feel so frightened beforehand, but then something hits your head and you're off! Everything speeds up, but you see things in slow motion, and you think "I'm going to fucking kick the shit out of you until you bleed out of your ears,"' an ex-gang member told me in the Cypriot holiday resort of Ayia Napa.

Both the policemen and the former gang member I spoke to had clearly left behind their violent tendencies, or at least had them under control. They were now older and wiser. However, I did meet a gang member in his late twenties who was definitely still addicted to violence. I met him in a club in the Loughton region of London. It was Saturday night and the place was crowded with suntanned girls in revealing, skimpy dresses, and guys wearing designer jeans and boots.

One such person was Pete, who was wearing a very smart, crushed cotton suit and blue shirt. His face was tanned, and his hair dyed. He would have looked like a pop star if it hadn't been for the scar on his cheek.

He explained to me outside the club that he was the club's 'dealer'. He was the person from whom all the punters bought their cocaine, ecstasy and heroin.

I was situated in a club in Leytonstone before this but the cops were keeping an eye on me and I thought I'd move out here. Moving out into any club where there are rich punters ain't easy 'cos you gotta get rid of the opposition, if you know what I mean? That means you gotta fight them. Usually, it's just knife fights, but sometimes it's worse. I stabbed the geezer who was here and took over his turf. He was crapping himself! I had to laugh. He didn't know who he was fucking around with.

The worst I ever stabbed anyone was down Ilford way, where I stabbed this bloke ten times or more. Just left him there for dead. I dunno if he died or not. I don't think he did 'cos I never heard about him.

But you gotta look after yourself. I've been stabbed loads of time. Once, a year ago, I nearly died. I was in hospital for a month. But I got out again, and with more of a reputation. Now people are getting to be really scared of me. The only people who aren't are the ethnics: those Kosovans and Albanians and Turks are right fucking nutters and they ain't to be messed with. They are really taking over the trade in north London. It's no joke.

I learnt afterward from a friend that Pete's earnings from his drug dealing were considerable. However, he didn't have a bank account, and carried a roll of banknotes worth thousands around with him, all tied together with a gold pin. Moreover, I became aware that it was Pete's love of fighting that drew him to the dealing, not the other way round. 'He wants to scrap,' his friend said. 'If he sees the chance for a fight, he will take it. Just the other day I was in a club with him and I watched him provoke a massive fight. It really kicked off. I've known him from since he was a kid, and he's always been like that.'

There are thousands of characters like Pete everywhere in Britain today. The fear and misery that they can inflict upon communities cannot be underestimated. A pupil of mine told me about his hellish experience with one such character in a deprived area in Basildon.

I live near a council estate lovingly referred to as Beirut, which is also near another council estate, known as Alcatraz. I started getting attacked by kids from these two estates at a very young age. I was eight when I suffered my first one. A group of kids from Beirut attacked my mum's garage, and she phoned the police. The yobs blamed me for getting nicked. They chased after me, and punched me in the face. After that, whenever I saw them coming I would run like hell, and get away.

The chief yob is a boy called George. His mum and step-father are alcoholics. He is a bitter and twisted individual who likes to randomly attack people. Last November, he threw a stick at my head as I was walking down the road.

I shouted at him that he was a cunt, and he returned with eight other people. I was with my martial arts teacher, coming back from a class. George ripped up a fence panel, and started clubbing my teacher. He drove a nail through his head. There was blood everywhere. The police and an ambulance were called. Fortunately, this time Goerge was charged, and put in prison for a lot things: GBH, common assault, disturbance of the peace.

George has done everything. Arson. Theft, mugging, joyriding, drug dealing. I am very, very frightened of him.

He's out of prison now, and wanting to get even.

But I don't want to move. Every area has its scumbags.

The battlefield comes to our rural towns

'I think she wanted to prove she's hard or something because she jumped on me when I was walking home from school and stabbed a fag in my eye.'

It isn't just the run-down areas in Britain that are afflicted with this sort of mindless violence. Even in the relatively affluent town of Chippenham, in the south-west, people's lives are affected by yobbery. One evening in June, I visited one of the well-known 'yob' areas in the town. Despite the rainy weather, some children were out for some fun. They were shouting, 'You fucking cunts' at each other, and throwing cans of Special Brew around. As I drew closer, I saw that they were obviously quite well off: their coats were clean and expensive, and they were carrying trendy, designer-label shoulder bags. They were also not older than 12, judging from their diminutive statures.

As I approached they eyed me gingerly, and then hastened away towards the centre of the town. I continued through the car park, and walked down an embankment beside the leisure centre. In front of me was an idyllic country scene. A tree-lined river, ducks and swans floating serenely down its glassy surface, and a lush, green stretch of parkland. However, the scene was punctuated with knots of youths, hanging around smoking and drinking.

I talked to a group of teenagers who were leaning against the leisure pool's air vent. The warm air blew into my face, and the adolescents grinned sheepishly at me. There were three boys, whose names turn out to be Joe, John and 'Kill', and two girls, Gemma and Vicki. They were both 16 years old. Gemma was dressed in a pink top and black T-shirt, and had a fair degree of make-up painted onto her face, while Vicki was altogether more gregarious in dress sense and manner. She was wearing eyeliner, and had on a revealing top that didn't do much to hide two burgeoning breasts.

Both of them were only too anxious to talk. A repeated refrain throughout the evening was that 'There is fuck all to do here.' Vicki's story unfolded as I talked to her. She was involved in a serious assault a few months ago.

You see, I started going out with this guy called John, and this girl, let's call her Sarah, didn't like this because she thought John was her boyfriend. Now Sarah, we know her well from school. She's quite respectable. She comes from a good home, but she's chippy. She doesn't like her mum, or something. But her parents live in a big house. I think she wanted to prove she's hard or something because she jumped me when I was walking home from school and stabbed a fag in my eye. I had to go to hospital. It was very blurry. Very uncomfortable.

I didn't go to the police, though. I just wanted to forget it. I had John, and that was what mattered. Anyway, my eye got better but Sarah didn't. She couldn't get over the fact that I got John. A few months after I was stabbed in the eye, I was walking home from Chickoland, late at night, and Sarah caught up with me. She had been drinking and was laughing about my eye so I ran at her, and pelted her in the shin, and I managed to pin her up against the wall by the side of Superdrug. John was there. He tried to stop me, and then he had to try and restrain her from punching me because she managed to twist me around and get me against the wall.

The police were called and we were both taken away. They told us off and then let us go. Stuff like this happens all the time around here. I think it's 'cos there's nothing to do except getting pissed and racing around town in cars. That's a favourite thing to do, I suppose. But you get sick of it after a while.

I found a similar situation in the nearby town of Calne. I walked across the lovingly tended green in Calne, tripped down a cobble-stoned street, passed an astonishing medieval house and gateway, and then strolled into a main shopping area. Opposite me there was a phone booth that had been completed smashed in. Great piles of glass lay heaped up on the pavement. Further up the road, in the library, a kindly, calm librarian told me about how there was a group of children in the town, aged between 12 and 15, who regularly come into the library and abuse the public. 'Just yesterday, a group of them came in and one of them starting shouting and swearing in the children's section,' she said, pointing to a brightly coloured seating area. 'The parents hate their children hearing that language. We asked him to leave but he wouldn't. That is quite common here – children causing mayhem, and not leaving. So we actually had to call the police.'

She told me that at night, outside the library, the children gathered and rode their skateboards up and down the ramps near the idyllic country stream. They smoked and drank, shouted obscenities at each other and then threw their rubbish into the stream. 'There isn't much else to do here,' the librarian said.

My best mate - death

'If we are not careful, yob culture will take over completely, and no one will be safe on the streets. If we don't do something quickly, society is going to break down and everywhere will become like the Wild West.' Jamie James

Jamie James, former gang member and self-confessed yob, feels that there is a real distinction to be made between a yob and a gang member.

A yob does things like phone the police or the fire brigade, and then when they arrive chucks stones at them. As a yob I loved the theatre of the whole thing. I loved being seen kicking the shit out of people. I wasn't frightened of being caught. It all added to my street cred. Added to which, you know the police aren't going to do anything if you're a juvenile. A proper gang member, on the other hand, is involved in organised crime. The last thing they want to do is get caught by the police. A gang member keeps his head down.

When I was a teenager, I had two identities. One as a yob, and one as a gang member. As a yob, I was called Gerry, and as a gang member, I was Jamie. The Gerry part of me was very reckless. I'll give you an example. When I was 14, I lent some money to someone who I thought was a mate. He ended up not paying it back. Now, the thing about being a yob is that you can never lose face. My mates were like, 'He's taken your money, and now he's laughing about it. You are going to have to do something about it.' So I got into a fight with this kid. I hit him over the head with a bottle. He, though, managed to kick me, and so the fight wasn't a clear-cut victory for me: I still hadn't got my money back, and he'd kicked me. So I stole his family's car, and drove it through their front door. The entire family was there in the living room, and I realised then that I could have killed them. I can still remember the looks on their faces. I realised that they had nothing to do with the feud, and that I could have killed some innocent people. I was arrested for the offence, but the police never got me because they couldn't prove it was me.

Although I was sick about what I had done, I carried on my life of crime. You see, I got into a way of doing things that was hard to get out of. I had never gone to school properly since I was 11. I used to register in the morning, bunk off for the day, then register in the afternoon and then bunk off again. It was a great scam because I could always tell the police I was in school – and had a legal document to prove it – and that left me to do whatever I wanted without ever getting charged. So I'd drive around with my mates, hold up a shop for the money, and then register at school for the afternoon. There was no way the police could get me.

I got into so many fights that I can scarcely remember them all. One of the worst and most traumatic for me was when I threw a tennis ball at someone's head, and that led to a massive showdown in a park in south London. Me and my best friend Mike fought together. I got stabbed by our enemies, this gang we were feuding with. Mike helped me out and got stabbed himself. We both lay gasping on the floor. We were sitting there just laughing about it, watching the blood leak out of our chests and stomachs. We couldn't believe that we had so much blood in our bodies. There were great pools of blood on the floor. An ambulance was called, and the other gang ran off. The paramedics turned up. I thought my friend had gone to sleep because only a minute ago I had been laughing with him about all our blood. His eyes were shut and he looked pretty white. But the paramedics said, 'No, he's dead.' I said, 'No, don't be stupid, I was just talking to him a couple of minutes ago.' The medics lifted him out of my hands. It took me ages to realise he was dead. I lay in hospital thinking he was still alive. I even got up to look for him. But he wasn't there. He was dead.

It took two weeks for me to register that he was dead. He was my best mate. If I was being nicked, he was being nicked. We did everything together. He was an only child, and I still see his mum. She isn't mad at me. She is pleased that I have got a proper job now, and am not involved in all the violence.

My whole body is scarred from the fights I have been involved in. My nose is broken because someone threw a paving slab against my nose. I was having a fight with this geezer, and it was a dead draw, and then he smashed a paving stone into my face. I thought I was going to die.

The silliest fight I ever got involved with was when this guy bumped into me on the bus, and he wouldn't say sorry, so I slapped him, he slapped me and then it was a fully fledged fight.

One of the biggest fights I ever got involved with was the Thamesmead boys versus the Abbey Wood boys. I was 15. It all started when I was walking through Abbey Wood and I was attacked by a Chinese boy, who hit me on the head. We fought, and I got the better of him. That meant that I was now pitted against the Abbey Wood boys.

There were other run-ins. Eight of my mates were walking along this hill in Thamesmead, and we bumped into some Abbey Wood boys. There were four of them on the hill but as we went down it, we saw there were masses of them in cars. They'd brought a whole load of grungy travellers with them. We were ready for a fight but we hadn't expected so many of them. So we got together our mates; there was a phone box and we quickly phoned around. Then there was a massive kick-off. In yob culture, you know all the people on your manor who will fight with you. There were scores of injuries. Someone lost their eye when a belt got hit in their face. We fought with baseball bats, bottles and knives. The travellers were the worst for knives: they were properly tooled up.

Another time, my cousin got tangled up with the boys in Bexley Heath because he went out with a white girl from Bexley Heath School, which made them want to kill him. People started talking to each other, and spreading rumours, and exaggerating things, and saying more bad things, and soon there was real war between the two tribes, who included a lot of family members. I took my cousin along with the Thamesmead boys to confront the Bexley Heath boys at a bar in Bexley Heath. The Bexley Heath boys had assembled a huge crew consisting of old men, young kids, heavy-duty blokes from the East End, boys from Woolwich and other kids from all over. Seeing that there was so many of them, I made a phone call, and got loads of people who were part of my gang to come along from Thamesmead. You had the yobs from Bexley Heath and the gang members from Thamesmead fighting against each other. It was a fatal combination. The Bexley Heath boys weren't rich-rich, but they were well off. They were classic yobs: kicking balls against cars, bullying people in the street, doing silly, petty crime stuff like muggings. They didn't realise that they were up against a major gang. We had warned them not to tangle with us, that they didn't know the consequences of taking on a properly organised gang.

So we all piled into the pub, which was a small, enclosed space. The Bexley Heath boys were on one side of the pub, and the Thamesmead boys on the other. There was another huge kick-off. We had a huge fight in the pub, and then it spilled out into the road outside. Someone was stabbed, someone was thrown in front of a moving car, people were being thrown all over the place. The road was covered with Bexley Heath boys.

The police turned up and the fight broke up. But after the cops had gone, we walked down into Bexley Heath centre, which was a ten-minute walk from the pub. More police came along, and so we all jumped onto the buses. At that point, someone shouted 'They're back.' We turned around and saw that the road was swamped with Bexley Heath boys. They went into McDonald's. The security guard had clocked what was going on, but he couldn't do anything. Everyone was now fired up for another fight. We screamed at them, 'Come out, come out, let's finish this off.' A chair flew out of McDonald's and all hell broke loose. We all surged into McDonald's.

The fight this time was even worse than before: the gangs were throwing chairs, tables and food at each other. The customers were so scared that they jumped over the counters and ran for cover among the ovens. There were stabbings, glassings, chairs broken over people's heads. I threw tables and chairs at people. I loved the huge rush of it all. It was very, very exciting. But it was scary. I thought that I might die at any moment, but I didn't care. I thought: 'If I die, I die.' I wasn't too fussed. Things hadn't been going well for me. I had got a girl pregnant but had lost the baby twins she was carrying a week before this, and the week before that one of my cousins had died. He'd died in a fight in east London, trying to protect me from some guys who wanted to get me. As I watched all those knives stabbing people in McDonald's I felt more or less fearless. They could stab me for all I cared.

But for some reason, I didn't get badly hurt. The police were called and there were a lot of arrests. A lot of people got injured. One boy got his lung punctured by a knife, and another had his skull fractured.

Jamie James, now 29, runs a youth organisation that tries to help gang members give up their lives of crime. Seeing what it is like for children on the street, James confessed to me, 'If we are not careful, yob culture will take over completely, and no one will be safe on the streets. If we don't do something quickly, society is going to break down and everywhere will become like the Wild West. The thing is, getting involved in real yob culture is a messy, dangerous business. I have lost too many friends as a result of it. The truth is that death is your best friend in a gang. If you die, you've got no comebacks. Death is not demanding. Death demands nothing from you. There is only silence and nothing to do. That is preferable to the life of a real gang member. In that respect, death is the best mate you'll ever have.'

The battle to be obscene

'Every day I walked past these boys and girls they would say that I was a fucking cunt, a wanker, a dickhead, a bastard.'

Obscenity has been part of the British identity for millennia. Swearing, the most all-pervasive form of obscenity, is one of the oldest concepts in the language. The Anglo-Saxons over a thousand years ago had the idea of an 'oath' enshrined in the language, and the notion of *andswarian*, of swearing against someone, was very important to them. To swear against someone was a very serious matter; the recipient had his honour at stake and, among the Anglo-Saxons' warrior class, was obliged to defend it.[52] There was also the ritual insult of *flyting*; here, people would engage in a verbal jousting match involving seeing who could insult each other in a more persuasive and technically efficient fashion.[53] Finally, there were the insults thrown at foreigners: to be called a 'Dane' was the equivalent of being sworn at.[54]

In the Middle Ages, the word 'horson' was the most wounding insult, meaning 'son of a whore'.[55] Recently, this word has returned to Britain's streets and schools as the worst conceivable insult. The worst fights I ever had to break up in school were where two children had shouted 'yer mum' at each other – 'yer mum' is an abbreviated form of 'your mother is a prostitute', i.e. you are the son of a prostitute. For me, an insult like this is properly obscene because it is deliberately said with the intention of causing public embarrassment and hurt by stating that the person closest to you indulges in 'taboo' sexual habits.

During the Renaissance, at a time of unprecedented religious upheaval, numerous common oaths became unacceptable, and were replaced by the more creative thinkers with some fabulous new words, many of which we find in Shakespeare's curses. Later on, during the Augustan period of the 18th century and the Victorian era of the 19th century, decorum ruled the roost, and most swear words were outlawed in print, culminating most famously in Dr Thomas Bowdler attempting to rewrite Shakespeare's plays without the swear words. This Victorian attitude prevailed in the upper echelons of the British establishment until the 1960s, when the rise of the hippy generation, together with a relaxation of the obscenity laws, lead to what Geoffrey Hughes calls 'a modern explosion' in swearing.

A resident of Salford living in an estate just off Liverpool Street explained to me how her life was made a misery by local youths swearing at her. 'Every day I walked past these boys and girls they would say that I was a fucking cunt, a wanker, a dickhead, a bastard. They were doing it to everyone, but it upset me a lot because I hadn't done anything and, at night, I would hear them in the street shouting you fucking this, you fucking that, and I wondered if it was about me. It was never any worse than the swearing. They never threw things at me, or threatened me. It was just swearing,' she said in a timorous voice, looking up and down the street as she did so.

In Bristol late one Friday night in July 2005, I witnessed a policeman being subjected to a drunken rant by a student with a middle-class accent wearing some very expensive designer gear. The student kept saying: 'Excuse me, but what the fucking hell do you think you fucking well were doing? Excuse me for swearing. I didn't mean to swear. But what the fucking hell were you fucking doing taking the girl out of the nightclub?' The student, it transpired, had nothing to do with the girl who had been escorted by some police out of the nightclub; he was just using that as an excuse to swear at the policeman. He clearly got a kick from swearing at him, and then pretending not to be swearing at him. The policeman, who was young and on his own, didn't know how to respond, and found himself being followed by the student for at least ten minutes, while being subjected to this drunken rant.

'I make it very clear to my police force,' said Superintendent David Baines of Swinton Police in Greater Manchester, 'that swearing repeatedly at a police officer is something that the miscreant should be put in the back of the van for. The officer should issue a warning and then, if it continues, it's the back of the van.'

Baines is relatively unusual in that he has an extremely low tolerance of swearing, which is considered a very minor offence unless it is used to create a public affray. 'If you're not careful it can be seen as the thin end of the wedge and, if a group sees that a police officer is tolerating a lot of swearing going on, they can think that they can get away with more. Call me old-fashioned, but people shouldn't be swearing around figures of authority.'

Baines told me that many schools appeared to have lost control over their more unruly pupils, and that this then leaked onto the streets. I certainly know this from my own experience as a teacher, having been sworn at a few times during my career, and having listened to a lot of swearing in my classrooms. Most of my pupils have known that swearing is unacceptable, but have done it in order to prove that they are 'hard' to their peer group. 'I was just bigging it up, sir,' one pupil said to me, adding, 'It's a way of getting on with everyone.'

One teacher in a small town in Scotland told me that in recent years, swearing has become so prevalent that she has started swearing too. 'It's the only way you don't look like an idiot,' she said, clearly dubious about what she was doing. 'If you don't swear, you look stuck up. It's everywhere on the TV, on the Internet. Everyone is swearing. I don't tolerate pupils swearing at me, but I do let them swear in the class now.'

Her experience is not unique. Up and down the country, anecdotal evidence suggests that swearing has become much more acceptable in the country's classrooms. As Baines himself recognised, teachers do not have the sanctions of the police. A gang member from London told me, 'At school, it's all a bit of a joke. You know that the teachers can't do anything to you, so you swear and laugh at them 'cos you can. It's funny watching them get so stressed out.'

Theodore Darymple feels that we have very significantly spoilt our way of life because the codes of public civility that used to be common to all classes a few decades ago are now gone.

In all walks of life, there is a failure to accept that some behaviour is better than others. Let me give you an example. I feel that swearing in public is extremely antisocial. When I was working in the prison, and in the ward of my hospital, I didn't allow my patients to swear. I felt that it was cowardly to let my patients get away with it. And do you know what? The most extraordinary thing is that nine out of ten people

– even the most hardened criminals – would apologise. People want a figure of authority. The terribly sad thing is that the prisons are full of men who want to be there – I know because I worked for many years as a prison doctor. It is notoriously difficult for the police to catch burglars, and yet the prisons are full of them. And why do you think that is? It's because those people wanted to be caught. The prisons are places where there are clear boundaries, very few responsibilities and no women. A very high proportion of prisoners have extremely chaotic relations with women and are frequently in prison because of violence that they have committed against their partners.

It is tempting to say that the language of the football terrace has pervaded our society: our schools, our hospitals, our streets. What is ironic about this is that swearing is no longer tolerated in most football grounds throughout the country. 'When I was running the Oldham police force, we made it very clear that swearing would not be tolerated on the terraces,' says David Baines. 'It was about the "respect" issue. It just isn't respectful to be swearing like that when there are children and families around. Our football supporters, Oldham and Preston ones alike, knew the score. They knew that they would be thrown out of the ground for swearing. And they stopped doing it after a few matches where a lot of them were kicked out.'

Baines managed to impose these standards of civility upon the tough working-class supporters of Preston and maintain them. 'Preston knew the standards. Going to a football match there was a pleasant experience because there wasn't a lot of foul language,' Superintendent Baines says. 'However, supporters from other sides sometimes got a shock. I remember one match where we started kicking out the Wigan supporters who were swearing. They turned to us and said, "What are you doing this for? We always swear at home!"

They didn't think that they were doing anything wrong.'

As is the case with pornography, the media has played a huge role in breaking down the codes of civility that used to bind our society together. Perhaps most insidious of all it has encouraged a form of 'self-righteous' swearing. The turning point occurred in 1985 on BBC TV, when Bob Geldof used the word 'fucking' to vent his frustration at the fact that the Live Aid appeal to save people starving in Ethiopa had not received enough money. He did not say 'Give us your fucking money,' as he is now credited for, but he did use the word 'fucking' to vent his indignation at the lack of charity of the British people. The public were shocked into action and the money started pouring in. Suddenly the word 'fucking' had a different context within the media; it wasn't simply used to be rebellious, but was there to express genuine outrage. It had become acceptable to hurl it at people when there was an important issue at stake.

It was in exactly the same way that Alistair Campbell would swear before his enemies. His swearing is always tinged with self-righteousness. When he swore at BBC executives, he was swearing feeling that he had right on his side. He said to Jeremy Vine, the BBC political correspondent, 'You will fucking report exactly what I tell you to report; you'll stick to my fucking schedule and nothing else.'[56] The tone is similar to Geldof's: the swearing is there to threaten but also to suggest that since he has right on his side, he has licence to swear like this. Whereas in previous eras, British political figures would have framed their threats in the most polite forms of address, thus emphasising their social superiority, now they employ the language of the street. The brawling thug who swears because he is certain he is right has replaced the aristocratic mandarin.

Just as attitudes towards verbal obscenities have changed hugely in the past few decades, attitudes towards visual obscenity have also changed. By the 1970s and 80s, mass-produced pornography, previously only sold in specialised sex shops or in covert fashion, was placed on the top shelves of corner shops. It was in this environment that Richard Desmond published titles like *Asian Babes, Horny Housewives, Readers' Wives, 40 Plus, Big & Black, Big Ones International, Spunk-Loving Sluts, Double Sex Action* – and telephone sex lines. In 1995 he launched Television X: the Fantasy Channel, a pornographic television channel (now supplemented by a range of websites).[57] In 2000 United sold the *Express* newspaper group to Desmond for £125 million; it included the national *Daily Express* and *Sunday Express* newspapers (each with a circulation of around a million) and the *Daily Star* (537,000).

Desmond and David Sullivan, who owns the pornographic daily 'newspaper' the *Sport*, have virtually cornered the market in magazine porn in Britain; their influence upon the way in which the British public views women and tolerates 'obscenity' cannot be overestimated. When Desmond donated £100,000 to the Labour Party in 2002, even the normally on-message Labour MPs protested. Ms Harman told the *Daily Telegraph*: 'I wouldn't take money from Richard Desmond for my own office, so I don't think the Labour Party should. It would be a pity if this issue undermined women's confidence in all the government has achieved for women in childcare, family-friendly employment and tackling domestic violence.'[58] The culture secretary Ms Jowell also said: 'You either talk equality or you act equality.'[59] Desmond sold many of his pornographic titles in March 2004, but still owns the most profitable 'adult' TV channel in the UK, the Fantasy Channel.

It was the ripped-up copy of *Spunk-Loving Sluts* I found floating around a playground near where I live that made me think again about the influence that pornography has over a culture. There it was, a woman leering lasciviously over a dildo, with her opened crotch depicted in anatomical detail. I kicked the pages away from the swings, and directed my four-year-old son's gaze towards the climbing frame. In

the distance, I saw a group of youths laughing at the fringes
of the park. Perhaps they had something to do with the scat-
tered obscene pages, perhaps they didn't. The point was that
someone had deliberately put them there, where young children might see them, knowing that it was highly antisocial
to do so. I felt there was a shameless yobbery about this act
that is part and parcel of the aggressive, in-yer-face culture
that the pornographers had created.

The obscenity for me was not so much the pornography –
I am liberal when it comes to such stuff – but the culture that
has made it so publicly and readily available. In the days of
the secretive sex shop at least it was kept away from people
who wanted to avoid such stuff, but now it is all-pervasive. It
is staring at you whenever you walk into a newsagents, naked
women are often on billboard posters, it pops up in emails
and is there at the click of a button on the Internet, and it is
very apparent in most high streets now. During my travels
around Britain, I was struck by the prevalence of the Ann
Summers chain in many 'respectable' towns: shop dummies
with stiletto heels and S and M outfits goading passers-by to
enter the 'naughty' realm of the shop. In Cardiff and Ayia Napa
in particular, I noted that there was a fetish among the women
– of all ages – for dressing up in Ann Summers-type outfits.
A recent survey of 2,000 15-19-year-old girls found that 67 per
cent considered 'glamour model' to be their ideal profession.[60]

Part of British drinking culture is linked with women
dressing up in sexy outfits that invoke the sluttiness of 'girly'
magazines. The people who celebrate these attitudes are chal-
lenging the rest of us to disapprove, knowing full well that
we can't stop them from 'expressing themselves'. Part of the
thrill of it for them is other people's disgust. They know that
images which are at the margins of being unacceptable
provoke as much admiration as revulsion because they
awaken the 'yobbish' element in the Brits, many of whom
want to stick two fingers up at other people.

CHAPTER SIX

Sitting Ducks

❝ I could see immediately that the family were "sitting ducks" because the path or raised deck which ran beside the houses could easily act as a "shooting range" from where missiles and abuse could be hurled at the intended victim. ❞

The asylum seeker's story

'It's not racist or anything, it's just that Nazi is a nice-sounding word.'

The yob is a theatrical creature, revelling in parading his power and influence, and fighting people he knows he will beat. As D.S. Simmons said to me, though, he is predominantly a coward, taking on people who he knows he can defeat. The yob's favourite victim is 'the sitting duck' – the innocent person who just happens to be in the wrong place at the wrong time, but is sitting in front of the baying mob, unable to move and incapable of retaliating.

A striking example of this was the tale of a Turkish Kurd, Mr Gezer, an asylum seeker who was placed with his family in the Toryglen estate in Glasgow in 2000. He was 50 years old and a victim of torture and other serious human rights abuses that resulted in severe psychiatric problems, and had been diagnosed with depression, including psychotic depression. He arrived in the UK with his 15-year-old daughter Esme in September 2000, and sought asylum on arrival. His wife and youngest child Ibrahim, aged 13, followed him at the end of September, and she also sought asylum upon arrival. Until August 2001, he was housed with his family in a one-bedroom flat in Tottenham – accommodation that was intolerably cramped. He was then told in no uncertain terms that his only option was to be relocated to Glasgow.

Although they were only housed in the Toryglen estate for just under two months, they were subjected to a horrifying series of attacks and intimidation. From September to October 2001, they were abused in the street and threatened with dogs by local residents. Stones were thrown at them, and they were spat on and surrounded by anti-asylum seeker graffiti and general hostility. Late on 27 October, the Gezer family were attacked in their home by three unknown white men. Gezer's son was threatened with a knife by one of the men. They kicked the door and smashed the windows. The family were terrified and their screams alerted a neighbour, also a Turkish asylum seeker who, because of previous attacks, had a panic button in his flat. A security guard then called the police. Gezer and his family were the victims of a racially motivated attack and the police recorded it as a 'racist incident'. The family were too terrified to remain and fled Toryglen forever.

The Gezer family's experience was not a one-off. The government's policy of dispersing thousands of asylum seekers to Glasgow has resulted in hundreds, possibly thousands of refugees being attacked.

When I visited the Toryglen estate in the summer of 2005, I spoke to a number of asylum seekers who were housed there. One woman, who had a four-year-old child, explained that she had fled from the civil war in the Congo, and was grateful to be out of that country. 'But I do not like it when the boys throw stones at me, and say go back home.' she said. 'I shout back at them that this is my home. I have nowhere else. This is my home.'

I asked her what the boys said back, and she shrugged her shoulders. 'They just laugh,' she said.

I spoke to a local resident, Jessie, who worked as a care worker for the immigrant community in Glasgow, and she explained to me that things had got a lot better since the Gezer family had moved. 'I knew the family. They were lovely. The little girl was such a sweet child. I shudder to think about what they endured,' she said. 'The thing is the council put them in a house which had deck access, and didn't put them in the tower blocks where most of the other asylum seekers were.'

She walked me across the estate to where the Gezer family had been housed. We crossed a barren patch of land, which was covered in broken glass and surrounded by predominantly boarded-up shops. Turning a corner, we saw the row of houses where the Gezer family had been situated. I could see immediately that the family had been 'sitting ducks' because the path or raised deck that ran beside the houses could easily act as a 'shooting range' from where missiles and abuse could be hurled at an intended victim.

'You only have to see it to know just how vulnerable an outsider is in those houses,' she said. 'We make sure that the asylum seekers are put in safe accommodation now.'

There were a number of gangs hanging around the estate. I spoke to one group of teenage boys, who were smoking spliff and drinking Buckfast in their tracksuits and trainers. They told me that they didn't fight the asylum seekers now. 'Only if they get on our tits,' one giggled. 'But mostly we give the Rutherglen gang a good hiding every Friday and Saturday night!'

There was a cheer from the boys. I asked them what else there was to do around the estate and they said that there were things like the youth club. 'But it is nae as much fun as kicking the shit out of the NEDs in Rutherglen,' one youth opined.

In Glasgow, 'chavs' are nicknamed 'NEDs', which is an acronym for 'Non-educated Delinquent'. Contempt for NEDs in Scotland is very prevalent. I attended a comedy evening in central Glasgow where all the jokes appeared to be about NEDs. There was real nervousness about them in Glasgow because gangs of youths were so prevalent. The Neddies that I spoke to were very cooperative; they told me about their lives of drinking Buckfast and getting into fights. They showed me their scars from knife fights, pointed out their battlegrounds and explained to me their intricate insignia.

In Toryglen, one nickname for the gang was the 'Nazi Circus'. 'It's not racist or anything; it's just that Nazi is a nice-sounding word,' one boy said. Subsequent research of the archive revealed to me that Toryglen is a predominantly white area of high social tension and deprivation. There are high levels of general violence and criminality on the estate involving gang-related violence. Toryglen has a long history, predating dispersal, of hostility towards ethnic minorities, and has traditionally been a 'no-go' area for ethnic minorities; the use of deck-access accommodation made asylum seekers particularly vulnerable to racist attacks in their homes.

During 2001–2, the Strathclyde police, whose jurisdiction includes Toryglen, had the highest incidence of recorded racial incidents (367) and the second highest recorded incidence of racist incidents against asylum seekers (72), with Toryglen being one of the worst areas for attacks. Scotland and Strathclyde in particular saw a dramatic rise in the incidence of reported racially motivated violence and abuse since the introduction of dispersal of asylum seekers to housing estates in Scotland. Reported incidents involving racial harassment increased from 866 in 1999–2000 to 1,495 in 2002. Asylum seekers were most likely to be victims of racially motivated incidents in their homes and on the streets – with almost 50 per cent of recorded racist incidents taking place in the street.

Perhaps not surprisingly, I found a very similar story in the other council estates in Glasgow. In the Sighthill area, I spoke to a number of asylum seekers who all spoke of being verbally and physically abused. At the root of the problem was the government's policy of rehousing these people in areas where the police knew there would be trouble. Added to this, the general hysteria about asylum seekers in the press had compounded the problem. All of them were sitting ducks: the victims of the government's thoughtlessness, the media's hysteria and the local community's malevolence.

Terrified in the chip shop

'They take my petrol. They smash my windscreen.
They pull off my mirrors. They pull up my bonnet
and put newspapers in there. This is the worst place
I have ever worked.'

August 2005. In a run-down part of Salford, the city attached to Manchester, I parked next to a vandalised community theatre and wandered around, asking people what they thought of the area. A number of residents told me from behind high railings that it was fine. 'Very quiet,' they said. They were older, white working-class people who had very few gripes with anyone.

I could, however, sense things were tricky by a row of shops because there was a gang of youths hanging around the corner, shouting and laughing. In the local fish and chip shop I talked to Dujuan, an immigrant from Hong Kong, who had been working in the shop for one and a half years. There was no one in the chip shop, and she felt free to talk. 'I am very, very frightened here,' she said in halting English.

Last month, the teenagers broke the window of the shop twice. But mostly, the problem is my car. They damage my car many, many times. I do not live here. I drive here. I come here every morning, and every night I find something happen. They scratch the car. They let the air out of the tyre. They take my petrol. They smash my windscreen. They pull off my mirrors. They pull up my bonnet and put newspapers in there. This is the worst place I have ever worked. I come from a very poor part of Hong Kong, but it was nicer there. And I have worked in Manchester, where it is nicer. But here it is the worst. They come at me as I go to my car, in their hoods, in their trainers. They make comments. They say you 'f-ing chink, chinky go home, chinky we kill you'. The police do nothing. There is no CCTV here. But I know who it is who smash up my car. I know their names. I know their addresses, I tell the police this, but still the police do nothing. It is very bad. I can't sleep. I am very worried.

I point out that there is a poster on her wall advertising the Antisocial Behaviour Unit, which can be called if people experience trouble like this. 'You should call them,' I say.

She shrugs her shoulders. 'If the police do nothing, what are they going to do?' she says.

Suddenly, I watch Dujuan's face transform. She had been quite relaxed with me, but now her face is full of fear. She stops talking. A small, rat-faced man in his late thirties enters the chip shop. He is very thin, with a David Beckham haircut: blond, spiky hair. He is wearing jeans, and looks tanned and relatively affluent. I ask him about what he thinks of the area.

'Love it mate. Absolutely fantastic. No complaints whatsoever,' he says, snapping his fingers at Dujuan and saying, 'Two portions and an Irn Bru, love.'

Dujuan busies herself with the chips, and he looks at me quizzically. 'No. It's great here. I wouldn't change it for the world.'

I left Salford feeling profoundly disturbed. Dujuan's story really moves me because she is so obviously vulnerable: she is an identifiable outsider. She is sensitive. She is emotional. And that makes her a target. The rat-faced man was probably indicative of the community in that he felt part of something larger; he clearly wasn't frightened of anybody in the area. Not the menacing hoodies hanging around outside the shop, or any other areas of the estate. He wasn't a target. He was possibly one of those who contributed towards choosing the target: his manner of talking to Dujuan indicated a master-slave relationship that he was very happy with. He certainly wasn't that concerned about her anxious expression, or her hurried, sycophantic subservience. It suited him just fine. Can antisocial behaviour be about body language? David Ramsbotham, the former chief inspector for prisons, thinks so. He told me that the way the prison officers looked at prisoners could be highly antisocial. 'It can be a look of contempt, of sneering disregard, it can be the way someone shuts a door, the way a plate is put on a table. These little things send unconscious signals which have a definite effect if they are done hour after hour, day after day,' he said to me.

I watched the rat-faced man drop his change casually onto the counter and then leave slamming the door behind him, and saw that Ramsbotham had a point. Antisocial behaviour was more than about throwing stones at cars; it was a whole attitude, a whole mode of being for some people.

Intolerable noise

'The worst incident was when the boys went joy-riding and crashed into my car.'

While in the majority of cases, it is the immigrants who are the victims of racist crime in our yob nation, things can work the other way round, particularly in London. As D.S. Simmons and Wildman pointed out to me, London is suffering from an explosion in street gangs, many of which are ethnic in origin. This is largely a result of youths coming from backgrounds and countries that are socially deprived and culturally quite different from ours. Too many youths from ethnic communities are tapping into the yob culture prevalent in Britain, and things are spiralling out of control.

Charles Baron is a liberal man who has devoted his life to acting and writing. Now in his sixties, unlike many of his contemporaries, he has not become a reactionary. However, it is not so much his prejudices, but his experiences, which have driven him and his family to move out of his home in north London.

> The behaviour outside our house for the last 18 months has been the catalyst for us moving house, which we are now in the process of doing. I suppose our troubles started when a housing association set up shop next door to us, over a year and a half ago. For some reason, which I still don't fully understand, a lot of Somali boys from north London decided that this was their hanging out place. This soon meant that these youths would sit on the steps to our house, lean on our railings and, if our car was parked outside, sit on the bonnet of the car. Most of them chewed a special type of tobacco called 'cat' and spat a lot because of this. They would also sneak around the side of the house to a concealed archway, and smoke spliff there, frequently kicking down the gates to the archway.
> They spread out, as well, and would use our fence, at the back of the house, as a goal, and would kick balls repeatedly against the fence, so much so that they broke our fence and a window. We got so many balls in our garden that we stopped giving them back in the end.
> They were very large teenagers, and very, very loud. Their voices would penetrate into our living room as they shouted at each other. Added to which, they would always be play-fighting, and this caused a lot of very noisy yelling.
> Gradually, as the months passed, we began to notice more and more drug dealing. Every time we went out we noticed the lads passing cash and drugs through car windows. It was at this point that the police began to become interested. I had been calling them nearly three times a night until that point and they hadn't seemed that interested, but once it was clear that there was some serious drug dealing going on, they started to arrive in numbers. Frequently, they'd arrest one or two members of the gang,

and then get the whole lot of them shouting abuse at them. But the police kept their cool. They never over-reacted. I admire them for that because I don't think I would have done the same in their situation.

That said, I was always scrupulously polite to the boys when I asked them not to spit and sit on my step, and they seemed to respect that. They would say sorry. However, I am aware that they weren't so nice to some other people. A male nurse who lives near us got punched in the face, and the man running the record shop along the road got badly beaten.

The worst incident for us was when the boys went joy-riding and crashed into my car. A younger brother had taken the keys of the car from his older brother, and invited all his mates along for a merry drive-about. He came round our corner rather too widely and too wildly and crashed into my car. There was a very lengthy court case because the older brother wasn't insured, and I think it is still unresolved.

I think they didn't like being disrespected. Once I asked one of them, 'Do I know you?' because he was sitting on my step and I had told him countless times before that it was not right for him to do that. He got very aggressive because he thought I was disrespecting him by suggesting that I didn't know him when I did.

The thing is they came from a different culture from mine. A culture whose codes I didn't understand, and there seemed to be no sense in which they felt obliged to fit into the norms of our society. Or perhaps they didn't even know that they should. They also seemed to revel in the yob culture that is around in certain sections of Britain. The two things seemed to merge together: their lack of real cultural understanding of middle-class values of politeness and their desire to participate in yob culture. It was a fatal combination for us.

The police must have had a CCTV trained on the area because soon they started to arrive before any real trouble started. And that had a real effect: the masses of teenagers that used to assemble outside the house began to disappear, until it was only twos and threes congregating.

My family and I just decided that we'd had enough and decided to move. We knew of people who had been badly attacked by youths like the ones who hung around our house. We just didn't want to be around for that to happen to us.

Much in the same way that the Gezer family were sitting ducks, Charles Baron's family were also the victims of their geographical location. There was absolutely nothing that his family could do to stop the quality of their life being ruined by the noise and antisocial behaviour of the Somalis situated right next door to him.

The street from hell

'What's happened here is like an episode of *Brookside* except that it's all true.'

Perhaps the most striking example I came across of a 'sitting duck' was the story of Phil Hughes and his family when I was travelling around Wales, investigating yob culture there. In Ebw Vale, in the Welsh valleys outside Cardiff, I was drawn to the estates perched high on the slopes of the valley. In particular, I was curious about a remarkable-looking estate in an area called Rassau. The land was verdant and spectacular: lush grass swept around the modern houses like waves of green. In contrast, the houses were undistinguished: two-storey, concrete blocks with only one tiny window at the back of each house.

In one street, Summerfield Road, I found that 44 houses out of 60 were boarded up. What was remarkable was that it looked like quite a pleasant place to live. The houses were nicer and bigger than the ones further back, and the street clearly had the potential to be a homely, pleasant place. At the moment, though, it felt like walking into a ghost town. There was no one here on this Saturday afternoon except for a few kids on BMX bikes racing down the valley, and a solitary teenager sitting morosely on a wall.

I approached him and asked him what had happened to the houses. He bowed his head and then shrugged. 'I dunno. They just did it,' he said.

I asked what his name was, and he told me that it was Rhys. I could tell that while he might not be one to offer any explanations, he was willing to talk to me.

'Did any kind of fighting happen here?' I asked.

'Yeah, I suppose so,' he said. At that point a much younger boy of about ten appeared, and both of them smiled at each other.

'What kind of fighting?'

'It's them Hilltop boys. They come up here, and we fight them. Then the cops come and say we done it, but it's them Hilltop cunts. We only have screwdrivers to stab them with, but they have knives.'

'Why do the fights start?'

He shrugged his shoulders. 'They just do,' he said. 'Down at Red Gravel.'

'What's that? A pub?'

'No. It's just this red gravel outside the school down there,' he said, pointing down the hill. A misty blue light shone in the distance over the polished rooftops of the town.

'It's always the Hilltops. They chase us and we run away.'

'You never chase them?'

'Nah. They chase us. They got knives and we got screwdrivers. You can't chase someone with a screwdriver.'

'Why don't you get some knives?' I suggested.

'Then we'd be just like them,' he said.

'So there's some honour in having screwdrivers?'

'Only Hilltops have knives,' he responded. 'Sometimes if the Hilltops see us in the town, they chase us. Last month, they chased us and I got my head stamped on. Now the police say that we can't speak to them, and they can't speak to us. They aren't allowed here, and we aren't allowed there.'

'So do you ever get into trouble with the police?'

'Nah, not really. I only got arrested two times. The police don't like us. They think we are starting on the Hilltops, when really the Hilltops are starting on us.'

Everything with him seemed to return to his enmity with the Hilltops. I asked if there was anything else to do in Rassau. 'There's fuck all to do. If you are lucky, you can get a ride in someone's car and race up and down for a bit. But mostly there's fuck all to do.'

'What about any youth clubs?'

'That's for the younger children,' he said. 'Sometimes we throw stones at the windows of it. They got computers in there.'

'What about drugs? Are there much of them?'

'They all went – them people went away,' he said, pointing at the boarded-up houses.

I knocked on a few more doors and didn't get much information, because nearly everyone who was there had just moved in. They'd heard that there had been some trouble there, but they didn't quite know what.

Fortunately, when I asked one man coming out of his house what had happened, his eyes lit up. He was kindly faced man with very muscular arms and a large chest poking out of a tight-fitting black T-shirt. He shook my hand warmly and said, 'It is a long story. Why don't you come in for a cup of tea?'

I accepted gratefully, and followed him into his house. He

was called Phil Hughes, and was chairman of the Rassau Tenants and Residents' Association. He introduced me to his wife, Julie, and his elderly mother, who was sitting in a chair next to the TV. He switched off the TV, and made some cups of tea in the adjacent kitchen. His living room was crammed with historical books – books about the 20th century mostly – and was decorated by woodcarvings, which I was to learn later were made by Phil.

Julie smiled wearily. 'Yes, you should certainly hear about this street if you are writing a book about antisocial behaviour. What's happened here is like an episode of *Brookside*, except that it's all true.'

Once we all had our cups of tea, Phil sat down in his chair and told me his remarkable story.

Julie and I have lived here for 27 years. When we moved into the street in 1978, it was a very nice place: it was the first project built in the area. There were lots of young families here, as well as people in their seventies and eighties. There was a fabulous atmosphere too. Everyone would pull together. We get some very serious weather here during winter since we are exposed on the slope of the valley. When the snow comes, it falls very thickly. But back in those days, everyone would work together and dig out the snow. There were a couple of lads with Land-Rovers who would help ferry people around if need be.

There was also a tremendous neighbourly feeling about the place. Everyone would help everyone else. We had a neighbour, an elderly man called Roy, who had no relatives to help him out, so we took care of him for about 20 years until he died: sorting out his food and his cleaning, and getting him out of the house.

Then about 15 or 16 years ago, the council started moving in the bad with the good. These were people who had been expelled from other council properties. There were a couple of ruffians who got three-bedroom houses to themselves. These guys were drug dealers who attracted lots of undesirable characters from all over. They didn't want to do any honest work. The pits had closed down at this point, and there wasn't much for them to do anyway. They would buy a lot of drugs from Bristol, and then sell them here on the street. They were menacing, difficult people: most of the residents were afraid to speak to them.

It was then that things like the car racing started to happen. They would use this road as a track and screech up and down it at top speed. Perhaps worse than that was the noise: the music that they played was very, very loud, and it didn't get switched off. It would play into the night, for weeks on end.

Most dramatically and tragically, there was a murder on the street. The council moved in a girl who had five or six children from different fathers. At the time she moved in here, she had a partner who had a track record of violence. The police and the council knew that he beat her up. She was stabbed to death by him: he stabbed her 24 times, and then went on to rape his female lawyer.

After this, another girl, let's call her Sarah, moved in opposite us. She had lots of men coming in and out of her house at all times of the day and night. Although she only had a two-bedroom house, there would frequently be 40 or 50 people in there.

We found out later that Sarah was chatting to people on the Internet, and inviting them over. So we would get guys from all over the country coming to the house. She had a young boy, a six-year-old, a lovely kid, who was expected to look after himself. One of the guys who slept with her told us that sometimes she would have the child in the bed as she was having sex with these strangers.

Once we found the little boy wandering down the street at midnight, calling out and crying, 'Where's my mummy?

Where's my mummy?' She had disappeared for the night. No one knew where. Anyway, a neighbour looked after the boy until she came back. We phoned the social services and the police, and told them about the situation. We said that he was at risk. But nothing was done. We suspect that because she had contacts in the local council, she was allowed to get away with anything.

Twenty-one of us signed a petition saying that the boy wasn't safe. The social services arrived, looked around and judged that we were lying. She'd put on a good act for the day, you see.

The most dramatic day in the street happened when I returned to Summerfield Road and found a policeman sitting on the bonnet of his police car, blocking the way into the street. He said that I wasn't allowed to go into the street, but didn't explain why. So I phoned our home number and the phone was answered by a PC. 'Everything is fine, sir. We are sorting out the situation,' he said.

'But this is my home number! Where are my family?'

'They are being taken care of, sir. At the moment, we are in the middle of an armed siege, and we are using your house as a lookout point. You will be pleased to know that there is no armed siege in your house.'

What had happened was that some lads had robbed a post office in Gloucester and taken the money, and then one of them had hidden the money, as far as we know. Then the other two robbers went looking for their mate who had hidden the money. When they found their so-called friend, they accused him of stealing the money, and shot him in the hand and cut him with Stanley knives. They left him and came up to Summerfield Road, and hid out in Sarah's house. Julie, my wife, had spotted them because one of them had a police baseball cap and was wearing camel army gear; he had a machete hanging off his belt and was carrying a rifle. The other one was carrying a handgun. Julie phoned the police immediately, and they then arrived en masse. They had armed officers in the gardens, cordoned off the street and had a command vehicle hidden away from the armed robbers.

Sarah behaved very irresponsibly by laughing about the whole thing. She put her kid in the window and made him shoot at the police with toy guns. The armed robbers thought the whole thing was a huge joke and didn't take it seriously. The police managed to negotiate their surrender, but the robbers demanded that they gave themselves up after they had finished watching *Coronation Street*. This sounds so ridiculous, but you couldn't make it up! It's completely true! Eventually, they came out with their arms raised above their heads. They were laughing and joking still.

When one of the policemen said that it was no joke, they just jeered. They didn't care at all. Mind you, it did get a bit more serious when the police pushed them to the ground and frisked them for weapons. Only then did it dawn upon them that they were in a lot of bother.

A couple of young people have died of drug overdoses in the street. One died at a party having taken too much heroin, and another committed suicide by hanging himself after he became an alcoholic.

The drugs began to take over the streets. Too many kids were high because there were so many dealers hanging around. Once we saw a black guy in a stretch limo pull up outside Sarah's house, and go into one of her interminable parties. This bloke, we learned later, had just been released from prison and was a big-time drug dealer, covered in bling-bling jewellery, and draped in scantily dressed girls. He'd come up to see if Sarah was all right. Sarah's husband, who was never around, was a drug dealer, and so she had a lot of connections in the drug world.

However, after the armed siege, the council realised that

they needed to do something with Sarah and she was relocated, taking her poor child with her.

The sadness continued, though. A neighbour of ours died of a heart attack after chasing some kids who had been chucking stones at his windows. He was a nice guy who wouldn't tolerate the nonsense that was going on in the street, but his health suffered greatly as a result, as everyone's health in the street has suffered. My health has suffered from it; there is no doubt about it.

It was not easy bringing up two children in this atmosphere. However, we were strict and firm with them, and taught them right from wrong. If they were grounded, they were really grounded.

Life, though, was very hard. During the miner's strike in 1984, I was in one of the few collieries that wanted to carry on working. However, the flying pickets soon put a stop to that, and we were expected to take handouts from the National Union of Mineworkers. I wouldn't do that. I went shooting rabbits for our food instead.

We also made sure that our kids didn't go without. We'd give them some money to buy a treat at school just like all the other kids had. It brings tears to my eyes to remember how my daughter, after a term of giving her these pennies for tuck, brought them all home so that we might have a bit more money. She'd saved up every single penny!

My children were not picked on at school, though. They had too much street cred from living on the dreaded Summerfield Road, which was in the local press a lot, usually because I had publicised the horrors that were happening here.

I suffered as a result of my petitions, my complaints to the council and my refusal to give in to those thugs. My life was threatened four times, my car was petrol bombed and we got all sorts of nasty stuff through the letter box. At one point, there was a £300 bounty on my head to give me a severe beating. But I was power lifting at the time, and I could look after myself.

Once, I looked out of our living room window to see these two massive guys sitting on the bonnet of my car. One was six foot eight, and the other was six-six. I was in a dilemma. I knew that if I let that happen, they would walk all over us. I told Julie, 'Call an ambulance, because I am going out there.'

I strolled out and said to one of them, 'Get off my car otherwise I will hit you. Whatever happens one of you is going to get hurt. I don't care if I die. I don't care what happens to me, I am going to hurt you badly. Very badly. I have had enough, and I am going to sort you out.'

The taller one thought about this for a minute, and got off the bonnet of the car. 'Sorry pal, but they're not paying me enough to do this,' he said. And then they both left.

I assume that they were the hired hoodlums of Sarah but I never got to the bottom of what was going on there.

Only two of the original occupants are in the road now. The council moved all the problem people out, but by then nearly everyone else had moved out as well. We can't move because we bought this place. After all, would you buy a house in this street?

Phil stopped here and looked me in the eye. I considered his question and gulped: No, I wouldn't.

The truth is, I don't want to move. We are beginning to change things around here. We've set up a youth club, and we've also got a drop-in centre for teenagers, which we are hoping to expand. We've got some plans to do this, and we are hoping to get money from the Welsh assembly to build it. Basically, it will happen because even if the assembly doesn't give us money, we'll build it ourselves. We've now got a 'life-support' centre, which is part of the community centre. We've bought the old surgery at the centre and now have computers with broadband and an excellent education centre to train people to a good enough standard so that they can go on to do a nursing degree or physiotherapy, or anything to do with the medical services. It's attended by a real variety of people, including single mothers, married women with children and a few young lads. It is open to everyone but is mostly attended by women.

Do you know what is fascinating? We get the kids down at the centre and show them the computers, and the art room, and do you know what they would rather do? Paint! They love it. There aren't enough opportunities for children to do this sort of thing. I have just started working with a local comprehensive because I am chairman of the local Ebw Vale crime-prevention panel. We have given the schools money for their after-school clubs to do community projects because we see that this is the best way of stopping crime. It is proactive rather reactive. There are a few after-school projects going on like drama clubs and school choirs, and some kids even play golf. I personally am helping some teenagers to decorate the Rassau community centre with very large Celtic shields. One young girl has designed two borders with a Celtic theme to decorate the entrance of the community centre.

The only thing I would say to someone who is suffering like my family suffered is 'Don't give up'. What doesn't kill you makes you stronger!

Of all the stories I heard during investigations into yob culture, that of the Hughes family was the most harrowing as well as the most uplifting. They had been 'sitting ducks' – victims of the council's rank stupidity in the way it relocated trouble-makers, victims of yob culture, victims of poverty and social deprivation – but despite everything they had stood and fought against it. And there they were, after all those years, still in Summerfield Road, and proud to be there.

Most importantly, they were doing things to change the yob culture of the area. They were the sitting ducks who sat up and fired back at their tormentors.

CHAPTER SEVEN

What Do We Do Now?

6 These middle-class lawyers who make vast sums of money and live in their big houses do not live on the estates where the mob rules. They don't know what it is like to get bricks through the window, to be insulted on a daily basis, to cower before a gang of drunken thugs. 7

The ASBO capital of Britain

'What about the rights of the victim? Aren't the vast majority of us entitled to live lives which are free from the fear of being abused and attacked?'

The magnificent Victorian buildings cast long shadows in the morning sunlight, and city workers dressed in expensive clothes move purposefully towards shining cliffs of glass. I climb the steps into the fabulous cathedral to public service that is Manchester town hall: a huge Victorian building full of Gothic arches and great echoing stone corridors. It is rather like Pugin's Houses of Parliament, but in my view the architect Waterhouse did a better job: the building is more imposing, less pompous. It makes me feel as though I am in Gotham City with its sinister alcoves, twisting staircases, dark recesses and marvellous Pre-Raphaelite wall paintings. Twisting shadows entwine faces as they walk past the statues of eminent men.

In many ways the building embodies what is best about the public spirit of the city of Manchester: it is generous, civic-minded, but also laced with menace in the pursuit of good. In order to beat the bad guys, you have to be a little like them, it seems to be saying.

No one better personifies this philosophy than Bill Pitt, the 58-year-old head of the Nuisance Strategy Unit for Manchester. He is a wiry, intense man who looks much younger than his years. There is something peculiarly Mancunian about his no-bullshit philosophy of getting things done. He started up the Nuisance Strategy Unit in the mid-1990s with only four people; now there are 62 people employed in the team. 'The yobs in Manchester are frightened of us,' he says proudly. 'We have a reputation for being callous, brutal, obsessive and single-minded. This is an important myth to cultivate when you are dealing with the guys we are dealing with. They are frightened of us. We want to keep it that way.'

Bill Pitt has been instrumental in bringing into being what is now known as the infamous 'ASBOs' (Antisocial Behaviour Orders). 'In the mid-1990s, I approached John Major's government to ask them to frame laws which would enable us to pre-empt trouble; this legislation has been refined by the New Labour government. Now we have a series of legislative tools which enable us to take out injunctions against people who create hell on the streets of Manchester,' Pitt says. 'The important thing is we pre-empt trouble. We give out injunctions which say to the so and so who has been chucking stones at the shops, who has been fighting, who has been riding his bike on pavements and mugging people, and so on, that you must not do this any more. If you carry on, you will go to jail. We publicise these orders, complete with photos, so that everyone in the community knows what is going on, and can report any breaches of the injunction.'

Pitt hands out some leaflets of the cases that the unit has dealt with. There is Darren Livesey, a handsome, dark-eyed miscreant, who has assaulted people, repeatedly used abusive and insulting language in public, threatened to destroy people's property and made the lives of the people on Railton Terrace, Moston very miserable. There are the teenagers Lois Carter and Zara Lewis, who have set fire to wheelie bins, made threats to local residents, harassed pupils and teachers at the local school, vandalised property, and harassed and verbally abused local residents. Their sweet, smiling faces shine up from the photos on the leaflet, giving no indication of what they have done. There is Daniel Garwell, who threw stones and verbally abused the residents of Cheetham, Manchester, kicked in the front door and attempted to ignite toilet paper wrapped around a residents' home and also damaged the window of a local

property with a ball and threatened violence to the occu-
pant if this was reported.

'We are the "ASBO" capital of Britain,' Pitt says. 'That's
because we are acting in the interests of the innocent victims
of Manchester. I expect complaints about antisocial behaviour to go up in the next 20 years because as more and more
residents get to hear about what we are doing, they will believe
that they can stop the yobs in their area. This legislation
works. And actually, it keeps a lot of kids out of jail. We
prevent trouble before it happens.'

'But what of the complaints by groups like Liberty that
this is charging people as guilty before they have been
convicted of anything in a court of law?' I say, remembering
a seminar I went to in London where numerous *Guardian*-
reading lawyers were fulminating about the ASBOs legislation because it was draconian and fascistic.

For the first time in the interview, Bill Pitt becomes visibly
angry. 'Liberty and ASBO Concern make me furious. They
are only interested in the rights of the perpetrator. What I
want to say to them is: "What about the rights of the victim?"
Aren't the vast majority of us entitled to live lives which are
free from the fear of being abused and attacked? These
middle-class lawyers who make vast sums of money and live
in their big houses do not live on the estates where the mob
rules. They don't know what it is like to get bricks through
the window, to be insulted on a daily basis, to cower before
a gang of drunken thugs. Our legislation is about the victim.
And actually, ultimately, it is about the perpetrator as well
because the vast majority of ASBOs mean that children and
adults – most ASBOs are taken out against adults – avoid
going to prison. They start behaving before getting slammed
up. When we get these people in our offices and TELL them
in no uncertain terms how to behave, they often blink at us
and say that this is the first time that anyone has ordered
them to do anything. We are often dealing with people who

have had no codes of behaviour imposed upon them. So I wouldn't listen to the libertarian claptrap of Liberty if I were you.'

But what of the complaint that having an ASBO is a badge of honour?

'I don't think it's a badge of honour if you are not allowed to ride in a vehicle, or if you can't talk to your friends,' he says sharply.

As Bill Pitt shows me out of the building, he talks very knowledgeably about the architecture of the town hall, and the philosophy of John Stuart Mill, the Victorian philosopher who was so influential in framing the laws of the modern world. 'I would direct anyone who complains about ASBOs to Mill's section "On Liberty", where he says that true freedom is the freedom of the many to live their lives free from fear.'

ASBOs in action

'My house, which should have been worth £100,000, was valued at £30,000 at this time.'

Bill Pitt told me that Lesley Pullman's story best illustrated the power of the ASBO to transform a blighted community. I interviewed Lesley a few days after a BBC *Panorama* programme was aired which suggested that ASBOs were being used in some cases to victimise the mentally ill and disabled.[61] Lesley was very annoyed about the liberal bias of this programme and the media in general and told me:

I know of so many cases now where ASBOs have made the lives of common, decent people so much better that I get very cross when the media try and suggest that ASBOs are unfair. The fact of the matter is that they empower communities who are suffering beyond belief. ASBOs give people a chance to fight back against the bullies and thugs who are destroying people's lives.

My own story is a case in point. I've lived in my house for 46 years, in New Moston, Manchester and for most of the time, I have never had a problem with my neighbours. I live in a privately owned house, but it is situated next to a council estate. There has never been a problem with the council estate though – contrary to the stereotype people have in their minds. No, there was never a problem until a family bought a property in my street in 2001 who turned out to be the family from hell. Within a month of them moving in, they had taken over the whole area. The mother had six children from four different fathers: there were two-year-old twins, a seven year old, an 11-year-old boy, and 15-year-old twins. The mother's boyfriend was disabled, and it was the compensation which he had got from being involved in some incident which left him disabled that then enabled them to buy the house.

This family was very unpleasant. They stoned my house, damaged my car, and attacked a number of people in my area with baseball bats and knives. I've got Multiple Sclerosis and they used to call me 'a MS cunt'. There was an Asian family on the street, and they – and some members of their gang – attacked them in their own home, brutally beating up a whole family, parents and children. When I went to see the mother who owned the property which attracted all these gangs, she told me to 'fuck off' . Then she said that the gang would 'burn me' – in other words burn down my house. I was terrified of these threats at first; then I got angry once I overcame my terror. The police were there at the time when I confronted her, but they were so busy dealing with the racist incident against the Asian family that they didn't have time to help me properly. So I wrote the whole story down in my diary for the council.

This confrontation was a real turning point because it identified me as a grass. And from then on, the gang always blamed me if the police turned up. I was the number one grass in their eyes.

I was later very frightened when the kids did a drive-by shooting on me. They were carrying guns and were sitting in a car pointing them at me. They drove past with one of them having his bottom on the wound-down window, both hands on a gun which was positioned over the roof of the car, repeatedly firing at me. The shots pelted across my door and window. It turned out that they were fake guns with metal pellets, but I didn't know that at the time.

Later on, a few of the teenage boys in the gang threatened me again, with one saying that he was going to rape me, and then burn me out. I was really unnerved. He said he would stick his cock in my mouth until I stopped grassing. He was just a kid in my mind, and for him to speak like this to me really made me think about how sick he was.

The whole community lived in fear of the gang.

I was one of the few people who dared to call the police; of course, they threatened anyone who grassed them up. The police though weren't much help. Going through the courts was not productive: I got two harassment orders imposed upon the two ringleaders of the family doing the worst damage. But they ignored the orders on a daily basis. Some of the offenders were tagged but they just ripped off their tags, and ignored the curfews imposed upon them. They intimidated witnesses so that no one dared testify against them. Added to which, the courts never notified the local community about what sentences had been imposed upon them.

Meanwhile, the situation on the street was getting worse. The mother was corrupting the local children by giving away drink and drugs, and was drawing more and more youths into the gang. My house, which should have been worth £100,000, was valued at £30,000 at this time. The gang was now threatening the shopkeepers, and a number of property owners wanted to get out. People on the council estate were begging the council to move them out.

I was in total despair at the justice system in general until I met the principal service manager for Manchester City Housing, Michael Lee, who was very interested and very angry about what was happening. You would have thought it was happening on his street, the reaction I got from him. He suggested trying an ASBO, which was just beginning to be trialed throughout the country then. The great thing about an ASBO is that you don't need to have identified witnesses, you can use 'hearsay' evidence from unidentified witnesses. We managed to get five people to testify in this way, and I testified in court as a witness. I faced my tormentors and I told what they had been doing to me.

As a result, we got an order which banned the ring-leaders from the area. Knowing that these ringleaders would breach the order, we were prepared for them: sure enough they came into the area, threatened one of the witnesses, and did a burglary. We reported them and they were jailed. One got six months and one got eight months in prison for breaching the ASBO. The family were evicted from their house, and the children were taken into care where they should have been years before. We have not heard from them since. The situation changed overnight.

Now, New Moston is one of the most popular areas in Manchester; my house has returned to its original value and is rising in value as more and more people can see what a nice place this is to live in.

ASBOs are about giving the victims of crime a voice. They put the needs of the victim first, not the needs of the perpetrator. They give people confidence to fight back against the yobs because the law-abiding majority can see them working very quickly. Civilised people don't want vengeance, they want justice and the ASBO can give this. The yobs repress communities and take away the communities' civil rights. Why should we sacrifice our lives for their enjoyment? These perpetrators actually have many agencies supporting them, and there's none for witnesses and victims. Organisations like Victim Support are very poorly funded and actually have very little power. I am fully in support of people getting help. There is a minority of families who are sticking two fingers up at us, and have chosen to revel in causing pain to other people. They have just got to be stopped. Finally, ABSOs have given us a way to get our lives back.

I now go into places where there are serious problems, and I meet with the law-abiding people who haven't got much but they want to live in peace and they want their children to live in peace and freedom. They haven't got that now. All their energy is taken up with avoiding being threatened and abused. Their children can't go out and play on the streets. It's a growing problem, but thankfully we have now got some legislative tools which enable us to fight back. The Witness Protection and Support Unit – which I run – helps these victimised people to fight back, and reclaim their communities. I would like to see some of these BBC journalists who think ASBOs are so bad to live on these estates themselves. They would not last five minutes. I am full of admiration for people who survive in these environments.

I have people sending me letters from all over the

country with just my name on it pleading for help. We need to send the message out to these wrongdoers that we are not going to give up, and they've got to change their lifestyle and not ours.

If you would like to learn more about Lesley's charity which supports the victims of anti-social behaviour, please log on to: www.communityfoundation.co.uk

Playing politics with ASBOs

'Doing things sober is no way to get things done.' Louise Casey, director of the government's Anti-Social Behaviour Unit.

I was impressed with Pitt's determined, sober approach to the problem. His attitude and character is in marked contrast to the 'anti-yob tsar' whom Tony Blair appointed to tackle antisocial behaviour. Louise Casey was appointed director of the Home Office's Anti-Social Behaviour Unit, but hit the headlines when it was discovered that far from condemning yobbery, she celebrated it. In front of a conference attended by senior civil servants, chief constables and criminal justice practitioners in May 2005, Ms Casey told her audience: 'I suppose you can't binge drink any more because lots of people have said you can't do it. I don't know who bloody made that up, it's nonsense.' On the tape, obtained by BBC News, she said some ministers might perform better if they 'turn up in the morning pissed'. 'Doing things sober is no way to get things done,' she added. She also threatened to 'deck' government advisers who spouted jargon at her.[62]

Much has been made of New Labour's attempts to stamp out antisocial behaviour, but as the Louise Casey incident reveals, a serious analyst has to doubt their sincerity. As Martin Sixsmith pointed out to me, the mere fact that the government didn't sack Casey on the spot indicated that it wasn't really determined to deal with the problem.

While I had no doubt that Bill Pitt's intentions for ASBOs were entirely honourable, I could see that this kind of pre-emptive justice could be used to muzzle legitimate political protest. ASBOs at their best are a much-needed remedy, but at their worst a thuggish government could use ASBOs to stop its critics from protesting on the streets.

Given our current problems, ASBOs are clearly worth experimenting with in order to see whether they cure some of our ills. Bill Pitt's approach was the most sensible; he told me that he felt the legislation should be constantly reviewed to see if it could be improved. ASBOs should always be viewed with a wary and critical eye.

'ASBOs are a terrible admission of failure,' Mike Batten, the magistrate, confessed to me. 'I am certainly not against using them in the courts because they appear to work, but I do feel that they are needed in a society where the common codes of decency and parental responsibility have broken down.'

Batten's point is incontrovertible. ASBOs do appear to stop the worst excesses of antisocial behaviour, but slapping a court order of this sort on someone is clearly only something to be done just before they are about to be given a prison sentence – and this is how they are usually deployed. They allow the courts to serve a warning upon a serial offender and give him or her a last chance before they are locked up.

Sorting out the trouble on the buses

'Unfortunately, the very residents who complain so bitterly about the antisocial behaviour are very reluctant to help out.'

G illian Ford, councillor for Cranham Ward and chair of the Upminster, Cranham and Emerson Park Area Committee in the London Borough of Havering, offered me another approach that circumvented the punitive nature of ASBOs. Her area is predominantly middle-class and affluent, but it has been afflicted in recent years, like many similar areas throughout Britain, by a rise in antisocial behaviour.

> We've had a particularly bad problem with children abusing buses in the Cranham area. Buses have been attacked with stones, bus bays have been smashed up, vehicles and property have been scrawled with graffiti. This suggested affluent area is actually suffering more than many of the poorer parts of the borough because about ten years ago the funding for youth clubs was withdrawn. And surprise, surprise, there has been an increase in antisocial behaviour. ASBOs have been taken out against the youth, but this is not solving the underlying problems.
>
> Some members of the council and the local community have realised that we have to give the young people something to do other than hanging around the bus stops and abusing people. Unfortunately, the very residents who complain so bitterly about the antisocial behaviour are very reluctant to see improvements in youth facilities.
>
> For example, our attempts to put a skate park in a small corner of a park met with objections from older residents. Many of the older generation just do not understand what

a skate park is; there is a massive gulf between them and the youth. After some fairly serious battles, we have secured a games area in one of the parks; a multi-games use area, where activities like basketball and football can be played. But it is always a battle because some of our residents, while wanting to stop antisocial behaviour, take the attitude of 'not in my backyard' with regard to things like skate parks.

We've realised, though, that the only real way to alleviate the problem is to target the children at a much younger age. By the time they are teenagers hanging around on the streets dabbling in drugs and getting involved in abusing people, it is too late. You have to stop them at a much younger age.

We need to engage with young people from the age of nine if not younger. We've got everyone from the police, to the bus companies, to the youth services engaged to go into schools and speak to 11–12-year-olds in the first instance about what is expected of them on the buses. The bus company has set up a reward scheme whereby youths can get as much as £100 for saying who is vandalising or abusing the buses and drivers. We've issued leaflets that clearly set out what is acceptable behaviour while commuting on buses. Video footage is to be shown to parents about how their children can be identified on the buses if they are behaving inappropriately. Any crime detected by the video is sent directly through to the local schools for identification purposes and the police. A lot of parents are totally unaware of what their children get up to. We've brought in victim support to help parents who have had children who are victims of bullying and harassment on the streets and buses. We hope to see slow but effective improvements soon.

However, without the youth service having proper funding, and without the support of a minority of parents who don't take responsibility for their children, things will not improve. The youth service in the borough is in the ridiculous position of having no base to work from. They have to walk the streets, doing their best to advise the young on drugs, pregnancy, behavioural issues, etc. This is not good practice and does not provide the youth with a good role model. A central contact point is needed, but this can only be achieved through appropriate funding.

The substance abuse worker's story

'At our best we are that extended arm of the parent, where we are guiding people in the right direction, making them aware that there are opportunities in the world out there which don't involve abusing drugs or your neighbours.'

Eric is a substance misuse worker who is funded by the NHS to stop young people from abusing drugs. He has worked for five years in the job, and knows very well that if young people are taking drugs they are also likely to be indulging in antisocial behaviour. Although he deals with teenagers who are from the most deprived homes, his solutions are very similar to Gillian Ford's. He told me:

> We're here in this inner city London office to give advice and information around substance misuse. The young person's substance misuse can lead to them offending, and can lead to them getting ASBO orders. We work with the Youth Inclusion Programme, and their remit is to work with anyone under the age of 13 and minimise their offending.
>
> We go onto the estates throughout north-east London, and speak to the young people there. We have specific

targets whom we try and reach out to: those who are excluded from school, those out of work, and inaccessible young people, people who have dropped out of the system. We will work with parents, professionals and anyone under the age of 19. We are all about advice and information; they don't necessarily have to have a substance misuse issue. It could be that they are thinking about trying drugs, or have got friends and family who are abusing drugs.

Education is the way forward. But not necessarily the education that kids get in schools. The education we provide is really around the peer pressure that is out there. What we say to them is 'If you're going to do it, be aware of the effects that it has'. We have two suitcases that contain drugs in silver cases and we show them what the drugs really do in different workshops on the estates, in the youth offending team, even in schools. We never say to them, 'Don't do it' except with solvents. Solvents are like playing Russian roulette: you do it, but you can kill yourself. Eventually you'll run out of luck.

I've spoken and helped a number of young people who have completely changed their lives because they've become educated about the issues. I've encountered young people who have been addicted to opiates, and I've shown them how to come off the drugs. I've referred them to other agencies, such as ASATS, the Adolescent Specialist Addiction Treatment Service, and seen some dramatic improvements. Once they come off the drugs, the anti-social behaviour usually stops: suddenly these youths are not running around off their heads, or trying desperately to get money for their next fix.

It's like a jigsaw puzzle: it's about making young people aware of how things could be better, and then showing a path through it all.

At our best we are that extended arm of the parent,

where we are guiding people in the right direction, making them aware that there are opportunities in the world out there which don't involve abusing drugs or your neighbours.

But there isn't the funding to really help all the problem kids who need helping. As it stands, we are always one step behind the dealers who are always coming up with new stuff. Dealers have started mixing heroin with cannabis and crack. It makes the cannabis a lot stronger, but it poses a real problem because it is extremely addictive. A kid might think they are smoking some spliff when actually they are smoking heroin and crack. This is a serious situation because you could have a whole generation of kids who are addicted without knowing it. It's been going on for about 18 months and like any drug problem, you've got the situation where some addicts will steal to get high.

If we are going to sort out this problem properly we need proper funding where schools, youth workers, substance misuse workers and anyone else who works with young people are truly educating them about life on the street. Kids need to know about all the issues; the diseases that can result from substance misuse, and the aggressive states of mind which the drugs – and the pursuit of them – can induce in someone.

Perhaps most importantly, we need to keep the difficult kids in schools, and not expel them for drug misuse because then they leave the system. This is why we have so many kids who can't read and write — they have been kicked out of school and their lives have spiralled out of control. We have to improve the provision for them in school. Drop the National Curriculum, and give them something interesting to do.

The biggest mistake that the government made was to get rid of the Youth Training Scheme, before Labour came into power, which trained up kids in trades like bricklaying, plumbing, engineering, car maintenance and so on. We've got kids now leaving school who are not smart enough to change a tap. It's a scary thing. My Dad had that old education where he learnt how to do so many different trades from plumbing to basic electronics. He left school wised up and employable. Now we hardly have any kids leaving school who do a proper trade and so we are in the position of having to hire Polish plumbers and Estonian car mechanics because there are not enough British kids to do this kind of work. They're too busy living on benefits, getting high on drugs, and causing mayhem to work – and besides they are not educated enough to do anything anyway. It is very, very scary problem. Sooner or later if we are not careful England is going to be the thickest place on earth.

A manifesto for change?

So if we were to draw all the lessons of these disparate experts together, we could broadly divide the areas that need to be addressed into three categories: cultural attitudes, education, and the justice system. These areas all overlap, but within them there are a number of recommendations which might make a difference to the quality of all our lives.

1. **Cultural Attitudes.** Most overwhelmingly, again and again in the testimonies I listened to, I heard how responsible adults no longer felt able to challenge yobbish behaviour. Perhaps most significantly, they no longer felt able to stop children from misbehaving in public. Clearly, there needs to be a significant debate about this; all of us need to feel more empowered to intervene if we see antisocial behaviour going on. Unfortunately, we are too often getting the message that it is OK to be yobbish. Our politicians, our leading sportsmen,

our celebrities are, for the most part, celebrated for behaving in highly antisocial ways. The most striking aspect of the testimony of older people was that their communities used to be self-policing, in a way that they definitely are not anymore. The media could play a leading role in this by being at the forefront of a public 'conversation' about the issue. It could also tone down the violent and semi-pornographic content of its programmes on TV, in magazines and newspapers, and, increasingly, the internet. In addition, we need to change cultural attitudes towards drugs, most particularly alcohol. We need to make it a much more shameful thing to get brazenly drunk or 'off your face' on any drug. The British are afflicted by cultural attitudes towards alcohol which threaten to destroy our culture.

2. **Education.** Many parents and children need to be better educated about how to behave in a civilised fashion. We need to bring parents into schools with their young children and together we all need to absorb some vital lessons about the values of civility and resolving conflict in a calm and rational way. Clearly, by giving schools more autonomy and by making sure that they are more involved in their local communities, more parental involvement will become possible. Schools need to feel part of their local communities, and to be accountable to them. They also need to be providing a much more meaningful education to pupils who don't want to participate in the National Curriculum; there needs to be a serious overhaul of our vocational education so that all pupils are literate, numerate and have a 'trade' of some sort by the time they leave school. If we are stuck for ideas, then perhaps it is time to bring back the YTS as Eric suggests.

We also need to significantly improve the youth service provision in many areas in the country – in working-class and middle-class areas – and improve the bureaucracy of such services so that these workers are properly funded and accountable.

3. The Justice System. As Lesley Pullman suggested, we need to improve the justice system so that it champions the rights of the victim, not the perpetrator. Charities like Victim Support and Lesley's Community Foundation need to be properly funded so that the justice system puts the needs of the victim first. The experiment with ASBOs needs to continue so that the legislation is rolled out across the country, widely publicised and refined so that it works in the best possible way. Overall, the justice system seems antiquated and unable to deal with the challenges of our new yob culture. It needs to be a lot more flexible and innovative in its approach so that it acts quickly when crimes happen, and dispenses punishments which match the crime.

Epilogue and Summation

'And what were the politicians doing about it? They were too busy indulging in their own kind of yobbery to really deal with the endemic social problems afflicting Britain's streets. '

The night bus home - 2005

'Had I turned into a bit of yob myself?'

T here I was again. It was midnight and I was back on
Leystonstone High Road waiting for a night bus – in
exactly the same situation I had been in six years before when
I had been attacked. I wasn't drunk now. I had been careful
not to drink too much in the pub in Wanstead: I knew that
I would be heading home this way – and that I would need
my wits about me.

My wife had advised me not to take the bus home. 'Just
get a cab from the pub,' she said. 'You don't want to get
smacked in the face again, do you?'

I hadn't taken the journey in six years. I was still, in truth,
a little bit traumatised by the event. I could still see those
youths approaching me on the bus, I could still feel the fear
surging through my alcoholic veins as they asked me for
money and I could still remember the boy's fist crunching
into my forehead.

'No, I am going to take it. I am not going to let those
bastards frighten me,' I said.

So here I was, standing by a deserted bus stop on the
empty Leytonstone High Road, waiting for the number 8
night bus. By now, though, I was regretting my decision to
turn down my friend's offer of a lift home. Unexpectedly, he
was heading my way and would have been able to drop me
at my door. He looked at me as though I was mad when I
said that I really wanted to take the 8 bus home. 'Are you
out of your mind?' he said. 'You don't want to get beaten up
again, do you?'

'Call it my pride. I want to prove to myself that I can do
it!'

As I watched a few drunken kids stagger out of the nightclub on the high road, I thought about my rejection of his

offer. What an idiot I was! I shouldn't be doing this. As I was thinking this, I saw several youths approaching me. I sensed danger: they were shouting loudly and had the obligatory sports' tops, baseball caps and white trainers. I thought about the words of a bouncer I interviewed in Bristol. 'We never let baseball caps and white trainers into the pub. They're always trouble.'

Was this a monstrous stereotype or was there a grain of truth in it? If it had been during the day, I might have had the nerve to talk to the kids – I had interviewed rougher looking kids in far worse spots throughout Britain during my investigations for the book – but I realised that midnight was not the best time to conduct such field research.

I started to walk away from the bus stop. I felt it was better to avoid trouble than cultivate it. As I hastened down the high road, I thought about what I had learned on my travels around our 'yob nation'. I was more frightened now than I had been in 1999. And with reason – many statistics showed that Britain was a much more violent place than it had been when I was a child: there was ten times more violent crime now. My local paper had just the day before revealed that a quarter of all crimes in my borough were assaults and beatings: a violent assault happened every minute in Tower Hamlets.[63] D.S. Simmons's words of warning echoed in my head as I hurried past the shuttered shops, 'These gangs are predatory. They stalk their prey. And they think nothing of using extreme violence.'

I looked around me. I could see no gangs around. There was no one lurking in the shadows watching me. Suddenly, though, as I was walking past a brightly lit window, a drunken boy plunged out of the door of a gaudy takeaway, nearly bashing into me in the process. Being very alert, I dodged out of his way, and ran to the next junction. I looked back. There was no sign of the bus. The drunk was leaning over the curb being sick. I gazed at the puking drunk and felt sorry for him. He was, like so many of us, a victim of the inability of the British to hold their liquor. He was also the victim, like many of us, of a merciless and remorseless campaign by the drinks' companies to profit from getting the British drunk. Politicians of left and right and the money men in the City had realised since the early 1990s that there were huge amounts of revenue to be generated by encouraging the growth of the drinks' industry: the politicians wanted the tax revenue and the City wanted a slice of the hefty profits. What was the net result? The treasury's coffers and the bankers' pockets were stuffed with money, while our town and city centres suffered a huge upsurge in alcohol-related violence.

I ran past a series of dreary high-rise flats and thought about my time spent in the bleak, socially deprived estates of London, Manchester, Glasgow and Belfast. Surprisingly, for all the terrible things I had learnt about in these places, I smiled when I remembered them because I had encountered friendly, chatty people who were only too willing to talk. I thought of Taj, the mixed-race gang member in Cumbernauld who had told me so much about the way in which these sink estates can trap even the most intelligent person into a life of crime and violence. I thought of his desire to escape from it all and felt sad. I reflected upon the gang that I had interviewed in the Toryglen estate in Glasgow: they had been exceptionally friendly. But again, my memories were tinged with sadness. Those young children were not being properly supervised: left to their own devices, they were drinking great quantities of alcohol, taking drugs and, by their own admission, beating up people. Where were the adults there? Locked away in their homes and their offices, wishing the problem would go away.

And what were the politicians doing about it? They were too busy indulging in their own kind of yobbery to really deal with the endemic social problems afflicting Britain's streets.

They were yet another symptom of the malaise: the abroga-
tion of adult responsibility for our young. I was sceptical now
about New Labour's drive against antisocial behaviour. I
knew too much about its own yobbery. I knew about the
party's deployment of spin doctors who specialised in bullying
their opponents and critics; I knew about its MPs, who lied
shamelessly to the public in order to further their own careers;
I knew about its ministers, who were allowed to be violent
without facing any consequences. I was convinced now that
it was the people like Bill Pitt, Gillian Ford and Phil Hughes
– the unknown people – who got results.

As I approached the roundabout next to Stratford
Maryland, I turned around and breathed a sigh of relief. Even
though I was about to enter the area where I had been
attacked, I was aware that I had passed through the most
dangerous part of my journey. Those high-rise estates were
poorly lit and there was no one around there. At least there
were other people milling around in Stratford. I knew that
unless I was a total idiot and went and sat at the top of a
bus next to a gang of youths – as I had done in 1999 – I
would be OK.

As I strode confidently towards the main bus stop at
Stratford, I grinned. I was now a much more self-assured
person than I had been in 1999. I now knew when it was
right to be frightened – and when it wasn't. No yobs were
going to attack me on these populous, well-lit streets unless
I invited them to. The way I was walking also marked me
out as someone who wasn't worth the bother of attacking: I
was strolling with my head up and looking steadily in front
of me. I wasn't drunk, and I wasn't chatting on my mobile
phone or listening to my MP3 player. In short, I wasn't a
target.

My travels and investigations had toughened me up. I felt
much more able and willing to attack my enemies. I remembered how after the publication of my first book *I'm a Teacher,*

Get Me Out of Here, a year or so before I had researched yob culture, I had been on a Radio 5 live phone-in and a caller had made some particularly unpleasant comments about my abilities as a teacher. They were ridiculous observations because she had never seen me teach. I had been cowed by her aggressive tone, and apologised for offending her. A similar incident had happened to me only a few days ago on another radio discussion about education. This time I felt armed and ready. I defended myself without apologising! I parried the other guest's aggression and responded with some of my own – without losing my temper. A steely calmness and confidence had entered my soul. I wasn't going to be turned over by anyone any more.

As I approached the main bus stop opposite the Stratford shopping centre, I wondered: had I turned into a bit of yob myself? I had bullishly criticised that woman on the radio, who had tried to ridicule my point of view. And here I was, with gritted teeth and hunched shoulders, bowling onto the night bus. I was fired up. I felt very aggressive. No one was going to mess me around any more. I found myself a safe seat at the bottom of the bus, next to a big African lady with a fabulous headdress, surreptitiously dug my Walkman out of my pocket – I knew it was safe to listen to it here – and switched on 'We Are The Pigs' by Suede.

This vituperative song with amazing electric guitar riffs and poisonous lyrics cured me of my aggression and I switched off the Walkman, properly reflecting on whether I was a yob or not. I realised that I now needed to analyse myself using my own schema.

1. Was I a victim of yobbery? In the course of my research for the first section of the book, I had conclusively found out that all yobs are originally victims of antisocial behaviour. From the posh officers in the army to the defence-less children in the playground, I had seen how yobbery

was passed on from bully to victim. I myself had certainly been a victim of yobbery, most particularly on this bus six years before. I was also aware that the media – cinema, TV, newspapers, books even – had made me coarser. I was someone who was prone to swearing like my favourite pop stars, and I did secretly admire and slyly laugh at the antics of characters like Grant Mitchell in *EastEnders*. And if I was really honest, if I was offered a place on *Big Brother*, would I turn it down? Perhaps for the benefit of the cameras, I wouldn't say no to indulging in a bit of theatrical yobbery myself. I didn't know.

2. But was I perpetrator of yobbery? I wasn't so sure about this. I knew that some people had not liked all the swearing in my previous two books, or their populist tone. Theodore Dalrymple would deplore my occasional tendency to put my feet up on the opposite seat on the train, and I was thoughtless about dropping litter on the odd occasion. In order to answer this question properly, however, I needed to look at the different facets of being a yob which I had explored in the book.

3. Did I enjoy parading myself in front of an audience? Did I enjoy making people feel embarrassed or frightened by making rude gestures or using bad language, or even worse by being publicly violent? In places like Cardiff, Glasgow and Ayia Napa, I had seen that the British loved to put on outrageous shows of public drunkenness. I had seen how this behaviour, while fuelled by alcohol, was not caused by it. No, the alcohol was like a green light that gave thousands of people permission to swear, puke and fight. Well, I certainly enjoyed speaking on the radio and writing articles, but my primary motive was not to instil fear or embarrass other people.

4. Did I actively seek out battlefields where I might vent my innate aggression? A defining feature of yobbery for me – from Alistair Campbell to Jamie James – was the yob's relish for a good ruck. It didn't matter what profession he was in; the yob would always gravitate to situations where there was a battle going on, and if there wasn't a battle, he would make one himself. Again, I had to answer in the negative here: I usually did my best to avoid any kind of confrontation.

5. And yet, I thought about the whole project of *Yob Nation* itself. I knew it was going to be a controversial book and I had written it in a deliberately provocative style. Did it covertly glorify the yobbery it sought to condemn? I thought about this. I felt my success with the interviews that I conducted was due to my reluctance to condemn my interviewees – particularly the more yobbish ones. They could sense my suspension of judgement as I interviewed them and that's why people like Taj and the Toryglen brigade, talked to me. The things they confessed to were horrifying; I was not seeking to glorify them, but to try and understand them, to listen to them, to see if any sense could be pulled from the chaos of their lives. My intention was the very reverse of glorification: it was a desperate attempt to comprehend.

Phew! So I wasn't a yob.

But then, I began to consider the reverse issue: was I a sitting duck? This was most people's fear in Britain today – that they would be victimised and harassed by the youths at the end of their street, mugged by a street robber or attacked by a drunken idiot in a pub or club. I had spoken to a number of such victims and, barring one, none of them was the typical victim: these were not wimpy, cowed people. They were precisely the opposite. Someone like Phil in Summerfield Road was a tough guy who was mercilessly plagued for years by the thugs in his street.

I knew that I couldn't be so complacent about this issue. I could become a sitting duck at any moment if I had a run of bad luck. If the youths in my street suddenly decided that they wanted to pick on me there wasn't much I could do about it.

Or was there? I had been uplifted by what Bill Pitt had told me. If my council was as efficient as Manchester City Council, where Pitt worked – which it wasn't – I felt confident that slapping an ASBO on some miscreants might make a difference, at least temporarily. However, I knew that the bitter truth was that while ASBOs seemed to be an effective stopgap, they certainly weren't the solution. Gillian Ford, Phil Hughes and Mike Batten were the only ones offering genuine answers: we need to re-educate parents about their responsibilities, and make sure that our young children are not indoctrinated by the older generations into yobbish behaviour, we need to make proper after-school provision for them so that they have more constructive things to do than throw stones at buses or victimise neighbours. We need to break the cycle of yobbery that is turning and turning in ever-widening circles across the land. The only real way we are going to do that is to curtail the worst excesses of our media, the money men in the City and our politicians, and get everyone – parents, teachers, policemen, bankers, bus drivers, football players – involved in inculcating the values of decency and civility in our children. We need not only to lead by example, but also to get involved in shaping the society we want instead of leaving it to everyone else. We need to get involved like Phil Hughes and Gillian Ford have done in helping our young people to be creative and not destructive. Above all, we need to be much more forceful with parents, with teachers – and ultimately with ourselves – about instilling certain standards of behaviour in our children. We need to catch them before it is too late. We need to ration the amount of TV they watch and demand that they are respectful of authority. We also need to put a heavier tax on the sale of alcohol; we'd only curtail Britain's violent binge drinking culture if the punters are thinking twice before buying a drink.

I got off the bus clenching my fists. Yes, we need to be aggressively liberal with our children and their parents: we have to force civility and decency down their throats!

I felt I had gone full circle. My own experiences in the classroom had been at the root of my desire to investigate our yob nation, and from there I had gone on to travel widely around the country to see what was really happening on our estates, in our suburbs, our offices and the corridors of power. Now I was back to the classroom: education could be at the heart of solving our problems. Not wishy-washy, take-it-or-leave-it education, but tough, demanding insistent education that grabbed people by the throats and ordered them to listen. Yes, if the decent people learned a few tricks or two from the yobs it could be done!

However, my triumphant spirits quickly dissipated when I saw what was going on at the top of the road. It was time to run again. I dodged out of the way of the drunks and prostitutes at the top of Brick Lane, crossed the road to avoid some inebriated clubbers coming out of the 24-hour bagel shop and flinging bagels at each other and raced all the way home, where I quietly slipped into bed. My wife, Erica, was sleepily pleased to see that I hadn't been beaten up.

'Of course, I wasn't,' I protested. 'That kind of thing doesn't happen to me any more!'

'I'm glad to hear it,' she replied, eyeing me doubtfully. She wasn't convinced. Unfortunately, nor was I.

Notes

1. Figures from British Crime Survey, Home Office, 2004. These figures are probably a gross underestimate. Many violent assaults go unreported.
2. Home Office Statistics.
   http://www.homeoffice.gov.uk/rds/pdfs/100years.xls
3. http://www.homeoffice.gov.uk/rds/pdfs05/hosb1105chap123.pdf
4. *Ibid*, page 16.
5. 'Antisocial behaviour and disorder', Findings from the British Crime Survey. http://www.homeoffice.gov.uk/rds/pdfs/r145.pdf
6. *The links between victimization and offending* by D.J. Smith, published by the Centre for Law and Society, University of Edinburgh, www.law.ed.ac.uk/cls/esytc
7. http://www.childline.org.uk/bullying-biggesteverriseincalls.asp
8. *Ibid*, page 15.
9. Page 64, *Alistair Campbell*, Peter Oborne and Simon Walters, Aurum Press, 2004 page 64.
10. *Ibid*, pages 82–3.
11. *Ibid*, page 125.
12. *Ibid*, page 127.
13. Porn king is caged at last', *News of the World*, 16 May 1982.
14. Mary Riddell Sunday 6 November, 2005 *The Observer*
15. *Sun*, Friday, 26 October 2005.
16. Justice for Linda Campaign website. This is my summarised version of the story on the website.
17. *Ibid*.
18. See my books *I'm a Teacher, Get Me Out of Here* and *Teacher On the Run* for more on these issues.
19. *Evening Standard*, Monday, 10 October 2005.
20. *The Times*, Wednesday, 28 September 2005.
21. *Guardian*, Friday, 7 October 2005.
22. *The Oxford Student*, 13 January 2005.

23. http://www.msnbc.msn.com/id/3340355/
24. *Mail on Sunday*, 2 October 2005.
25. *Daily Telegraph*, 29 September 2005.
26. *Daily Telegraph*, 30 September 2005.
27. *Mail on Sunday*, 2 October 2005.
28. *Mail on Sunday*, 18 September 2005.
29. *Evening Standard*, Wednesday, 9 November 2005.
30. *Daily Telegraph*, 15 October 2005.
31. *The Times*, 27 October 2005.
32. *Guardian*, Adrian Levy and Cathy Scott-Clark, Saturday, 20 November 2004.
33. *Ibid.*
34. *Observer*, 23 October 2005.
35. *Daily Mail*, Monday, 29 August 2005.
36. *Mail*, Sunday, 28 August 2005.
37. *An Inebriated History of Britain*, Foreword to the 2005 edition, by Peter Haydon, Sutton Publishing 2005.
38. *Alcohol Problems in the Family*, Publication by European Union in 1998.
39. *The Guardian*, 17 November 2005, page 9.
40. Home Office statistics, 2004–5. Crown copyright.
41. *Daily Telegraph*, Tuesday, 2 August 2005.
42. *Ibid.*
43. *Sun*, 20 August 2005.
44. *The Times*, 27 August 2005.
45. *Daily Telegraph*, Tuesday, 2 August 2005.
46. Warbuton A.L. and Shepherd J.P., 'An evaluation of the effectiveness of new policies designed to prevent and manage violence through an interagency approach. A final report for WORD (Grant number R/98/037)'. February 2004.
47. *Bath and North East Somerset Crime and Disorder Audit.*
48. The Institute of Alcohol Studies. http://www.ias.org.uk/publications/alert/05issue1/ alert0501_p8.html
49. *East London Advertiser*, 4 August 2005.
50. *East London Advertiser*, 4 August 2005.
51. *Sun*, 19 September 2005, page 19.
52. *Swearing, A Social History of Foul Language, Oaths and Profanity in English*, by Geoffrey Hughes, Blackwell, 1991, page 44.
53. *Ibid*, page 48.
54. *Ibid*, page 50.
55. *Ibid*, page 89.

56. *Alistair Campbell*, Peter Oborne and Simon Walters, op. cit., page 127.
57. http://www.ketupa.net/beaverbrook1.htm
58. *Daily Telegraph*, Wednesday, 12 June 2002.
59. http://news.bbc.co.uk/1/hi/uk_politics/2039988.stm
60. *The Guardian*, G2, Kira Chochrane 'Is this your idea of glamour?' 15 November 2005
61. Panorama BBC 1 Sunday, 20 November 2005 http://news.bbc.co.uk/1/hi/programmes/panorama/4447228.stm
62. Story from BBC News: http://news.bbc.co.uk/go/pr/fr/2/hi/uk_news/politics/4656305.stm Published: 7 June 2005, 13:08:32 GMT.
63. *East London Advertiser*, 27 October 2005.

Index

on public transport 5–9,
8–9
rising levels of 12–13
Mulvay, George 112
murder 43, 241
Murdoch, Rupert 53, 54, 63

national character, British
30–2
National Curriculum 81, 264,
266
National Health Service
(NHS) 172, 198, 262
Nazi Circus *see* Toryglen
estate gang (Nazi
Circus), Glasgow
NEDs (Non-educated
Delinquents) 230
see also chavs
networking 131
New Labour 20, 53, 61, 63,
96, 152–8, 159–61
anti-social behaviour
policies 251, 258–9, 273
briefing rooms 100–1
and bullying 155, 157–8,
160–1, 273
and the drinks industry
175, 176, 197–8
political parades of 135–7
Newcastle 113
Newport, Wales 170–4
News International
Corporation 52–3
News of the World
(newspaper) 56–7,
129
Nigeria 10
night buses 5–8, 9, 270–8
nightlife 108–26

battlefields of 170–3,
182–4, 187–200
financial costs of 171–2
noise pollution 241
Nomura 176
Northern Ireland 132–4
Northern Irish Police Force
133–4
Nuisance Strategy Unit 250–3

Observer (newspaper) 58, 175
Ofsted 80, 82
Oldham 222
organized crime 12–13
Osborne, George 129
Oxford University 128

paedophilia 56–7
Page 3 girls 54, 57
pain, enjoyment of inflicting
11, 13–14
Paki Panthers 14–15
Panorama (TV programme)
253
parades 96, 107–40, 275
parents
authoritarian 42–3
boundary setting by 40, 44
of bullies 37
categories of 42–3
of delinquents 37–42
effective 277–8
ineffective 39–40, 78
paranoid 40–2
and teenagers 78
who defend their
children's bad behaviour
81–2
Pitt, Bill 70, 250–3, 258, 259,
273, 277